Guide to the State Historical Markers Of Pennsylvania

George R. Beyer
Regional Introductions by Harold L. Myers

Commonwealth of Pennsylvania
Pennsylvania Historical and Museum Commission
Harrisburg, 1991

This is the fifth edition of *Guide to the Historical Markers of Pennsylvania, Erected by the Pennsylvania Historical and Museum Commission.* Previous editions were published in 1948, 1952, 1957 (reprinted in 1967, in addition to supplements), and 1975.

CONTENTS

INTRODUCTION

The three hundredth anniversary of the charter from King Charles II that established Pennsylvania — and made William Penn its colonial proprietor — was celebrated by the Commonwealth in 1981. Three centuries of Penn's devoutly proclaimed "Holy Experiment" find their meaning in the founder's unfolding legacy of liberty and justice. The history of this legacy is filled with the names of persons, places and events of lasting significance. There have been settlers and soldiers, politicians and reformers, churches and colleges, roadways and canals, treaties and constitutions, beginnings and endings. A rich and unfinished tapestry, Pennsylvania's history is daily brought to public attention through the hundreds of historical markers erected throughout the Commonwealth by the Pennsylvania Historical and Museum Commission.

It was in 1913 that the Pennsylvania Historical Commission was established, and one of its major responsibilities was the marking of historic places within the boundaries of the Commonwealth. During the next twenty years, nearly 150 commemorative plaques were erected. Having been affixed, usually, to large boulders and dedicated in conjunction with local historical and patriotic societies, their permanence seemed assured. Many of the plaques were notably handsome, but with their small lettering and lack of contrast they were not easy reading in an increasingly fast-paced automobile age. After 1933 the Historical Commission ceased their erection and devoted its attention to other programs.

In 1945 the Historical Commission, the State Archives and the State Museum were united to form the Pennsylvania Historical and Museum Commission. A major initiative of the new Commission was the creation of a program to erect historical markers with a thoroughly modified design. The first of the new roadside-type markers were placed the following year, and by 1948 more than seven hundred had been installed. The next several years saw the erection of the first city-type markers, so that by 1952 the number of historical markers was over one thousand. Although rising costs have slowed the rate at which markers have been added in more recent years, the total now is approximately fifteen hundred.

The roadside-type marker

The city-type marker

Since 1946 the markers have been emblazoned with bright gold letters on a background of blue — the State colors — and topped by the coat of arms of the Commonwealth. Mounted on sturdy metal posts, they are more readable and easily maintained than the older plaques. They present history to the public in an understandable form.

The first comprehensive list of these new markers was the *Guide to the Historical Markers of Pennsylvania,* published by the Historical and Museum Commission in 1948. Its fourth edition (published in 1975) presented the texts and locations of more than 1,350 markers. The present edition — the fifth — adds some 160 erected during the past fifteen years. These include the tercentenary markers dedicated at the county seats (usually at the courthouse) — the earliest ones in 1981 — to honor the sixty-seven counties. In addition, this *Guide* reflects a renewed interest in the plaques erected by the former Historical Commission and provides the title, text and location of each of those still in place. This is the first comprehensive listing of these to be published.

Another innovation is the grouping of the counties, for the purpose of this *Guide,* into twelve regions. These regions are arranged in a more-or-less clockwise sequence, beginning with the southeast (''where Pennsylvania began'') and concluding with the picturesque northeast. Each region is introduced with a short historical survey and maps that locate each marker by number. The marker texts themselves are arranged in geographic sequence within each county, and all titles are alphabetized in an index.

The reader may wish to keep this book in a pocket or car for easy reference. We hope that it will enhance an understanding of a precious heritage which has been more than three hundred years in the making — a creation of the beliefs and actions, the hard work and heroism, the struggles and accomplishments of men and women who have passed this way before us, here in the Keystone State.

You Have A Role

You, in fact, can help in commemorating historic persons, places and events in Pennsylvania.

First, you can inform the PHMC of a damaged or missing historical marker. (Markers in each county are removed for short periods every several years for refinishing, and it is PHMC policy to inform the local news media when this is to be done.) Any incident involving a marker should be reported as soon as possible, since this may lessen the possibility of further damage and increase the likelihood of recovery. Please phone such information to (717) 783-1971, or write to **Historical Marker Maintenance,** Pennsylvania Historical and Museum Commission, P.O. Box 1026, Harrisburg 17108-1026. It should be noted that the repair of even a severely damaged marker can usually be accomplished more speedily and at less cost than can the manufacture of a replacement.

Second, the PHMC is always pleased to receive suggestions for new markers that will commemorate subjects of historical significance to the State. A suggestion may be submitted by any person or organization, public or private, inside or outside Pennsylvania. For a copy of the suggestion form and related materials, phone the **Historical Marker Program,** (717) 783-9871, or write to the address above. Following submission of a completed form, the proposal will be evaluated by a historical marker review panel appointed by the PHMC. Approval of new markers takes place annually.

The number of historical markers produced with State funds is now limited to a few each year. However, there is provision for the private funding of new markers **that meet the same guidelines and are approved by the same process as for other State historical markers.** Ruined or missing markers may also be replaced through private or other alternative funding. For details of the procedure, phone or write the **Historical Marker Program** as above. After an approved, privately funded marker has been erected, it will become an integral part of the official statewide system and will be maintained just as are the other roadside and city-type markers in Pennsylvania's sixty-seven counties.

How To Use This Guide

Each section of this *Guide to the State Historical Markers of Pennsylvania,* devoted to a region, is introduced by a map or maps that show the counties of the region, many of the principal highways, and the routes that may be used in finding the marker locations. A circled number indicates on the map where one or more historical markers are located. Furthermore, a circled letter at the county seat represents the marker dedicated for that county during Pennsylvania's tercentenary.

By region, the counties are arranged alphabetically. Within each county the special tercentenary marker, bearing the name of the county and indicated by a circled letter, is listed first. This is followed by the geographically arranged texts of the other markers in the county, their arrangement reflected in the circled numbers on the map. In cases where two or more markers are essentially at the same point on the map — for example, in the same city or town — they are given the same number; we have nevertheless tried to arrange them in the text geographically.

Each marker entry begins with its circled location number taken from the map, and the marker title. The next several lines compose the marker text, in most cases shown exactly as it appears on the marker itself. Each entry concludes with the marker's location and the date of its dedication — if one was held — or of its erection. If the marker is of the city type, or if it is one of the old plaques (see below), that fact is noted. If such is not indicated, the marker is of the roadside type.

As has been noted, the *Guide to the State Historical Markers* — unlike its previous versions — lists the plaques of the old Pennsylvania Historical Commission, erected during the period from 1914 to 1933 and, at the time of the compilation of this *Guide,* still in place. These plaques are listed with the more recent historical markers and not in a separate section; the information about them is presented in the same format. Their inscriptions, however, are usually quite different in arrangement, capitalization and punctuation from those on the more recent markers; these have been modified in this *Guide* to conform more closely to the newer usage, but the wording has not been altered. In those few cases where it has seemed advisable to condense a particularly lengthy text, every omission has been identified by ellipses (...). Likewise, if a plaque has no simple title, a title is suppled in brackets.

Perhaps some future book will accomplish what is impractical for this *Guide,* namely the listing of other plaques and memorials in Pennsylvania that were erected neither by the old nor by the present Commission. Most of the plaques listed here were placed in cooperation with historical and civic organizations, but the participation of the Pennsylvania Historical Commission was essential to each, and its name is inscribed thereon. The marking of historic sites was a key program of the old Commission until 1933, just as it is today for its successor, the Pennsylvania Historical and Museum Commission.

Note on Marker Locations

In the information given beneath the marker texts, the designations **I, US** and **PA** refer to the familiar systems of Interstate, U.S.-numbered and State-numbered traffic signs. (Although no historical marker is directly located on an Interstate highway, a few are situated close to exits.)

Certain historical markers are located on or close to State highways without traffic-route numbers. Such highways are generally designated in this *Guide* by the **SR** (State Route) numbers introduced in 1986; these four-digit numbers now appear on small to medium-size signs which have been erected at intersections and at the beginning of particular segments along these highways. For certain of these roads, this *Guide* also indicates the old **LR** (Legislative Route) numbers, which have been superseded by the new designations but which still appear on some maps.

State Entrance Markers

State entrance markers, with the title "Pennsylvania," are located on many of the older main highways entering the Commonwealth from the six neighboring states of New Jersey, Delaware, Maryland, West Virginia, Ohio and New York. Erected between December 1948 and November 1949, all of these markers are of the roadside type and bear the following inscription:

PENNSYLVANIA
Founded 1681 by William Penn
as a Quaker Commonwealth.
Birthplace of
THE DECLARATION OF
INDEPENDENCE
and
THE CONSTITUTION OF
THE UNITED STATES.

Regional Organization of this Guide

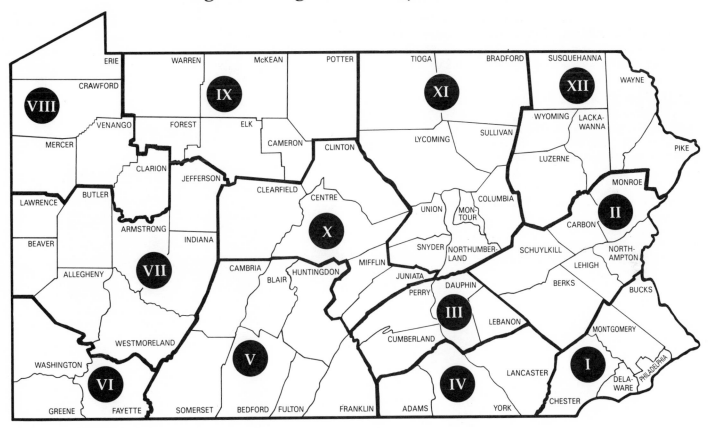

REGION I

Freedom's Port of Call

The southeast corner of Pennsylvania comprises *Bucks* and *Chester* counties and the county and city of *Philadelphia* — all established by William Penn in 1681 — and two counties formed from them, *Montgomery* in 1784 and *Delaware* in 1789.

In October 1682, Pennsylvania's founder and proprietor by royal charter, after an ocean crossing, disembarked at Upland village (now Chester), joining thousands of the members of the Religious Society of Friends — settlers from England and Wales. For them, who had known persecution, a new society was forming, a plantation by God's own hand, he said — an opening to Godly life and good government, and to freedom and opportunity for other churches and nationalities as well.

The city of Philadelphia was laid out at Penn's direction in 1681. It thrived as a major seaport with a lively culture, its enlightened citizens — Benjamin Franklin and others — were leaders in learning, science and civic improvement, and it was the seat of Pennsylvania's government until 1799. The most populous city in the young republic, where the Declaration of Independence was resolved in 1776 and the Constitution in 1787, Philadelphia was the national capital only until 1800.

Planted firmly in Pennsylvania soil, the vision of freedom, though clouded at times, lived on. In 1688 German-born Quakers, in Germantown, had issued the first public protest against the ownership of slaves, the forerunner of growing opposition in the region to slavery. In time, freed by the State of Pennsylvania in an act of gradual emancipation, descendants of slaves were to gain distinction in religion, education and culture.

Delaware County, south of Philadelphia and in the beginning a part of Chester, is among the oldest as a historic region. Here was settled a part of the colony of New Sweden, 1638, and the settlement of Tinicum, 1643, from which the Swedish colony was governed. Today, the 1724 Old Chester Courthouse, early houses of worship, and ancient burial grounds distinguish the region, as does its history of truck farming, shipbuilding and heavy industry.

Just as its neighbors, Chester County awakens memories of the American Revolution, in particular the Battle of the Brandywine. Though it achieved some distinction from iron and steel, much of the county retains its rural landscape. Montgomery County likewise recalls Revolutionary events, such as at Whitemarsh and Valley Forge. Just as felicitously, old houses and venerable landmarks remind us of John James Audubon, Lucretia Mott, Henry Melchior Muhlenberg, Woodrow Wilson and other notables.

Pennsbury, the Bucks County home of William Penn, was built facing the Delaware River. Resolute as the founder had been in dealing justly and peacefully with the Native Americans, the notorious Walking Purchase of Indian lands was begun not far from there in 1737. Nevertheless, the cry of war was not heard here until 1776 when Washington and his troops crossed the Delaware and surprised their slumbering foe. This river still supplies water to the Delaware Canal, a carrier of freight as late as 1931 and a delight to visitors even today.

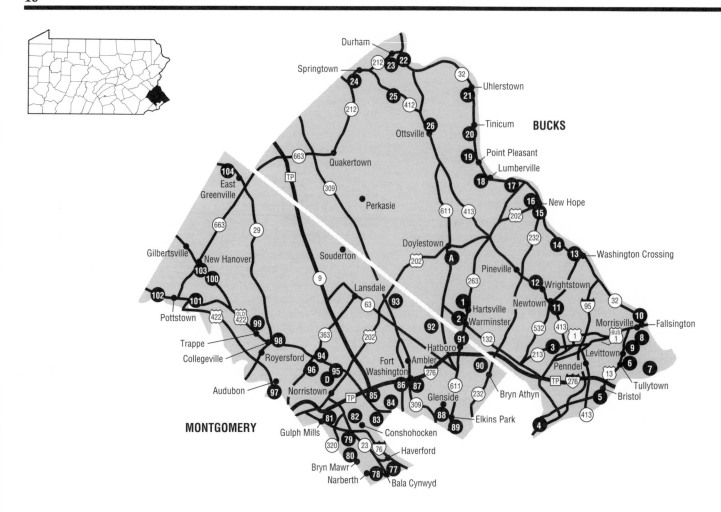

Durham
Springtown
212 23 22
32
24
Uhlerstown
25 412
21
212
Ottsville 26 20 Tinicum
BUCKS
663 19 Point Pleasant
104 Quakertown Lumberville
East 309 18 17
Greenville TP
611 413 16 New Hope
663 15
29 202
Gilbertsville Perkasie 232 14 Washington Crossing
New Hanover 202 Doylestown 13
103 Souderton A Pineville
100 9 263 12 Wrightstown
102 101 Lansdale 1 Newtown 11 95 32
422 OLD 63 93 Hartsville 10
Pottstown 422 99 92 2 Warminster 532 413 BUS Morrisville Fallsington
Trappe 363 91 132 1 8
98 202 3 9 Levittown
Collegeville 94 Hatboro 213 6
Royersford 96 95 Ambler Penndel 7
Audubon D Fort 90 TP 13 Tullytown
97 Norristown Washington 86 87 611 232 Bryn Athyn 5 Bristol
85 Glenside 309 88 Elkins Park 413
MONTGOMERY 81 82 84 89 4
Gulph Mills 83 Conshohocken
320 79 76
80 23 Haverford
Bryn Mawr 77
Narberth 78 Bala Cynwyd

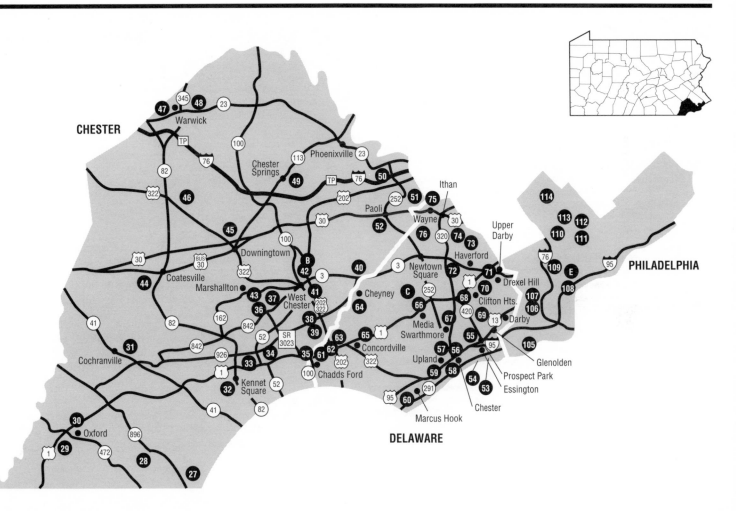

CHESTER

DELAWARE

PHILADELPHIA

Warwick

Chester
Springs

Phoenixville

Paoli

Ithan

Wayne

Upper
Darby

Haverford

Downingtown

Coatesville

Marshallton

West
Chester

Cheyney

Newtown
Square

Drexel Hill

Clifton Hts.

Darby

Media
Swarthmore

Upland

Glenolden

Prospect Park

Essington

Cochranville

Concordville

Chadds Ford

Chester

Marcus Hook

Kennet
Square

Oxford

Bucks County

A BUCKS COUNTY
One of Pennsylvania's three original counties. Formed 1682 by William Penn and site of his home, Pennsbury Manor. Name is derived from abbreviation for Buckinghamshire in England. Doylestown, chosen as county seat in 1812, was incorporated 1838.
City type: Courthouse, E. Court St., Doylestown. Dedicated Oct. 29, 1982.

1 HEADQUARTERS FARM
The Moland House was Gen. Washington's headquarters. August 10-23, 1777, while his army camped nearby. Here Lafayette joined the American army.
Old York Rd. (old PA 263) N of Hartsville. Erected Oct. 22, 1947.

2 JOHN FITCH'S STEAMBOAT
Fitch tested near here a model steamboat in 1785. Before his death in 1798, he built 4 mechanically successful steamboats. The first in the U.S., they proved financial failures, leaving final success of the idea to Robert Fulton.
Junction PA 132 & 263 in Warminster. Erected Oct. 23, 1947.

3 PLAYWICKY INDIAN TOWN, 1682
Was located to the south in the vale by the run and springs. The chief Tammany of the Unami Group (their totem — the tortoise) of the Lenni Lenape or Delawares sold to William Penn the land between Neshaminy and Pennypack Creeks, June 23, 1683. Marked by the Pennsylvania Historical Commission and the Pennsylvania Society of the Colonial Dames of America, 1925.
Plaque: PA 213 (Bridgetown Pike) .5 mile from Neshaminy Creek & 2.5 miles W of Langhorne. Dedicated Oct. 17, 1925. While the *Guide* was in preparation, this plaque was found to be missing. Hope remains for its recovery or replacement.

4 ROCHAMBEAU ROUTE (NARRAGANSETT BAY TO YORKTOWN)
On Sept. 2, 1781, French and American armies crossed the Delaware River near Trenton and moved toward Philadelphia by way of Bristol. Part of the march was along this highway called, then, the King's Path. Troops encamped here for the night. Officers used Red Lion Inn as headquarters.
US 13 near Philadelphia city line. Erected Oct. 18, 1954.

5 BRISTOL
Early river port laid out as Buckingham, 1697. The third oldest borough in Pennsylvania, chartered Nov. 14, 1720. County seat of Bucks, 1705-26. Travel and trade center for over two hundred years.
Main highways leading into town. Erected 1947 & 1949.

5 ABRAHAM LINCOLN
On Feb. 21, 1861, the train carrying the President-elect from Springfield, Ill., to his Inauguration in Washington, D.C., stopped briefly near this point. Mr. Lincoln appeared on the rear platform and spoke to the assembled crowd, estimated at more than a thousand people.
City type: near intersection Bristol Pike & Pond St., Bristol. Dedicated 1991.

6 PENNSBURY MANOR
William Penn's country home in Pennsylvania, built 1683-1700. Here he often resided while in America. Re-created by the State as a historic shrine. Follow this road for 3.5 miles.
SR 2055 (old US 13), Tullytown, near junction SR 2059 (Bordentown Rd.). Erected Nov. 11, 1949.

7 PENNSBURY
William Penn's country home, built in 1683-1700. Administered by the Pennsylvania Historical and Museum Commission.
At site, E of Tullytown. Erected [1948].

(8) PENNSBURY MANOR

William Penn's country home in Pennsylvania, built 1683-1700. Here he often resided while in America. Re-created by the State as a historic shrine. Location is about 3 miles to the SE.

SR 2020 (Tyburn Rd.) S of Fallsington; SR 2059 (New Ford Rd.) at SR 2020. Erected Oct. 8, 1951.

(9) HISTORIC FALLSINGTON

One of the places first settled in Pennsylvania, this village has retained a great many of the fine houses of its provincial period. The Friends meeting organized in 1683 was attended by William Penn in 1701. The original building of 1692 stood near the site of the present Friends meetinghouse.

Business US 1 at SR 2020 (Tyburn Rd.); SR 2020 at SR 2006 (New Falls Rd.). Dedicated June 3, 1961.

Stagecoach Tavern, Historic Fallsington

(10) SUMMERSEAT

Washington's headquarters, Dec. 8-14, 1776. Built in 1773 by Thomas Barclay; restored in 1931. Owners included Robert Morris and George Clymer. Located at Legion and Clymer Aves.

At site, Legion Ave. near Hillcrest Ave., Morrisville. Erected Jan. 27, 1949.

(11) DURHAM ROAD MILESTONE

Bearing the inscription "1 M to N" (one mile to Newtown) this milestone is believed to have been placed before 1741. It is one of two such markers still located on the historic 43-mile road from Bristol to Durham Furnace. Newtown, an important stop along this road, was the county seat from 1726 to 1813.

PA 413, 1 mile S of Newtown. Dedicated Oct. 28, 1988.

(12) WALKING PURCHASE

Measured 1737, according to a supposed Indian deed of 1686, granting lands extending a day-and-a-half walk. Using picked men to force this measure to its limit, Thomas Penn reversed his father's Indian policy, losing Indian friendship.

PA 413 at Wrightstown. Erected Jan. 10, 1949.

(12) WALKING PURCHASE

Starting here at sunrise, Sept. 19, 1737, Marshall, Yeates, and Jennings set out on the "Indian Walk." In one and a half days. Edward Marshall reached a point beyond present Mauch Chunk, some 65 miles to the north and west.

Accompanies marker above. Erected Jan. 10, 1949. Mauch Chunk is now borough of Jim Thorpe.

(13) PENNSYLVANIA CANAL

A system of State-built public works to connect Philadelphia, Pittsburgh, Lake Erie. The Delaware Division, Bristol-Easton, begun 1827; operated by the State 1831-58, and by private owners to 1931. A State Park since 1940.

PA 532 W of Washington Crossing. Erected Dec. 14, 1948.

13 WASHINGTON CROSSING

Here Washington and his men braved ice and sleet Christmas night, 1776, to cross the Delaware and to surprise and defeat the Hessians at Trenton. The victory gave new life to the patriot cause.

PA 532 at Washington Crossing. Erected Nov. 17, 1947.

14 DELAWARE CANAL

The highway crosses the canal midway in a level extending from the locks near Yardley to those at New Hope. Near by is the Jericho Creek aqueduct, one of nine such structures in the 60-mi. canal from Bristol to Easton.

PA 32, 2.3 miles N of Washington Crossing at Jericho Creek. Erected Jan. 19, 1949.

15 DELAWARE CANAL

Opened from Bristol to this place in 1831; and completed to Easton in 1832. Outlet lock to the river built here in 1854. The nearby River House, built 1794, was a popular barge stop on the canal.

PA 32, just S of PA 232 at New Hope. Erected Jan. 20, 1949.

15 DELAWARE CANAL

Here are Locks No. 8-11 of the 23 lift locks on this canal. New Hope also had one of the nine aqueducts, and the only toll station between Bristol and Easton. Coal was the largest item of shipping.

PA 32, 50 ft. N of PA 232 at New Hope. Erected Jan. 10, 1949.

16 SAMUEL D. INGHAM

Statesman, industrialist, born here Sept. 16, 1779. Secretary Treasury, 1829-1831, under Jackson and holder of other State and National offices. Active in the early anthracite coal industry; canal advocate.

US 202, 1.5 miles W of New Hope. Erected Oct. 22, 1947.

17 PENNSYLVANIA CANAL

Same text as Pennsylvania Canal above.

PA 32, 3.5 miles N of New Hope. Erected Jan. 11, 1949.

18 PENNSYLVANIA CANAL

Same text as Pennsylvania Canal above.

PA 32 at Lumberville. Erected Jan. 11, 1949.

18 DELAWARE CANAL

Here is Lock No. 12 in a series of 23 lift locks, numbered from Bristol to Easton. Just above here is one of the nine aqueducts by which the canal and its traffic crossed courses of small streams.

PA 32 at Lumberville. Erected Jan. 20, 1949.

19 TREASURE ISLAND RESERVATION

Consisting of Treasure Island and Marshall Island. Home to one of the nation's oldest Boy Scout camps, established by the Philadelphia Council, B.S.A., in 1913. Birthplace of the Order of the Arrow, a national campers' honor society founded upon Native American traditions. Its Unami Lodge No. 1 was created here in 1915 by the camp's first director, E. Urner Goodman, and his assistant, Carroll A. Edson.

PA 32, 3.5 miles N of Point Pleasant. Dedicated June 25, 1989.

20 DELAWARE CANAL

On the 60-mile canal from Bristol to Easton, nine aqueducts, including this at Tinicum Creek, carried boats of 71-ton capacity across small streams. The initial cost of aqueducts averaged about $7,000.

PA 32 at Tinicum. Erected Jan. 21, 1949.

21 DELAWARE CANAL

Uhlertown, known as Mexico at an earlier date, was named for Michael Uhler, boatbuilder and operator of a line of canal boats. Lock No. 18 and well-kept buildings are interesting reminders of canal days.

PA 32 at Uhlerstown (Uhlertown). Erected Jan. 21, 1949.

22 PENNSYLVANIA CANAL

Same text as Pennsylvania Canal above.

PA 611 at Durham Furnace. Erected Jan. 7, 1949.

22 DELAWARE CANAL

Here is Lock No. 21 in a series of 23 lift locks, numbered from Bristol to Easton. The aqueduct over Cooks Creek is one of nine which carried water and shipping across branches of the Delaware River.

PA 611 at Durham Furnace. Erected Jan. 24, 1949.

22 DELAWARE CANAL

This canal encouraged a revival of the local iron industry, neglected since 1789; and the new Durham Furnaces, which operated here from 1848 to 1908, made this an important point for canal shipping.

PA 611 at Durham Furnace. Erected Jan. 24, 1949.

23 DURHAM FURNACE

Built 1727. Original site at Durham. In blast until 1789, it made cannon and shot in the colonial wars and Revolution. One-time owners included James Logan and George Taylor.

PA 212 at Durham. Erected Nov. 21, 1947.

24 WALKING PURCHASE

Starting here at sunrise, Sept. 19, 1737, Marshall, Yeates, and Jennings set out on the ''Indian Walk.'' In one and a half days. Edward Marshall reached a point beyond present Mauch Chunk, some 65 miles to the north and west.

PA 212 & 412, .6 mile S of Springtown. Erected Jan. 7, 1949. Mauch Chunk is now borough of Jim Thorpe.

25 GALLOWS HILL

Here Edward Marshall and his associates of the famous Indian Walk of a day and a half, September 19-20, 1737, left the old Durham Road on the first day and followed the well-beaten Indian path which led northwesterly through present Hellertown, Bethlehem, Northampton and the Lehigh Gap. Marked by the Pennsylvania Historical Commission and Citizens of Bucks and Northampton counties, 1925.

Plaque: intersection PA 412 & SR 4075 (Gallows Hill Rd.), Stony Point. Dedicated Nov. 21, 1925.

26 WALKING PURCHASE

Same text as Walking Purchase just above.

PA 611, .5 mile N of Ottsville. Erected Jan. 4, 1949.

26 WALKING PURCHASE

Solomon Jennings, one of the three walkers, fell out of the race near here, having covered about 18 miles from Wrightstown. He followed the others to a point near his home on the Lehigh River.

Accompanies marker above. Erected Jan. 4, 1949.

Chester County

B CHESTER COUNTY

One of Pennsylvania's three original counties, formed 1682 by William Penn. Name derived from Cheshire in England. West Chester, the county seat since 1788, was incorporated in 1799. County was the scene of important military activities in 1777-1778.

City type: County Courthouse, N. High St., West Chester. Dedicated Oct. 26, 1982.

27 MINGUANNAN INDIAN TOWN

Was located here. The chief Machaloha or Owhala and his people of the Unami group (their totem — the tortoise) of the Lenni-Lenape or Delawares sold to William Penn the lands between Delaware River and Chesapeake Bay to the Falls of Susquehanna River, October 18, 1683. Marked by the Pennsylvania Historical Commission and the Chester County Historical Society, 1924.

Plaque: intersection SR 3006 (Yeatman Station Rd.) & SR 3034 (London Tract Rd.) 1.5 miles NE of Strickersville. Dedicated Oct. 18, 1924.

28 THOMAS McKEAN

The signer of the Declaration of Independence, Chief Justice of Pennsylvania and Governor, from 1799 to 1808, was born on this farm on March 19, 1734. Also active in the politics of Delaware, he encouraged Caesar Rodney to cast the deciding vote for American Independence.

PA 896 NW of PA 841, Franklin Twp. Dedicated Oct. 26, 1974.

29 EVAN PUGH

Born 1828 on Jordan Bank farm 3 miles south. First President, Penn State University, 1859 until death, 1864. Put his college at fore of movement toward mass education in science for farming, industry.

City type: PA 472 (Market St.) near 5th St., Oxford. Dedicated Sept. 26, 1964.

30 LINCOLN UNIVERSITY

Chartered as Ashmun Institute, April 29, 1854. Founded by Rev. John Miller Dickey for the purpose of providing liberal higher education for people of African ancestry in America. In 1866, it became Lincoln University, interracial and international.

SR 3026 (old US 1) 2 miles NE of Oxford. Erected Jan. 25, 1967.

31 JOHN F. FRITZ

His absolute integrity, mechanical ability, inventive genius, and practical resourcefulness brought about improved processes and products in the iron and steel industry in America. He introduced the three-high rolls into the Cambria mill, applied the Bessemer process to American practice, improved the manufacture of armor plate. Fritz was born 1.3 miles NE of here in 1822.

PA 41, 2.8 miles SE of Cochranville. Erected Aug. 17, 1954.

32 [STEYNING MANOR]

The Manor of Steyning, of 15,500 acres patented by William Penn for ''fatherly love'' and one beaver skin yearly to his daughter Laetitia Penn at Philadelphia, October 23, 1701, is here marked on its western line adjoining a tract of 14,500 acres which the Proprietor patented to his son William Penn, Junior, May 24, 1706. Marked by the Pennsylvania Historical Commission and the Chester County Historical Society, 1926.

Plaque: SR 3048 (old US 1) southbound, .5 mile W of Kennett Square. Dedicated Oct. 23, 1926.

33 BATTLE OF BRANDYWINE

On Sept. 11, 1777, an American force of about 11,000 men, commanded by Washington, attempted to halt a British advance into Pennsylvania. The Americans were defeated near Chadds Ford on Brandywine Creek by approximately 18,000 British and Hessian troops under Howe.

US 1, 1 mile E of Kennett Square. Erected Mar. 18, 1952.

33 BATTLE OF BRANDYWINE

Howe planned two separate attacks against the American line. In early morning, the British Army divided here, Knyphausen's troops went east to engage the center of the line at Chadds Ford, while a force under Cornwallis marched approximately 6 miles north, then 3 miles east, to outflank Washington's right wing and attack from the rear.

Accompanies marker above. Erected Mar. 18, 1952.

34 INDIAN HANNAH (1730-1802)

The last of the Indians in Chester County was born in the vale about 300 yards to the east on the land of the protector of her people, the Quaker assemblyman William Webb. Her mother was Indian Sarah and her grandmother Indian Jane of the Unami group (their totem — the tortoise) of the Lenni-Lenape or Delaware Indians. Marked by the Pennsylvania Historical Commission and the Chester County Historical Society, 1925.

Plaque: PA 52 (E side) .2 mile N of junction US 1. Dedicated Sept. 5, 1925; lost ca. 1961; duplicate placed 1976.

35 [AMERICAN LIGHT INFANTRY]

The American Light Infantry near this place vigorously resisted the advance of the British at the Battle of Brandywine, September 11, 1777. Erected by the Pennsylvania Historical Commission and the Chester and Delaware County Historical Societies, 1915.

Plaque: US 1 (N side) 1 mile W of Chadds Ford. Dedicated Sept. 11, 1915.

36 TRIMBLE'S FORD

September 11, 1777, while on the march to the Battlefield of Brandywine, the British Army under Howe and Cornwallis crossed the Brandywine at the ford just south of this point. Erected by the Pennsylvania Historical Commission and the Chester and Delaware County Historical Societies, 1915.

Plaque: SR 3023 (Camp Linden Rd.) .2 mile E of SR 3058. Dedicated Sept. 11, 1915.

37 BATTLE OF BRANDYWINE (Sept. 11, 1777)

After fording the branches of the Brandywine, British troops under Cornwallis turned SE here early in the afternoon to attack the rear of the American right wing under Sullivan, 3 miles downstream. Conflicting intelligence reports on this movement prevented formation of a proper defense by Sullivan.

PA 842 at intersection SR 3061 (formerly LR 15198) SW of West Chester. Erected Mar. 18, 1952.

37 SCONNELLTOWN

Cornwallis' division of the British Army halted here September 11, 1777, on its march to the Battlefield of Brandywine. Erected by the Pennsylvania Historical Commission and the Chester and Delaware County Historical Societies, 1915.

Plaque: near intersection SR 3061 & SR 2001, just off PA 842 SW of West Chester. Dedicated Sept. 11, 1915.

38 OSBORNE'S HILL

From this ridge General Howe directed the movements of the British Army at the Battle of Brandywine, Septembler 11, 1777. Erected by the Pennsylvania Historical Commission and the Chester and Delaware County Historical Societies, 1915.

Plaque: SR 2001 (Birmingham Rd.) at driveway to Osborne Hill, 1 mile S of Strodes Mill. Dedicated Sept. 11, 1915.

38 BATTLE OF BRANDYWINE (Sept. 11, 1777)

The British attack on the American right wing began here late in the afternoon. After heavy fighting, the defense line which Sullivan formed hastily near Birmingham Meeting House was forced to retreat to Dilworthtown, 2 miles SE. Reinforcements from Chadds Ford delayed the British as Sullivan's men fall back.

PA 926 at intersection SR 2001 (Birmingham Rd.) W of Darlingtons Corners. Erected Mar. 18, 1952.

38 [THE BRITISH ATTACK]

The British attack upon the American right wing under Sullivan at the Battle of Brandywine, September 11, 1777, began here. Erected by the Pennsylvania Historical Commission and the Chester and Delaware County Historical Societies, 1915.

Plaque: PA 926 at intersection SR 2001 (Birmingham Rd.) near marker immediately above. Dedicated Sept. 11, 1915.

38 BIRMINGHAM FRIENDS' MEETING HOUSE

Erected in 1763. Used as a hospital after the Battle of Brandywine, September 11, 1777. Erected by the Pennsylvania Historical Commission and the Chester and Delaware County Historical Societies, 1915.

Plaque: wall of meetinghouse, SR 2001 (Birmingham Rd.) .5 mile SE of PA 926. Dedicated Sept. 11, 1915.

39 DILWORTHTOWN

The Battle of Brandywine, September 11, 1777, ended a short distance southeast of this place. Erected by the Pennsylvania Historical Commission and the Chester and Delaware County Historical Societies, 1915.

Plaque: SR 2001 (Birmingham Rd.) & Old Wilmington Pike, Dilworthtown. Dedicated Sept. 11, 1915.

40 OKEHOCKING INDIAN TOWN

The chiefs Pokhais, Sepopawny and Muttagooppa with their people of the Unami group (their totem — the tortoise) of the Lenni-Lenape or Delawares were moved from Lower Ridley and Crum creeks by William Penn to a square tract of 500 acres on the north side of this road east of Ridley Creek . . .1701. Marked by the Pennsylvania Historical Commission and the Chester County Historical Society, 1924.

Plaque: PA 3 (West Chester Pike) .5 mile E of PA 926 & 4 miles W of Newtown Square. Dedicated June 21, 1924.

41 GREAT MINQUAS PATH
An important Indian trail, key to Pennsylvania's fur trade in the 17th century, crossed the present highway near here. It linked trading posts on the lower Schuylkill with Indian towns to the west. The Dutch, Swedes, and English fought one another for control of the path.
Business US 322, 1 mile SE of West Chester. Erected June 26, 1951.

41 [GREAT TRAIL OF THE MINQUAS]
The Great Trail of the Minquas or Susquehanna Indians from the Susquehanna to the Schuylkill crossed the present road about this point. It was the path prior to 1670 for their conquest of the Lenni-Lenape or Delaware Indians and for trade with the first Dutch and Swedish settlers on the Delaware River, thousands of beaver skins yearly being carried down over this "beversrede" or beaver road to Fort Beversrede on the site of Philadelphia and to other neighboring trading posts. Marked by the Pennsylvania Historical Commission and the Chester County Historical Society, 1925.
Plaque: Business US 322 at Church Ave. just S of West Chester. Dedicated Nov. 14, 1925.

Entering West Chester

42 GENERAL LAFAYETTE
After visiting Brandywine Battlefield on July 26, 1825, General Lafayette came to West Chester. From a point about a half block west from here, he reviewed troops parading in his honor.
City type: N. Matlack St. at Lafayette St., in park. Erected Aug. 13, 1952.

42 JOSEPH T. ROTHROCK
Conservationist, father of the State Forest idea in Pennsylvania, lived in this house from 1876 until his death in 1922. He pioneered in the development of forest fire control, reforestation, and scientific forestry.
City type: NW corner, N. Church & W. Lafayette Sts., West Chester. Erected June 9, 1952.

42 LINCOLN BIOGRAPHY
The first published biography of Abraham Lincoln was printed in this building on Feb. 11, 1860. It was prepared from Lincoln's own notes, and served to introduce him to the public as a potential presidential candidate.
City type: 28 W. Market St. between High & Church Sts., West Chester. Erected Sept. 17, 1952.

42 WILLIAM DARLINGTON
Physician, congressman, began a service of 33 years as president of Bank of Chester County, in this building, 1830. Especially noted for his many contributions to the science and study of botany in the early 1800's. He died in 1863.
City type: 13 N. High St. between Market & Gay Sts., West Chester. Erected April 11, 1952.

42 HORACE PIPPIN
Born in West Chester in 1888, Pippin occupied this house from 1920 until his death in 1946. A self-taught black artist, he painted while living here such acclaimed works as "Domino Players," "John Brown Going to His Hanging," and the "Holy Mountain" series.
City type: 327 W. Gay St., West Chester. Dedicated June 9, 1979.

Leaving West Chester

43 JOHN BEALE BORDLEY
The noted agriculturist purchased land just north of here in 1792 and named it "Como Farm." Here he conducted numerous experiments on crop rotation and maintenance of soil fertility. Bordley planned new devices for seeding and reaping wheat. His works on Rotation of Crops, and Husbandry and Rural Affairs were widely read. Died, 1804.
SR 3062 (Strasburg Rd.) just off PA 162, 1.6 miles W of Marshallton. Erected Mar. 25, 1953.

44 JOHN G. PARKE
Born in this vicinity on Sept. 22, 1827, the noted Army Engineer is remembered chiefly for having set the exact boundary between the Oregon Territory and Canada. His survey, begun in 1857, was halted by service in the Civil War and was not completed until 1869. He later became Superintendent of West Point.
Business US 30 at Veterans Hospital just E of Coatesville. Erected July 22, 1968.

44 PETER BEZELLON
Famed Indian trader and interpreter bought a tract of 500 acres in this area in 1736. This site is a part of the tract. He died in 1742. Bezellon and his wife, Martha, lie buried in St. John's churchyard at Compass, Penna.
City type: SR 3064 (West Chester Rd.) at Oak St., S end Coatesville. Erected Oct. 15, 1954.

44 BRANDYWINE MANSION
Historic Fleming house, purchased by Moses Coates in 1787. Acquired in 1810 by Jesse Kersey and Isaac Pennock, founders of the Brandywine Iron Works. Occupied 1816-1825 by Pennock's son-in-law, Dr. Charles Lukens, whose widow Rebecca continued and expanded the firm's operations following his death. Rebecca Lukens, who lived here until her death in 1854, gained renown for her vision and business capability.
102 S. 1st Ave. (SR 3043), Coatesville. Dedicated July 25, 1985.

45 THOMAS B. READ
The painter and poet was born Mar. 12, 1822, a mile away. Author of well-known "Sheridan's Ride." Spent mature years in Europe, but died in New York City, May 11, 1872, and is buried in Philadelphia.
US 322 at intersection SR 4037 NW of Downingtown. Erected May 12, 1948.

46 SPRINGTON MANOR
The largest reserved estate of the Penns in Chester County. It was first authorized by William Penn as a 10,000-acre tract in 1701. After resurvey in 1730, it contained 8,313 acres, including most of present Wallace Township. The southern boundary line of the Manor was near this point.
SR 4023 (Springton Rd.) & Highspire Rd., 1 mile N of US 322, Wallace Twp. Dedicated Oct. 5, 1984.

47 HOPEWELL VILLAGE
Forge built 1744 by Wm. Bird; furnace built 1770 by his son Mark. Furnace and other remains of an ironmaking community of the era, administered by the National Park Service, are about 3 miles away.
PA 345 at Warwick, just N of junction PA 23. Erected Aug. 5, 1948.

48 WARWICK FURNACE
Built 1737 by Anna Nutt and Co. Made first Franklin stoves, 1742. Supplied shot and cannon for American revolutionists. Furnace a mile and a half away on side road; iron mines a mile west on the highway.
PA 23 between Warwick & Knauertown. Erected May 12, 1948.

49 CHESTER SPRINGS
Earlier known as Yellow Springs. Resort since 1750. Washington's headquarters, Sept. 17, 1777, after Battle of Brandywine. Hospital for his soldiers during the winter encampment at Valley Forge, 1777-1778.
PA 113 at Chester Springs. Erected May 13, 1948.

50 VILLAGE OF VALLEY FORGE
Village settled by the workers at iron forge begun in 1742. The forge and part of village were burned by the British army in 1777. Washington's quarters during the winter of 1777-78 were in the Isaac Potts house, a part of the original village.
PA 23 E & W of village. Dedicated Sept. 17, 1960.

51 THE BAPTIST CHURCH IN THE GREAT VALLEY
Organized in 1711 by Welsh families, it is the third Baptist church in the State and the mother of eight congregations. The present building, the second, was erected in 1805.
SR 1007 (Valley Forge Rd.) .4 mile SE of PA 252, Tredyffrin Twp. Erected Apr. 21, 1951.

52 GEN. ANTHONY WAYNE
The house in which the Revolutionary leader and Indian fighter was born, Jan. 1, 1745, stands about a mile away. Died at Erie, Dec. 15, 1796; now buried at St. David's Church, four and a half miles away.
US 30 at junction PA 252 E of Paoli. Erected May 13, 1948.

Delaware County

C DELAWARE COUNTY

Formed September 26, 1789 out of Chester County. Named for the Delaware River and site of William Penn's first entry into Pennsylvania, 1682. Old Chester Courthouse (1724) is one of America's early public buildings. County seat, Media, incorporated 1850.

City type: Courthouse, Front St. & Veterans Sq., Media. Dedicated Oct. 3, 1982.

53 TINICUM

First permanent settlement in present-day Pennsylvania, founded 1643 by Col. Johan Printz, governor of New Sweden. Seized by the Dutch in 1655, and by the English in 1664.

PA 291 eastbound, just NE of Essington. Erected Oct. 13, 1947.

54 GOVERNOR PRINTZ PARK

Site of the first permament settlement in present Pennsylvania in 1643, and of the Swedish Capitol, the Printzhof. Administered by the Pennsylvania Historical and Museum Commission.

At site, 2nd St. & Taylor Ave., Essington. Erected June 28, 1948.

54 NEW SWEDEN

In 1643 the colony's Governor, Johan Printz, established its capital here on Tinicum Island. Earlier, in 1638, New Sweden had been founded at the site of present Wilmington. Although the colony was captured by the Dutch in 1655, many Swedish and Finnish settlers remained. This was the region's first permanent European settlement, some four decades before William Penn's 1681 founding of Pennsylvania.

At Governor Printz Park near marker immediately above. Dedicated Apr. 9, 1988.

55 MORTON HOMESTEAD

Begun about 1654 by Morton Mortonson, ancestor of John Morton, Pennsylvania signer of the Declaration in 1776. Administered by the Pennsylvania Historical and Museum Commission.

At site, PA 420 at Darby Creek, Prospect Park. Erected Sept. 9, 1966.

56 JOHN MORTON

Site of the birthplace of John Morton (1724-1777), signer of the Declaration of Independence. As delegate to the Continental Congress, his ballot, with that of Franklin and James Wilson, committed Pennsylvania to the cause of independence by one vote.

420 E. Ridley Ave., Ridley Park. Erected Jan. 27, 1967.

57 LEIPER RAILWAY

Built, 1809-10, by Thomas Leiper; surveyed by John Thomson. It was the first railway in Pennsylvania, and the first in America to be surveyed. The railway was used to transport stone from quarries on Crum Creek to the landing on Ridley Creek, a distance of 3/4 mile. It crossed the highway here.

SR 2008 (Bullens Ln.) E of PA 320, Nether Providence Twp. Erected Feb. 7, 1955.

Entering Chester

58 CHESTER

Second oldest settlement in Pennsylvania. Named Upland by the Swedes, Chester by Wm. Penn. Seat of Pennsylvania colonial government 1681-1683.

US 322 at NW end of city. Erected Oct. 13, 1947.

58 ROCHAMBEAU ROUTE (NARRAGANSETT BAY TO YORKTOWN)

After an encampment of several days in Philadelphia where French troops passed in review before Congress, the French and American armies moved toward Wilmington by the Chester Pike known then as the King's Highway. They encamped here on September 5, 1781.

US 13 (Morton Ave.) near Melrose Ave., E end of Chester. Erected Oct. 18, 1954.

58 GREEN-BANK

Name given to house built on this site in 1721 by David Lloyd. At one time, it was the home of Admiral Porter and Commodore Porter with whom Admiral Farragut often visited. Razed in Feb. 1882, by "Jackson Explosion."

City type: 2nd St. near Welsh St., Chester. Erected May 15, 1954.

58 OLD SWEDISH BURIAL GROUND

Site of first St. Paul's Episcopal Church, built in 1702. The grave of John Morton, a signer of the Declaration of Independence, is located just south of here.

City type: 3rd St. E of Ave. of the States, Chester. Erected May 15, 1954.

58 COLONIAL COURTHOUSE

Georgian Colonial design. Built in 1724, restored in 1920. In use for Chester County till 1786, for Delaware County, 1789-1851. Later used as City Hall. Oldest public building in continuous use in United States.

City type: Ave. of the States near 5th St., Chester. Erected May 14, 1954.

58 [WILLIAM PENN AND THE FIRST ASSEMBLY]

William Penn sat with the first Assembly of Pennsylvania, which passed the great fundamental laws in the House of Defense or Court House on this site, December 4-7, 1682. Marked by the Pennsylvania Historical Commission and the Delaware County Historical Society.

Plaque: inside wall of Old Courthouse, Ave. of the States near 5th St., Chester. Dedicated Oct. 28, 1932.

58 WASHINGTON HOUSE

Built in 1747 on this site. Was known as "Pennsylvania Arms" until after Washington stopped here following the Battle of Brandywine in 1777. Noted stopping place on the old Post Road. Building stood here until 1952.

City type: Ave. of the States near 5th St., Chester. Erected May 15, 1954.

58 PENN LANDING

Oct. 29, 1682, soon after finishing a two months' voyage, William Penn first set foot on his colony of Pennsylvania granted by Charles II the year before. The site is a block south.

SE corner 2nd (PA 291) & Penn Sts., Chester. Erected Oct. 13, 1947.

58 [ESSEX HOUSE]

William Penn (1644-1718) first lodged in America in "Essex House" on this site, October 28, 1682, the guest of Robert Wade, here the earliest Quaker settler on this side Delaware River, 1676, purchaser of the property, then called "Printzdorp," from the earlier occupant, Armegot, widow of Johan Papeogoja, Vice-Governor of New Sweden, 1653-1654, succeeding to ownership from her father, Johan Printz the Swedish first Governor, 1643-1653, in present Pennsylvania. Marked by the Pennsylvania Historical Commission and the Delaware County Historical Society, 1932.

Plaque: wall at 102 Penn St., Chester. Dedicated Oct. 28, 1932.

58 MARTIN LUTHER KING, JR. (1929-1968)

King lived three years in this community and ministered under the mentorship of J. Pius Barbour. He graduated from Crozer Theological Seminary, 1951. A leader of the 1963 March on Washington, King won a Nobel Peace Prize, 1964.

City type: Calvary Baptist Church, 1616 W. 2nd St. (PA 291), Chester. Dedicated Jan. 14, 1984.

58 FINLAND

Name given to tract along Delaware River from Marcus Hook to Chester River. Grant for tract was given Captain Hans Ammundson Besk, a native of Finland, by Queen Christina in 1653. Site of first Finnish settlement in America.

City type: Concord Ave. at monument in Chester. Erected May 21, 1955.

Leaving Chester

59 CALEB PUSEY

An English-born Quaker and lastmaker, Pusey (1651-1727) purchased 250 acres from William Penn in 1681. As agent and grist mill manager for him, and colonial office holder, he was visited by Penn here.

City type: Race St. at City Rd., Upland. Erected June 9, 1967.

60 MARCUS HOOK

First port of call for Philadelphia shipping. First settled by Swedes, it was named by the Dutch, 1655-64, Marreties Hoeck.

US 13 at Municipal Bldg., Marcus Hook. Erected Oct. 13, 1947.

61 CHADD'S FORD

The Battle of Brandywine took place in this vicinity, September 11, 1777. Within sight of this point, the Americans under Washington and Wayne engaged the British and Hessians under Knyphausen, who had advanced from the westward. The main battle took place about two miles to the northward, where the British under Howe and Cornwallis flanked the American right wing under Sullivan and compelled the retreat of Washington's Army toward Chester. Erected by the Pennsylvania Historical Commission and the Chester and Delaware County Historical Societies, 1915.

Plaque: US 1 (S side) near junction PA 100, Chadds Ford. Dedicated Sept. 11, 1915.

61 JOHN CHAD[D]'S HOUSE

Proctor's American artillery occupied several redoubts near this house at the Battle of Brandywine, September 11, 1777. Erected by the Pennsylvania Historical Commission and the Chester and Delaware County Historical Societies, 1915.

Plaque: lawn of Chadd homestead on PA 100 just N of US 1. Dedicated Sept. 11, 1915.

62 BATTLE OF BRANDYWINE

On Sept. 11, 1777, an American force of about 11,000 men, commanded by Washington, attempted to halt a British advance into Pennsylvania. The Americans were defeated near Chadds Ford on Brandywine Creek by approximately 18,000 British and Hessian troops under Howe.

US 1 southbound, just E of Chadds Ford. Erected May 12, 1952.

62 BATTLE OF BRANDYWINE

The center of the American line, Wayne commanding, was near Chadds Ford and faced west. In late afternoon as Cornwallis was making the main assault on the American right wing, 3 miles north, Knyphausen's division of British and Hessians crossed Brandywine Creek, attacked Wayne and forced him to retreat.

Accompanies marker above. Erected May 12, 1952.

62 CASIMIR PULASKI

Polish volunteer, commanded cavalry detachment helping to cover Washington's retreat from Brandywine, Sept. 11, 1777. As brigadier general, served Sept. 1777-March 1778 as first overall commander of the Continental Army's cavalry. He was mortally wounded at the siege of Savannah, Oct. 9, 1779.

US 1 E of Chadds Ford near entrance Brandywine Battlefield State Park. Dedicated Sept. 13, 1975.

63 BATTLE OF BRANDYWINE

On Sept. 11, 1777, an American force of about 11,000 men, commanded by Washington, attempted to halt a British advance into Pennsylvania. The Americans were defeated near Chadds Ford on Brandywine Creek by approximately 18,000 British and Hessian troops under Howe.

US 202 & 322 just S of Dilworthtown Rd., 1.6 miles N of US 1. Erected May 12, 1952.

63 BATTLE OF BRANDYWINE

The battle ended just southwest of hear at nightfall. With Howe and his troops holding the field, Washington's force withdrew to Chester. Although he was wounded, Lafayette helped to reorganize the retreating troops, and Pulaski's cavalry protected them from attack.

Accompanies marker immediately above. Erected May 12, 1952.

64 FANNY M. JACKSON COPPIN (1837-1913)
Educator, writer, humanist, missionary. A former slave, she graduated from Oberlin College in 1865. Principal, Institute for Colored Youth, 1869-1902. (I.C.Y. became Cheyney University, 1983.) Coppin pioneered industrial arts and teacher education.

City type: Cheyney University campus, off Dilworthtown & Cheyney Rds., Cheyney. Dedicated Feb. 12, 1986.

65 COLONIAL GRISTMILL
The stone gristmill at this site was built in 1704 by Nathaniel Newlin, a Quaker who emigrated from Ireland in 1683. The mill, restored to working order, is a fine example of vital segment of Colonial economic life.

US 1, 1 mile E of Concordville. Erected May 5, 1959.

66 MINQUAS' PATH
Near here the trading path leading westward to the Susquehannock Indians crossed Ridley Creek. Thousands of beaver skins were sent yearly to the first Dutch and Swedish posts on the Delaware by this route.

SR 3019 (Rose Valley Rd.) just S of Media borough line. Erected Oct. 13, 1947.

66 [GREAT TRAIL OF THE MINQUAS]
The Great Trail, Minquas or Susquehanna Indians, Susquehanna to the Schuylkill, crossed Ridley Creek at Long Point, 484 yards to the south. Thousands of beaver skins yearly were carried down to the first Dutch and Swedish settlers on the Delaware. Marked by the Pennsylvania Historical Commission and the Borough of Rose Valley, 1926.

Plaque: W side, SR 3019 (Rose Valley Rd.) .5 mile S of Moylan-Rose Valley railroad station near Media. Dedicated June 5, 1926.

(The "Great Trail" monument, featuring a bronze statue of a beaver near its base, was the work of the Philadelphia sculptor Albert Laessle. A large plaque, 41 inches high and 24½ inches wide, includes a bas-relief depiction by Charles H. Stevens of a procession of Minqua Indians carrying beaver skins on the trail.)

67 BENJAMIN WEST
Famous American painter; born in this house, Oct. 10, 1738. Best known for the picture, "Penn's Treaty with the Indians." Died 1820, in Europe, where he had lived since 1759.

PA 320 in Swarthmore. Erected Mar. 3, 1948.

67 J. EDGAR THOMSON (1808-1874)
Here was born the first chief engineer, Pennsylvania Railroad, 1847-52, and its third president, 1852-74. He was responsible for construction of the main line, Harrisburg to Pittsburgh, and for the system's expansion to the Mississippi River.

City type: junction SR 2016 (Baltimore Pike) & SR 2027 (Thomson Ave.) just NE of Swarthmore. Dedicated June 25, 1991.

68 SPRINGFIELD FRIENDS MEETING
Site of Friends' meeting since 1686. Present building erected, 1851. A school and library were established here in 1832. Benjamin West, noted American artist, attended this Meeting when he was a boy.

SR 2009 (Old Sproul & W. Springfield Rds.), Springfield. Erected Oct. 27, 1951.

69 LOWER SWEDISH CABIN
The only remaining log cabin of its type, among several once located on Darby Creek. Evidently built by Swedish settlers who came to this area after 1638. Used by the early Philadelphia filmmaker, Siegmund Lubin, as the site for several pre-1910 motion pictures.

City type: at site on Creek Rd., Clifton Heights. Dedicated Oct. 21, 1989.

70 DR. GEORGE SMITH (1804-1882)
A doctor, judge, scientist, and State Senator, Smith came to Collenbrook in 1829 upon his marriage to Mary Lewis, heir to this eighteenth-century family estate. He was a founder of the Delaware County Institute of Science and author of the 1862 "History of Delaware County." While a Senator, as chairman of the Education Committee, he drafted the 1836 law providing for this State's first public school code.

W end Marvine Ave., Drexel Hill. Dedicated Oct. 25, 1985.

71 SELLERS HALL
First permanent home in Upper Darby, built about 1684 by Samuel Sellers who occupied it with his bride, Anna Gibbons. Their son, Samuel Sellers, Jr., was the first of many family members active in mechanical and scientific pursuits. Birthplace of John Sellers, a founder of the American Philosophical Society. In 1769 he served on a select committee that observed the planet Venus in its passage across the sun.
N side Walnut St. between Copley & Glendale Rds., Upper Darby. Dedicated Oct. 25, 1985.

71 ABRAHAM L. PENNOCK
This prominant abolitionist and patron of the arts resided here at Hoodland until his death in 1868. The home had been built in 1823 by his father-in-law, John Sellers II. A leader in the Pennsylvania Anti-Slavery Society, Abraham Pennock also was an advocate of woman suffrage and active in the temperance movement. Notable visitors to his home included John Greenleaf Whittier and James Russell Lowell.
76 S. State Rd. (SR 2026), Upper Darby. Dedicated Oct. 25, 1985.

72 THOMAS MASSEY HOUSE
A fine example of early Pennsylvania rural architecture. Brick section was built before 1708 by Thomas Massey, who by 1696 was owner of a 300-acre "plantation" here. An earlier central wooden section was replaced by stone about 1730 by his son. Original wood kitchen replaced by stone about 1800. Room above kitchen added sixty years later. The house was deeded in 1964 to Marple Township and was restored.
467 Lawrence Rd. (SR 1020), .5 mile NE of PA 320. Dedicated May 9, 1986.

73 OLD HAVERFORD FRIENDS' MEETING
This site has been a center for Friends' activities since 1684. The older section of the present structure, since remodeled, was built in 1700 as an addition to the original log meeting house where William Penn worshiped in the eleventh month, 1699.
SR 1005 (E. Eagle Rd.) at St. Denis Ave., Havertown. Erected Oct. 24, 1975 (revised 1947 marker).

74 JOSHUA HUMPHREY
Designer of the frigate Constitution, "Old Ironsides," lived 1803-38 in the Pont Reading House, which stands opposite. The present house was built at dates from 1683 to 1813.
SR 1001 (Haverford Ave.) near Haverford. Erected Oct. 13, 1947.

75 RADNOR MEETING HOUSE
A center of Friends' activities since 1686. The second house, built about 1721, served as an officers' house and a hospital for the Valley Forge encampment.
Junction PA 320 & SR 1019 (Conestoga Rd.), Ithan. Erected Oct. 13, 1947.

76 ST. DAVID'S CHURCH
Erected 1715 by Welsh Episcopalians, renovated 1871. Commemorated by Longfellow's poem. Final burial place of Gen. Anthony Wayne, whose remains were brought from Erie in 1809.
SR 1046 (St. David's Rd.) at SR 1017 (Church Rd.) 2 miles SW of Wayne. Erected Oct. 13, 1947.

Montgomery County

D MONTGOMERY COUNTY
Formed September 10, 1784 from Philadelphia County. A famed Revolutionary site of 1777-1778 was Valley Forge. Norristown, the county seat, was laid out 1784; incorporated in 1812. Noted for its industries, Montgomery became a major suburban county.
City type: Courthouse, Swede & Airy Sts., Norristown. Dedication pending.

77 JAMES A. BLAND
Buried in this cemetery is the famous minstrel, composer of "Carry Me Back to Old Virginny" and many other songs. Born on Long Island in 1854, he traveled widely but died in obscurity at Philadelphia in 1911.
City type: PA 23 (Conshohocken State Rd.), Bala Cynwyd. Erected Sept. 26, 1961.

78 EARLY TAVERN

Opened in 1704, this tavern was known in Colonial times as the William Penn Inn, the Tunis Ordinary and Streeper's Tavern. Familiar to Franklin and Washington, the inn was renamed, shortly after the Revolution, in honor of Gen. Wayne, who had lodged here.

General Wayne Inn, 625 Montgomery Ave., Narberth. Dedicated Sept. 14, 1972.

78 MERION FRIENDS MEETING

Continuously used since its erection in 1695 by Quakers, this Meeting House is thought to have been visited by William Penn. Welsh carpenters are believed responsible for its highly unusual cruciform architecture.

City type: 651 Montgomery Ave., Narberth. Erected Sept. 15, 1967.

79 CHARLES THOMSON

Secretary, for fourteen years, of the Continental Congress. Born in County Derry, Ireland, 1729. Died at his home, Harriton, 1824. The house stands a short way up this road.

SR 3034 (Morris Ave. at Harriton Rd.) NE of Bryn Mawr. Erected Sept. 10, 1947.

79 HARRITON

Built 1704 by Rowland Ellis; named by Richard Harrison, next owner. His son-in-law, Charles Thomson, Secretary of Continental Congress, lived here 1774 until his death in 1824.

City type: SR 3034 (Morris Ave. at Harriton Rd.) NE of Bryn Mawr. Erected June 12, 1963 (revised 1947 marker).

80 WOODROW WILSON

Educator, statesman, President. Here, at Bryn Mawr College, Wilson held his first teaching position. From 1885, when the college opened, until 1888, he taught history and politics in nearby Taylor Hall.

City type: New Gulph Rd., entrance to college, Bryn Mawr. Erected Nov. 1958.

81 GULPH MILLS ENCAMPMENT

The Continental army marched from Whitemarsh to Gulph Mills by way of Swedes ford, and encamped on nearby hills, Dec. 13-19, 1777. From here, the army moved to Valley Forge.

City type: PA 320 near intersection SR 3030 at Gulph Mills. Erected May 2, 1955.

81 GULPH MILLS VILLAGE

This house, built about 1780, was the old Bird-in-Hand General Store. Originally this area was named "Bird-in-Hand" for sign of a tavern that stood nearby. A building just SW of here was a forge. Like the store it later was converted into a residence.

City type: intersection PA 320 & SR 3039 (Gulph Rd.), Gulph Mills. Erected Nov. 9, 1982 (revised 1955 marker).

81 EARLY GRIST MILL

Just west of here is the site of mill built in 1747 by Abram Nanna. It supplied flour for the Continental army during its encampment at Valley Forge. Mill operated till 1895 when it was razed by fire.

City type: PA 320 at Gulph Mills. Erected May 2, 1955.

82 EDWARD HECTOR

Private in Captain Hercules Courtney's Company, Third Pa. Artillery, Continental Line, in the Battle of Brandywine. His home was in Conshohocken. He is symbolic of the many unknown Black soldiers who served in the American Revolution, but whose race is not mentioned in muster rolls.

Intersection SR 3016 & 3013 (Fayette & Hector Sts.), Conshohocken. Dedicated Sept. 19, 1976.

83 LAFAYETTE

On May 19-20, 1778, Lafayette, in his first independent command, occupied this position during reconnaissance with 2,000 troops, which were driven off by Howe's overwhelming British forces. On Howe's departure, Lafayette reoccupied Barren Hill until his recall to Valley Forge on May 23.

801 Ridge Pike (county highway), Barren Hill. Erected Oct. 7, 1980.

84 ST. PETER'S CHURCH

Lutheran, founded 1752 by Henry Melchior Muhlenberg. From steeple of original church, May 20, 1778, Gen. Lafayette gave orders for battle against British in old churchyard. Here he organized his famous retreat to Matson Ford, saving himself and 2200 Continental troops from capture.

Church Rd., off Germantown Pike (old US 422) 5 miles E of Norristown. Erected Nov. 9, 1963.

85 PLYMOUTH FRIENDS MEETINGHOUSE

In continuous use as a house of worship since about 1708, it served as a hospital and campsite for Washington's forces on way to Valley Forge. Eastern wing, added in 1780, replaced original log school. Site was a center of activity during Abolition Movement.

Germantown Pike (old US 422) & Butler Pike at Plymouth Meeting. Erected May 15, 1969.

86 HOPE LODGE

Built in mid-18th century, house is fine example of Georgian-period architecture. Administered by the Pennsylvania Historical and Museum Commission.

At site, Old Bethlehem Pike (SR 2018), Fort Washington. Erected Feb. 16, 1966.

87 WHITEMARSH

Here in the Emlen House Washington had his headquarters from Nov. 2 to Dec. 11, 1777, just before moving to Valley Forge. The last battle of this year was a British attack repulsed here on Dec. 5-6.

SR 2027 (Pennsylvania Ave.) just E of PA 309, SE of Fort Washington. Erected Dec. 22, 1947.

88 VILLAGE OF LA MOTT

Originally called Camptown, this village was laid out at the close of the Civil War on the site of former Camp William Penn. The camp was a training station for Negro troops enlisted in the U.S. Army from 1863 to 1865.

PA 309 (Cheltenham Ave.) just NW of PA 611, La Mott. Erected June 1973.

89 LUCRETIA C. MOTT

Nearby stood "Roadside," the home of the ardent Quakeress, Lucretia C. Mott (1793-1880). Her most notable work was in connection with antislavery, women's rights, temperance and peace.

PA 611 N of Cheltenham Ave., Elkins Park. Erected May 1974.

89 WALL HOUSE (THE IVY)

Original section, dated from 1682, was built by Richard Wall on land granted by William Penn. An early meeting place of the Society of Friends, 1683-1702. Additions were built about 1725 and 1800. Sarah Wall married George Shoemaker, 1694, and their descendants lived here to 1847. Purchased from the Bosler family, 1932, by Cheltenham Township.

Wall Park Dr. & Church Rd., Elkins Park. Dedicated Nov. 21, 1982.

90 BRYN ATHYN CATHEDRAL

This Swedenborgian center is noted architecturally. Buildings in 14th-century Gothic and 12th-century Romanesque styles. Built by cooperative craft guilds in medieval way. Endowed by John Pitcairn.

PA 232 in Bryn Athyn at Cathedral. Erected Sept. 10, 1947.

90 HAROLD F. PITCAIRN

The noted aeronautical pioneer established his first flying field on this site in 1924. The 1930 Collier Trophy, an award for accomplishments in aviation, was presented to Pitcairn and his associates for developing the American autogiro, first introduced here.

Buck & Paper Mill Rds., Bryn Athyn. Dedicated Apr. 29, 1972.

91 CROOKED BILLET

Named for a tavern once standing nearby. Scene of Revolutionary War clash during British occupation of Philadelphia. Militia of Gen. John Lacey, assigned to cut off British supplies, encamped here on May 1, 1778, when, surprised by British troops, they were defeated and driven off with heavy losses.

Meadowbrook Ave. at Crooked Billet Elementary School in Hatboro. Dedicated May 1, 1965.

92 KEITH HOUSE
Built 1722 by Sir William Keith, Lieutenant Governor of the Province of Pennsylvania, 1717-1726. Also called Graeme Park, for Dr. Thomas Graeme, owner after 1737.

SR 2038 (County Line Rd.) 1 mile NW of PA 611. Erected [1947].

92 GRAEME PARK
Estate, 1718-1737, of Sir William Keith, Pennsylvania Governor. Administered by the Pennsylvania Historical and Museum Commission.

At site SR 2038 (County Line Rd.) 1 mile NW of PA 611. Erected [1965].

93 WINFIELD S. HANCOCK
Outstanding Civil War general and hero of the Battle of Gettysburg, was born here Feb. 14, 1824. After 1828 he lived in Norristown, where he is buried.

PA 309 S of Montgomeryville. Erected Sept. 11, 1947.

94 RITTENHOUSE FARM
David Rittenhouse, born in 1732, lived here until 1770. Here he began his distinguished scientific career; and computed and observed the transit of Venus, 1769. Spent later years in Philadelphia, where he died in 1796.

Germantown Pike (former US 422) at Valley Forge Medical Center, 6 miles SE of Collegeville. Erected Mar. 14, 1949.

95 GEN. ANDREW PORTER
Revolutionary War officer; surveyor of western and northern State boundaries, 1784-87; Surveyor-General, 1809-13. Born near here, 1743; died at Harrisburg, 1813. His home, "Selma," is marked, a block distant.

W. Main & Selma Sts., Norristown. Erected Mar. 11, 1949.

95 SELMA
Home of Andrew Porter, Revolutionary general. Birthplace of his sons: David R., Gov. of Penna., 1839-45; James M., Sec. of War. 1843; George B., Gov. of Michigan Territory, 1831-34.

W. Airy St. in Norristown. Erected Mar. 15, 1949.

96 RITTENHOUSE FARM
David Rittenhouse, colonial scientist, astronomer, and instrument maker, lived on a nearby farm, where he built a telescope, said to be first made in America, and observed the transit of Venus in 1769.

PA 363 E of Eagleville, intersection SR 3009 (Ridge Pike) & 3002 (Trooper Rd.). Erected Sept. 3, 1947.

97 MILL GROVE
Originally built in 1762, the mansion later became the first home in America of the noted artist, naturalist and author John James Audubon (1785-1851). Here, he began his studies of American birds and wildlife, which he portrayed so vividly in his numerous realistic paintings. The site is now owned and operated by the County of Montgomery.

Entrance Audubon Wildlife Sanctuary, Audubon & Pawlings Rds. (SR 4041 & 4004), Audubon. Erected Oct. 9, 1970.

97 COL. TIMOTHY MATLACK
Noted for his fine penmanship, Matlack probably inscribed the Declaration of Independence on parchment in 1776. Commanding the "Shirt Battalion" during the Revolution, he engaged in battle against the troops of England. Matlack died April 14, 1829, and is buried nearby.

Pawlings Rd. (SR 4004) near Audubon Rd. (SR 4041) at Audubon. Erected June 4, 1969.

98 PERKIOMEN BRIDGE
Built in 1799, it is one of the oldest bridges still in use in the State. A lottery was authorized by a 1797 law to raise $20,000 for its construction.

SR 4031 (old US 422) at bridge E end Collegeville. Erected Sept. 4, 1947.

99 MUHLENBERG HOUSE
In this house Henry Melchior Muhlenberg, great Lutheran leader, lived from 1776 until his death in 1787. His son Peter Muhlenberg, a noted general of the American Revolution, lived here 1783-1802.

City type: 201 Main St. (old US 422), Trappe. Erected Apr. 28, 1960.

99 MUHLENBERG HOME
Large house to the SE built by Henry Melchior Muhlenberg, 1745. Of 11 children, 8 were born here, among them Peter, Revolutionary General, Congressman; Frederick A., 1st Speaker, U.S. House, 1st Judge, Montgomery County Court; Henry Ernest, botanist, 1st President of Franklin College, Lancaster.
E. 7th Ave., Trappe, .3 mile from Main St. (old US 422). Erected Oct. 3, 1963.

99 AUGUSTUS LUTHERAN CHURCH
Oldest unchanged Lutheran church in America. Built in 1743 by Dr. Henry Melchior Muhlenberg, who died in 1787 and is buried in the graveyard.
Main St. (old US 422) in Trappe. Erected Sept. 3, 1947.

100 JOHN F. HARTRANFT
The birthplace of John F. Hartranft, Civil War hero and Pennsylvania Governor, 1873-79, is to the right on the side road. He reorganized the State Militia as part of the National Guard.
Sanatoga Rd. (former LR 46007) SW of Fagleysville. Erected May 6, 1947.

101 JOHN F. HARTRANFT
Governor of Pennsylvania, 1873-79, and Civil War general, was born Dec. 6, 1830, about three miles distant. The house is still standing.
SR 4031 (High St., old US 422), Sanatoga. Erected Sept. 4, 1947.

102 FIRST IRON BRIDGE
The first iron truss bridge in the U.S. was built in 1845 in the Philadelphia & Reading Railroad blacksmith shop, just south of here. It was designed for the railroad in 1844 by Richard B. Osborne.
City type: SE corner, High & S. York Sts., Pottstown. Erected May 21, 1953.

102 POTTSGROVE
Built in 1752 by John Potts, Ironmaker, Washington's headquarters for five days — Sept. 1777. Administererd by the Pennsylvania Historical and Museum Commission.
At site on W. High St., Pottstown. Erected [1948].

103 FALKNER SWAMP REFORMED CHURCH
This congregation is the oldest in continuous existence in the Evangelical and Reformed Church. Organized October 15, 1725, by Rev. John Philip Boehm, founder of the German Reformed Church in Pennsylvania. Present building was constructed in 1790.
Swamp Pike (county highway, Limerick to Gilbertsville) .5 mile SE of New Hanover. Dedicated Oct. 9, 1960.

103 NEW HANOVER LUTHERAN CHURCH
The first German Lutheran Church in America; organized by Daniel Falckner about 1700. From 1742 to 1761 Henry Melchior Muhlenberg served as pastor. Present building, one-quarter mile NE, was erected in 1767.
Swamp Pike (county highway, Limerick to Gilbertsville) .2 mile SE of New Hanover. Erected Sept. 9, 1950.

104 NEW GOSCHENHOPPEN REFORMED CHURCH
Organized as a congregation in 1727 with George Michael Weiss as first pastor. Of the Reformed Churches in the U.S., it has the oldest existing register. Ancestors of Gov. John S. Fisher are among the many pioneer settlers buried in the first churchyard.
SR 1042 (Church Rd.) W of East Greenville. Erected Aug. 26, 1952.

Philadelphia County

E PHILADELPHIA
Founded by William Penn. Laid out in 1682. Chartered a city, 1701. Pennsylvania's capital until 1799; the nation's to 1800. County was one of Pennsylvania's original three, formed 1682 and consolidated with city in 1854. Name means "City of Brotherly Love."
City type: N. Broad St. (PA 611) & John F. Kennedy Blvd., just N of City Hall. Dedicated Dec. 6, 1982.

105 FORT MIFFLIN
Laid out in 1771 by the engineer John Montresor. Heroically held by the Americans under British siege until they were forced out, Nov. 15, 1777. Rebuilt 1798-1800 according to L'Enfant's design and enlarged in the 19th century. A U.S. military post until the 1950s.
City type: at site near Fort Mifflin Rd. Dedicated May 10, 1990.

106 JOHN BARTRAM (1699-1777)
Famed natural scientist. Had the first botanic garden in the U.S. for receiving plants of America and exotics. He was American botanist to king of England and member of several royal societies. House and garden are ¼ mile east.
City type: Lindbergh Blvd. at 54th Dr., West Philadelphia. Erected June 6, 1955.

107 PHILADELPHIA COLLEGE OF PHARMACY AND SCIENCE
Founded in 1821 at historic Carpenters' Hall by prominent apothecaries to improve the standards of pharmacy, the College was incorporated the following year. It is the oldest institution of its kind in the United States.
At entrance, 43rd St. & Kingsessing Ave., West Philadelphia. Dedicated Jan. 4, 1971.

107 PAUL ROBESON (1898-1976)
A Rutgers athlete and Columbia law graduate, Robeson won renown as a singer and actor. He was a noted interpretor of Negro spirituals. His career suffered because of his political activism, and he lived his last years here in retirement.
City type: 4951 Walnut St. Dedicated Apr. 8, 1991.

108 GLORIA DEI CHURCH (OLD SWEDES')
Oldest church in Philadelphia. Founded, 1677, by Swedish settlers. This edifice, of Swedish architectural design, was erected 1698-1703. The earlier place of worship was a blockhouse.
City type: 916 Swanson St., near Delaware Ave. & Christian St. Erected Dec. 17, 1954.

108 U.S.S. UNITED STATES
First vessel completed for new U.S. Navy. Frigate was launched near here May 10, 1797. Flagship of Capt. John Barry; builder was Joshua Humphreys. In 1812, under Capt. Stephen Decatur, Jr., occurred its celebrated capture of H.M.S. Macedonian. Vessel scrapped at Norfolk, 1866.
City type: S end Penns Landing (S of Port of History Museum). Dedicated Oct. 16, 1983.

108 STEPHEN DECATUR
Famed U.S. Navy officer. Born 1779 in Maryland, he grew up in a house on this site. Celebrated for his role in the Tripolitan War, 1804; capture of H.M.S. Macedonian, 1812; and the subduing of the Barbary powers, 1815. Killed in a duel in 1820. Buried, St. Peter's Church.
City type: 600 block, S. Front St. Erected Oct. 21, 1988.

108 ROBERT SMITH
Here stood the home of colonial Philadelphia's leading architect and builder. Born Jan. 14, 1722 at Dalkeith, Scotland, he died Feb. 11, 1777. Among his buildings are the Christ Church steeple, St. Peter's Church, the Walnut Street Prison, and Carpenters' Hall.
City type: 606 S. 2nd St. Dedicated Jan. 14, 1983.

108 FEDERAL STREET BURIAL GROUND
Congregation Mikveh Israel's second cemetery, founded 1849. Here are buried Abraham Hart the publisher; Alfred Mordecai, soldier and engineer; Dr. Sabato Morais, rabbi and educator; Judge Mayer Sulzberger; and noted Civil War veterans.
City type: Federal St. between 11th & 12th Sts. Dedicated Oct. 4, 1990.

108 HENRY GEORGE
The famous American economist was born here, September 2, 1839. His book "Progress and Proverty" sold in the millions. Tax socially produced land values, he urged, instead of individually produced labor and capital. He died 1897 in New York.
City type: 413 S. 10th St. Dedicated Nov. 18, 1984.

PENNSYLVANIA HOSPITAL
This is the first hospital in the U.S. Chartered by Colonial Assembly in 1751 for "relief of the sick poor." Benjamin Franklin and Dr. Thomas Bond were its chief founders. First building, erected in 1755, is still used.
City type: Pine St. between 8th & 9th Sts. Erected Dec. 17, 1954.

Pennsylvania Hospital, Philadelphia

 ## MIKVEH ISRAEL CEMETERY
Founded 1740. Notables buried here include Nathan Levy, whose ship brought the Liberty Bell to America; Haym Salomon, Revolutionary patriot; the Gratz family; and Aaron Levy, founder of Aaronsburg.
City type: Spruce St. between Schell & Darien Sts. Erected 1957.

 ## THADDEUS KOSCIUSZKO
After serving as a military engineer during the American Revolution, he later led an uprising in his native Poland. Exiled, the General resided in this house from November, 1797, to May, 1798.
City type: NW corner 3rd & Pine Sts. Dedicated Oct. 22, 1967.

 ## JAMES FORTEN (1766-1842)
A wealthy sailmaker who employed multi-racial craftsmen, Forten was a leader of the African-American community in Philadelphia and a champion of reform causes. The American Antislavery Society was organized in his house here in 1833.
City type: 336 Lombard St. Dedicated April 24, 1990.

 ## [JOHN PENN'S HOME]
On this site was the home, 1766-1771, of John Penn (1729-1795) last colonial Governor of Pennsylvania, son of Richard Penn and grandson of William Penn the Founder. Also the home, 1771-1810, of Benjamin Chew (1722-1810) last colonial Chief Justice of Pennsylvania. Marked by the Pennsylvania Historical Commission and the Colonial Dames of America Chapter II, Philadelphia, 1932.
Plaque: 242 S. 3rd St. Dedicated [October] 1932.

 ## BENJAMIN FRANKLIN (1706-1790)
Printer, author, inventor, diplomat, philanthropist, statesman, and scientist. The eighteenth century's most illustrious Pennsylvanian built a house in Franklin Court starting in 1763, and here he lived the last five years of his life.
City type: Chestnut St. between 3rd & 4th Sts. at Independence National Historical Park. Dedicated June 30, 1990.

 ## THE PHILADELPHIA CONTRIBUTIONSHIP for the Insurance of Houses from Loss by Fire
Oldest fire insurance company in America. Founded in 1752 by Benjamin Franklin and his friends.
City type: 212 S. 4th St. Erected Dec. 17, 1954.

108 AFRICAN ZOAR METHODIST EPISCOPAL CHURCH

Founded here in 1794 by 15 men and three women from St. George's Church, led by Rev. Harry Hosier. Zoar was active in the Underground Railroad and moved to 12th and Melon Streets in 1883. It is United Methodism's oldest Black congregation.

City type: 4th & Brown Sts. Dedicated June 2, 1990

108 ST. THOMAS' AFRICAN EPISCOPAL CHURCH

Organized in 1792 as an outgrowth of the Free African Society, formed 1787. The original church edifice stood here. Under the ministry of the Rev. Absalom Jones (1746-1818), a former slave, this became the nation's first Black Episcopal church.

City type: 5th St. S of St. James Pl. Dedicated Sept. 30, 1984.

108 MOTHER BETHEL A.M.E. CHURCH

Founded on ground purchased by Richard Allen in 1787, this congregation is the mother church of the African Methodist Episcopal denomination. The present structure, erected 1889, replaces three earlier churches on this site.

City type: 6th & Lombard Sts. Dedicated Mar. 19, 1991.

108 RICKETTS' CIRCUS

America's first circus building was opened here at 12th and Market Streets, April 3, 1793. On that day the English equestrian John Bill Ricketts gave America's first complete circus performance. President Washington attended his show later that season.

City type: 12th & Market Sts., PSFS Plaza. Dedicated July 15, 1983.

108 OLDEST PHOTOGRAPH

America's earliest surviving photograph was made here about Sept. 25, 1839. Using a cigar box and crude lens, Joseph Saxton of the U.S. Mint created an image of Central High School (now demolished) shortly after Daguerre had announced his process in France.

City type: Market & Juniper Sts. Dedicated Sept. 25, 1989; erection pending.

108 KAHAL KADOSH MIKVEH ISRAEL

In 1782 this congregation built Philadelphia's first synagogue at this site. Established about 1740, it had first worshiped in rented quarters here. The congregation erected a larger building in 1824 and has been elsewhere in the city since 1860.

City type: Cherry at Orianna St., between 3rd & 4th Sts. Dedicated late 1991.

108 FRIENDS MEETING

This meetinghouse was erected in 1804. It is used for weekly, Monthly, Quarterly, and Yearly Meetings of Friends. The ground was first used for burial purposes under patent issued by William Penn in 1701.

City type: Arch St. between 3rd & 4th Sts. Erected Dec. 17, 1954.

108 PRESBYTERIAN CHURCH IN THE U.S.A.

Here, in its first General Assembly held May 21-24, 1789, the Presbyterian denomination in America was formally organized on a national basis. This took place in the city's Second Presbyterian Church, which was at this site from 1750 to 1837.

City type: Arch St. near 3rd St. Erected July 1989 .

108 CHRIST CHURCH

Founded, 1695. Erection of present building begun in 1727. Bells were brought from England in 1754. Among the noted persons buried here are James Wilson and Robert Morris, signers of the Declaration of Independence, and Bishop White.

City type: 2nd St. between Market & Arch Sts. Erected Dec. 17, 1954.

108 PENN TREATY PARK

Traditional site of a treaty between William Penn and the Indians, this park is maintained by the City of Philadelphia in commemoration of the Proprietor's peaceful relations with the Indians.

At park on Delaware River, foot of Cecil B. Moore (Columbia) Ave. Dedicated Sept. 18, 1976.

108 ST. JOHN NEUMANN

Here lie the remains of the first male American saint, canonized in 1977. Born 1811 in Bohemia, he came to the U.S. in 1836. A devoted Redemptorist priest, he became fourth Bishop of Philadelphia, 1852, and set up nation's first Catholic diocesan school system. Died, 1860.

City type: 5th St. & Girard Ave., St. Peter's Church. Dedicated Mar. 28, 1981.

109 FREEDOM THEATRE

Formerly the home of actor Edwin Forrest, later Philadelphia School of Design for Women. Became Heritage House, then in 1968, Freedom Theatre, a community-based Black theater for professional instruction in the theatrical arts.

City type: 1346 N. Broad St. (PA 611). Dedicated May 16, 1991.

109 BEREAN INSTITUTE

Founded in 1899 by Rev. Matthew Anderson, pastor of Berean Presbyterian Church and founder of Berean Savings Association, this school taught Blacks skilled trades not available elsewhere. Later the curriculum was expanded to meet changing student needs.

City type: 1901 W. Girard Ave. Dedicated Oct. 17, 1990.

109 OPPORTUNITIES INDUSTRIALIZATION CENTERS

Established here in an abandoned jailhouse in 1964, O.I.C. was founded by Rev. Leon H. Sullivan and achieved worldwide recognition as a self-help vocational training center for Blacks which opened job opportunities formerly closed to them.

City type: 19th & Oxford Sts. Dedicated Nov. 23, 1990.

109 JULIAN FRANCIS ABELE (1881-1950)

The first Black graduate of the University of Pennsylvania's School of Architecture, Abele was the chief designer for the nationally known architectural firm of Horace Trumbauer, whose commissions during Abele's career included the Philadelphia Museum of Art and the Free Library of Philadelphia on Logan Square.

Philadelphia Museum of Art, 26th St. & Franklin Pkwy. Dedicated Feb. 12, 1991.

109 JOHN W. COLTRANE (1926-1967)

A pioneering African-American jazz musician, composer, saxophonist. Coltrane used African and Indian elements to create a distinctive style which at first shocked audiences but ultimately gained wide acceptance. He lived here, 1952-1958.

City type: 1511 N. 33rd St. Dedicated July 17, 1990.

109 HENRY O. TANNER (1859-1937)

While living here, Tanner studied at the Pennsylvania Academy of the Fine Arts. His earlier works portrayed the ordinary lives of African-Americans. After moving to Paris, Tanner painted religious subjects and won international acclaim.

City type: 2908 W. Diamond St. Dedicated Jan. 19, 1991.

110 PHILADELPHIA COLLEGE OF TEXTILES AND SCIENCE

Present campus of America's first textile college. Founded as the Philadelphia Textile School in 1884, it provided needed technical education to improve the manufacture and quality of domestic fabrics.

Campus, School House Ln. near Henry Ave., Germantown. Erected May 16, 1969.

110 RITTENHOUSE TOWN

William Rittenhouse, first Mennonite minister in America, erected here in 1690 the colonies' first paper mill. Successive generations of Rittenhouses built additional mills, establishing this region as the center of American papermaking. By the 1850s this village had over 40 buildings, and seven early buildings survive from this once prosperous industrial community. Scientist David Rittenhouse was born here in 1732.

Lincoln Dr. at Rittenhouse St. just off Wissahickon Ave., Fairmount Park. Dedicated Apr. 8, 1991.

111 PRINCE HALL GRAND LODGE
Masonic lodge named for Rev. Prince Hall, founder of Freemasonry among
African-Americans. The first Grand Master of African Masonry was Absalom
Jones, organizer in 1797 of Philadelphia's first lodge, the African Lodge of Free
Masons.
City type: 4301 N. Broad St. (PA 611). Dedicated Sept. 8, 1990.

112 FIRST PROTEST AGAINST SLAVERY
Here in 1688, at the home of Tunes Kunders, an eloquent protest was written by
a group of German Quakers. Signed by Pastorius and three others, it preceded
by 92 years Pennsylvania's passage of the nation's first state abolition law.
City type: 5109 Germantown Ave. Dedicated Oct. 8, 1983.

113 [WILLIAM RITTENHOUSE]
The Mennonites arrived in Germantown, October 6, 1683. William Rittenhouse
was chosen their first minister in 1688. In 1689 he drew this number 19 lot, and
on it in 1691, he and his fellow-members built the "Little Log Church." In 1702
he donated part of lot, and later the present church lot and burial ground. He
was the first paper maker in America. Died in 1708, aged 64 years. Erected by the
Pennsylvania Historical Commission and the Rittenhouse Memorial Committee,
1919.
Plaque: Germantown Ave. between Herman & Pastorius Sts., Mennonite burial
ground. Dedicated July 12, 1919.

114 WISSAHICKON INN
Opened May 30, 1884 by the industrialist Henry H. Houston as a 250-room
summer resort hotel. The architects were G.W. and W.D. Hewitt. Since 1898 the
Inn has served Chestnut Hill Academy (founded 1850) which acquired
ownership, 1940.
City type: Springfield Ave., front of Inn, Chestnut Hill Academy. Dedicated June
14, 1988.

Under a specially funded project, State historical markers pertaining to
various aspects of African-American history are being erected in the city of
Philadelphia. Texts for several of these markers — dedicated through May
1991 — appear in this edition of the *Guide.* The others will be included in
future editions.

REGION II

The First Line of Defense

Astride the Blue and Kittatinny mountains, easternmost of the Appalachians in Pennsylvania, are *Carbon, Monroe* and *Schuylkill* counties (on the north) and *Berks, Lehigh* and *Northampton* (on the south), two tiers of counties joined by the Schuylkill and Lehigh rivers.

The early record, particularly that of the communities of Bethlehem and Nazareth, reverberates with the history of the Moravian Church and its mission to the Indians, and with the journeys of peace envoys on the Tulpehocken Path between the house at Womelsdorf of Conrad Weiser, ambassador to the natives, and the Indian town of Shamokin (now Sunbury), where Chief Shickellamy, their representative, had his seat.

Although the peace was skillfully contrived by William Penn and by the Provincial government, guided by the peace witness of the Society of Friends, it was overclouded after 1737 by the Indians' notorious land cession known as the Walking Purchase. Finally, in 1755 the French-led upheaval and the killings of Moravian Indians at the town of Gnadenhuetten evoked a militant change in Provincial policy, leading to the erection of the frontier forts.

Long after the Indian treaties (signed at Easton from 1756 to 1762) and General Sullivan's punitive Revolutionary War expedition (launched from Easton in 1779) had removed the

possibility of Indian attack, people from various nations began to enter Schuylkill and Carbon counties to mine the rich deposits of anthracite coal. Meanwhile, Monroe, the most southeastern county of the Pocono region, received its settlers mostly from New England; apart from lumbering and a modicum of farming, its principal commodity became recreation.

To the south, in Berks, Lehigh and Northampton, farming has combined with manufacturing and the extraction of natural resources to drive the economy. Iron furnaces and forges have given way to the quarrying of limestone, the manufacture of portland cement — begun in Lehigh County in 1871 — and the extraction of slate. These counties were first settled by the English, many of them Quakers, and then in greater number by Germans, many of them of the plainer sects.

To reach markets, such canals as the Union, the Delaware, and the Lehigh and such railroads as the Lehigh Valley and the Reading were built. Industry brought fame to such founders as Thomas Rutter in iron; David O. Saylor in portland cement; and Robert M. Jones in slate; to Asa Packer, builder of the Lehigh Valley Railroad and Lehigh University; to Charles E. Duryea, Reading's automobile inventor and builder; and to others.

Homesteads of the families of Daniel Boone and Abraham Lincoln, and the Friends Exeter Meeting, which they attended, are landmarks. Berks County was the home also of three governors and Northampton of another, all of whom reflected the Jeffersonian/ Jacksonian politics of the early republic. From Lehigh came a signer of the Declaration of Independence. Other notables also have distinguished the history of the region.

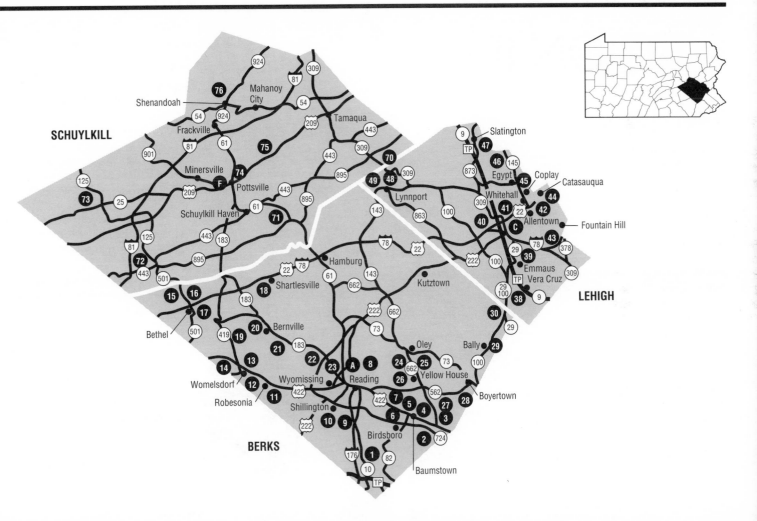

SCHUYLKILL

Shenandoah
Mahanoy City
76
Frackville
54
924
901
81
61
75
Minersville
74
F
Pottsville
73
25
209
Schuylkill Haven
71
125
81
125
443
183
895
72
443
501
15
16
895
183
18
Shartlesville
17
Bethel
501
419
20
Bernville
19
21
13
183
14
22
12
23
Womelsdorf
11
A
Robesonia
Wyomissing
8
Reading
Shillington
222
10
9
Birdsboro
176
1
82
10
TP
Baumstown

BERKS

924
81
309
54
54
Tamaqua
209
443
443
309
895
70
895
143
49
48
309
Lynnport
863
100
143
78
22
Hamburg
22
78
61
662
143
Kutztown
222
662
73
24
25
662
Oley
73
26
562
7
422
5
6
4
27
3
2
724

9
TP
47
Slatington
46
145
873
Egypt
Coplay
45
Catasauqua
Whitehall
44
41
22
42
40
309
C
Allentown
Fountain Hill
43
78
378
29
39
222
100
Emmaus
TP
Vera Cruz
29
100
309
38
9
30
29
Bally
29
100
28
Boyertown
Yellow House

LEHIGH

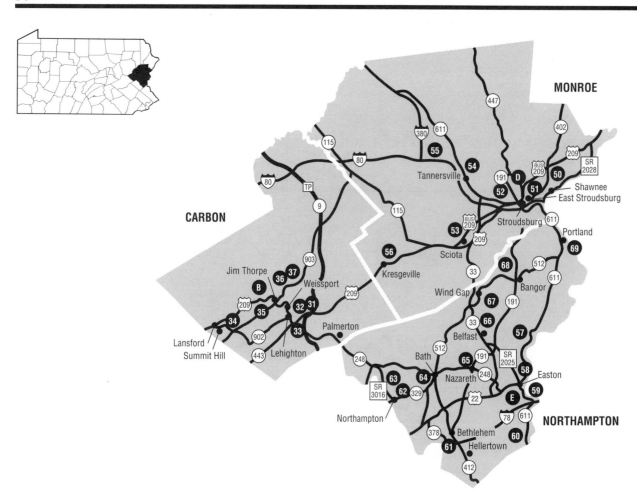

MONROE

CARBON

Tannersville

Shawnee
East Stroudsburg

Stroudsburg

Portland

Sciota

Jim Thorpe

Weissport

Kresgeville

Wind Gap

Bangor

Lansford

Summit Hill

Palmerton

Lehighton

Belfast

Bath

Nazareth

Easton

Northampton

Bethlehem
Hellertown

NORTHAMPTON

Berks County

(A) BERKS COUNTY

Formed March 11, 1752 from parts of Chester, Lancaster and Philadelphia counties. Named for Berkshire in England. County seat of Reading was made a borough in 1783, a city of 1847. The county's early ironworks gave rise to Pennsylvania's iron industry.

City type: Courthouse, N. 6th & Court Sts., Reading. Dedicated May 12, 1982.

(1) HOPEWELL VILLAGE

Forge built 1744 by Wm. Bird; furnace built 1770 by his son Mark. Furnace and other remains of an ironmaking community of the era, administered by the National Park Service, are about 7.5 miles away.

PA 10 S of Plowville. Erected Aug. 28, 1948.

Hopewell Village National Historic Site

National Park Service

(2) SWEDISH PIONEERS

First European settlers in present Berks County, on land granted by William Penn, 1704-5. The home of Mounce and Ingeborg Jones, built 1716 and the oldest house in the county, stands at the opposite end of the river bridge.

PA 724, 5 miles SE of Birdsboro. Erected Feb. 20, 1949.

(3) ANTHONY SADOWSKI

Polish pioneer, Indian trader, settled along Schuylkill River in this area, 1712. He served the Provincial Government as a messenger-interpreter during negotiations with Indian tribes in 1728. He was buried, 1736, in graveyard of St. Gabriel's Church.

US 422 eastbound near graveyard, Douglassville. Dedicated Sept. 18, 1966.

(4) DANIEL BOONE (1734-1820)

Famous pioneer and wilderness scout, who lived in this area his first 16 years. Born 3 miles northwest on site of Daniel Boone Homestead, State historical shrine.

Plaque: US 422, 2 miles SE of Baumstown. Replacement erected 1957.

(5) DANIEL BOONE HOMESTEAD

Site of the birthplace of Daniel Boone on Nov. 2, 1734, and his home until 1750. Administered by the Pennsylvania Historical and Museum Commission.

SR 2041 (former LR 06107) N of Baumstown at site. Erected [1948].

(6) [WILLIAM PENN'S FARTHEST NORTH]

William Penn on his first visit to America, 1682-1684, came farthest north on Schuylkill River fifty miles up from the Falls of Schuylkill to or near the mouth of Monocacy Creek three fourths of a mile south-west of this marker. Marked by the Pennsylvania Historical Commission and the Historical Society of Berks County, 1926.

Plaque: US 422, .8 mile SE of Baumstown. Dedicated Nov. 13, 1926 ca. 1 mile E of present site; relocated Oct. 6, 1945.

6 ## DANIEL BOONE
Greatest American pioneer and wilderness scout. Born Nov. 2, 1734. Spent the first 16 years of his life on the Boone Homestead a few miles north. Now a State historical shrine dedicated to American youth.

US 422 westbound at SR 2041 just E of Baumstown; US 422 eastbound at Baumstown Union Sunday School. Erected Apr. 1, 1947.

6 ## HOPEWELL VILLAGE
Hopewell Forge, 1744, and Furnace, 1770, were seven miles south. The furnace and the remains of an ironmaking community of the era are administered by the National Park Service, with recreation areas.

US 422 east & westbound at PA 82, Baumstown. Erected Mar. 29, 1947.

7 ## LINCOLN HOMESTEAD
Abraham Lincoln once said, ''My ancestors were Quakers from Berks County, Pennsylvania.'' The stone house, still standing, built by his great-great-grandfather in 1733, is just south of here.

US 422 at twp. road (former LR 06185) E of Mount Penn. Erected Mar. 29, 1947.

Entering Reading

8 ## READING
Laid out 1748 by direction of Thomas Penn. Seat of Berks County since 1752. Incorporated borough, 1783. Soon became, and has remained, center of the Pennsylvania-Dutch area. An old and progressive industrial community.

On main highways leading into city. Erected 1948.

8 ## HESSIAN CAMP
After Burgoyne's surrender, 1777, German mercenaries, mostly Hessian, were held prisoners at various places until end of war. Those brought to Reading, 1781, were encamped until 1783 in huts on the hillside a quarter-mile to the north.

Mineral Spring Rd. (Business US 422 westbound) at 18th St., Reading. Erected Oct. 1949.

8 ## DURYEA DRIVE
Named in honor of Charles E. Duryea, inventor and builder of first successful hill-climbing gasoline automobile in U.S. Duryea Drive, extending from City Park to the Pagoda, is the course used by Duryea for testing his cars, 1900-1907.

Intersection Clymer & 13th Sts. at Park Dr., Reading. Erected May 17, 1951.

8 ## PENN'S COMMON
Given in common to the citizens of Reading, in 1748, by the family of William Penn.

City type: Perkiomen Ave. (Business US 422 westbound) at 11th & Penn Sts., Reading. Erected Feb. 16, 1951.

8 ## THOMPSON'S RIFLE BATTALION: CAPT. GEORGE NAGEL'S COMPANY
With men enlisted from Berks County, Nagel's Company was a part of the first battalion in the colonies authorized by Congress, in June 1775. After gathering at Reading the following month, this company and other companies of the battalion marched approximately 350 miles in order to join the American siege of Boston.

Historical society, 940 Centre Ave. (Pa. 61), Reading. Dedicated Nov. 4, 1989.

8 ## SKEW BRIDGE
Regarded best example of skew bridge in U.S. Designed by Richard Osborn for the P.&.R. Railroad in 1857. Each course of the arch of forty feet is laid in ellipsoidal curve, each stone properly curved. There is no keystone.

City type: N. 6th St. at railroad bridge, Reading. Erected Mar. 1951.

8 ## HUNTER LIGGETT
Born here March 21, 1857. A graduate of West Point, 1879. He held commands in the Philippines, 1899-1901 and 1915-17, and rose to the rank of Lt. Gen. in 1918. On Oct. 16, 1918, he succeeded Gen. Pershing as head of the American First Army in Europe. Died, San Francisco, 1935.

City type: 145 S. 6th St., Reading. Dedicated Dec. 30, 1984.

8 DR. JONATHAN POTTS

On this site was the house occupied by Dr. Jonathan Potts; Deputy Director General, 1777-1780, of Northern and Middle Departments of the Continental Army.

City type: 545 Penn St., Penn Sq., Reading. Erected Feb. 16, 1951.

8 DR. BODO OTTO

Site of the home of Dr. Bodo Otto, Military Surgeon in Continental Army, 1775-82. Served as Surgeon-in-Chief at Valley Forge, 1777-78. Physician and Surgeon of the Continental Hospitals. Died, 1787.

City type: 525 Penn St., Penn Sq., Reading. Erected Feb. 16, 1951.

8 CONRAD WEISER TRADING POST

A hewn-log building, erected on this site about 1750; operated until 1760 by Conrad Weiser, distinguished pioneer settler, treaty maker, Indian agent and interpreter, and first Berks County lay judge.

City type: 505 Penn St., Penn Sq., Reading. Erected Feb. 16, 1951

8 WILLIAM STRONG

Eminent jurist; Member State Supreme Court, 1857-1868; Associate Justice of the Supreme Court of U.S., 1870-80; Member Electoral Commission, 1877. His law office and home stood on this site. Died, 1895.

City type: NW corner, 5th & Court Sts. just N of Penn St., Reading. Erected Feb. 16, 1951.

8 FEDERAL INN

Site of Federal Inn, erected about 1754. George Washington, with military escort, was a guest here, October, 1794, when on his way to muster an armed force to suppress the Whiskey Rebellion.

City type: 445 Penn St., Penn Sq., Reading. Erected Feb. 16, 1951.

8 HIESTER HOME

Site of house occupied by Joseph Hiester from about 1792 until his death, 1832; a Lt. Col. in Continental Army, Delegate to Provincial Convention in 1776; Member of Congress for 14 years; Governor of Pennsylvania, 1820-23.

City type: 439 Penn St., Penn Sq., Reading. Erected Feb. 16, 1951.

8 HENRY A. MUHLENBERG

Pastor of the Trinity Lutheran Church from 1803 to 1829; member of Congress, 1829-38; first U.S. Minister to Austria; candidate for governor of Pennsylvania at the time of death in 1844. His home was on this site.

City type: 400 Penn St., Reading. Erected Feb. 16, 1951.

Leaving Reading

9 UNION CANAL

In use, 1828-1884. It connected the Schuylkill at Reading with the Susquehanna at Middletown. About a mile east, at tip of Fritts Island, are remains of easternmost lock. It passed boats travelling to and from Philadelphia by way of Schuylkill Navigation.

Junction PA 10 & 724, 2 miles S of Reading. Erected Apr. 22, 1950.

10 THOMAS MIFFLIN

Member of the Continental Congress, a Revolutionary soldier, first Pennsylvania governor, 1790-99, lived at his estate Angelica from 1774 to 1794. The Berks County Farm and Home now occupies the site.

US 222 (E. Lancaster Ave.) at Mifflin Blvd., Shillington. Erected Mar. 27, 1947.

11 ROBESONIA FURNACE

Founded 1794 as Reading Furnace by ironmaster George Ege. In 1845 Henry P. Robeson expanded the furnace, spurring establishment in 1855 of the town of Robesonia. Although the furnace itself ceased operation and was razed in 1927, the Georgian-style ironmaster's mansion, Italianate office building, workers' houses, and other structures survived. The district is located just south of here.

US 422 (Penn Ave.) at Freeman St., Robesonia. Erection anticipated late 1991 (revised 1947 marker).

12 CONRAD WEISER

Pioneer, Indian interpreter, treaty maker from 1732-1760. The Indians called him the ''Holder of the Heavens.'' He lived, died, and is buried on this property, now a State Park devoted to his memory.

US 422, Weiser Homestead E of Womelsdorf. Erected Apr. 29, 1947.

12 TULPEHOCKEN PATH

An Indian Path from Shamokin (Sunbury) came over the mountains by way of Klingerstown and Pine Grove to Weiser's place in the Tulpehocken Valley. Chiefs of the Six Nations, carrying ''words of wampum'' to Brother Onas (Penn) at Philadelphia, traveled this path.

US 422, Conrad Weiser Homestead E of Womelsdorf. Erected July 16, 1951.

13 CHARMING FORGE

Erected in 1749; once owned by Baron Stiegel. Operated by ironmaster George Ege, 1774-1824. Hessians were employed in Revolutionary days to cut a rock channel for water supply. Site is to the north of Womelsdorf.

US 422, Womelsdorf. Erected Apr. 30, 1947.

14 JOHN A. SHULZE

Governor of Pennsylvania, 1823-1829. Born, 1775, in the old parsonage behind Christ Lutheran Church. During his terms, the State inaugurated its extensive program of internal improvements. He died at Lancaster in 1852.

US 422 outside Stouchsburg. Erected Sept. 6, 1951.

15 PILGER RUH

''Pilgrim's Rest'' was the name given to this spring on the Tulpehocken Path by Count Zinzendorf, the Moravian missionary, on his journey to the Indian towns of Shamokin and Wyoming in 1742.

PA 501, 4 miles N of Bethel. Erected Apr. 22, 1950.

16 FORT HENRY

Built 1756; garrisoned during the French and Indian War by troops under Capt. Christian Busse. Pennsylvania's major frontier defense east of Ft. Augusta (Sunbury). The site is $^3/_4$ mile to the northwest.

PA 501, 2 miles N of Bethel. Erected June 18, 1959 (replaced 1950 marker).

17 TULPEHOCKEN PATH

An Indian path connecting the Iroquois provincial capital at Shamokin, now Sunbury, with the Tulpehocken Valley, ran northwest through here. It was used by ambassadors to ''Brother Onas,'' i.e., Wm. Penn and his successors.

PA 501, 1 mile N of Bethel (just N of I 78/US 22. Erected Mar. 19, 1952.

18 NORTHKILL AMISH

The first organized Amish Mennonite congregation in America. Established by 1740. Disbanded following Indian attack, September 29, 1757, in which a Provincial soldier and three members of the Jacob Hochstetler family were killed near this point.

Old US 22, 1 mile W of Shartlesville. Erected June 26, 1959.

19 TULPEHOCKEN PATH

An Indian Path from Shamokin (Sunbury) came over the mountains by way of Klingerstown and Pine Grove to Weiser's place in the Tulpehocken Valley. Chiefs of the Six Nations, carrying ''words of wampum'' to Brother Onas (Penn) at Philadelphia, traveled this path.

PA 419 N of Host. Erected July 16, 1951.

20 CHRIST LITTLE TULPEHOCKEN CHURCH

Organized 1729, this is one of the early Lutheran churches founded by Rev. John Caspar Stoever, Jr., who started the parish records in 1730. A log church, erected before 1749, was replaced by the present stone building in 1809. Since 1853, Lutheran and Reformed services have been held here.

SR 4010 (former LR 06020) W of Bernville. Erected June 12, 1953.

21 UNION CANAL

This canal, suggested by William Penn in 1690, was in use from 1828 to 1884. Following the Tulpehocken, its course crossed Northkill Creek at South Bernville, about a mile northwest. There, two locks remain.

PA 183, .9 mile SE of Bernville. Erected May 12, 1950.

22 JOSEPH HIESTER

Revolutionary soldier, Congressman, Governor, 1820-1823, lived in the Hiester Mansion. Now a part of the Berks County Welfare Farm.

PA 183 at SR 3051 & 3053 (former LR 06039) near Leinbachs. Erected Mar. 27, 1947.

23 UNION CANAL

This canal was operated from 1828-1884. It connected the Schuylkill at Reading with the Susquehanna at Middletown. Remains of the tow path can be seen .3 mile southeast of here, along the Tulpehocken Creek.

Upper Van Reed Rd. near Tulpehocken Creek, ca. 1 mile S of Leinbachs. Erected Oct. 1950 (originally on PA 183 at Mount Pleasant).

24 DE TURK HOUSE

Built in 1767 by John de Turk, son of Isaac de Turk, a Huguenot who settled here in 1712 and was one of a number of French Protestants who were pioneers in this part of Berks County.

Junction PA 73 & 662 just S of Oley. Erected Dec. 4, 1948.

24 OLEY MORAVIANS

A building erected about 1748 by Moravians, for use as church and school, stands on the side road, about 1.5 miles away. They conducted a boarding school here, 1745-51; and built a later schoolhouse, since demolished, in 1776.

PA 662, 1 mile S of Oley. Erected Aug. 28, 1948.

25 DE BENNEVILLE HOUSE

Built 1745 by Dr. George de Benneville, preacher in this area 1743-55, and founder of Universalism in America. He died in Philadelphia in 1793. The house is 2.25 miles away on a side road.

PA 662, 1.5 miles N of Yellow House. Erected Dec. 4, 1948.

25 FISHER HOUSE

This home, built 1801 by Henry Fisher, is a fine example of late Georgian architecture. Brought from the British Isles, this style is reflected in old homes of eastern and southern Pennsylvania.

PA 662, 1.4 miles N of Yellow House. Erected Aug. 28, 1948.

26 EXETER FRIENDS MEETING

Established 1725 as Oley; name changed to Exeter, 1742. Present stone meeting house built 1759 near site of two previous log structures. Buried here are members of the Boone, Ellis, Hughes, Lee, and Lincoln families. Meetings discontinued 1899; building reopened for worship in 1949.

Meetinghouse Road, .5 mile S of PA 562 & 2 miles W of Yellow House. Erected May 7, 1979 (revised 1948 marker).

27 THOMAS RUTTER

Pioneer ironmaster and opponent of slavery who died 1730. Built Pennsylvania's first ironworks nearby, 1716. In ensuing decade he erected Pine Forge and built this mansion; in 19th century it was an Underground Railroad stop. Academy was founded here, 1945.

City type: Pine Forge Academy off SR 2063 (former LR 06102), Pine Forge. Dedicated Oct. 4, 1982.

28 COLEBROOKDALE FURNACE

Established on Iron Stone Creek, one half mile to the east, by James Lewis, Anthony Morris, Thomas Potts, and Thomas Rutter. Called after Colebrookdale Furnace in England, it is considered the first blast furnace to be erected in Pennsylvania, c. 1720.

PA 562 near SR 2040 (former LR 284) SW of Boyertown. Erected 1967.

28 CARL A. SPAATZ

Aviation pioneer. Born in Boyertown, June 28, 1891. A graduate of West Point, 1914, and a pilot in France in World War I. He rose to the rank of Brigadier General, 1940, and General, 1945. During World War II he was commander of the U.S. 8th Air Force and the U.S. Strategic Air Forces in Europe. First Chief of Staff of the newly independent U.S. Air Force, 1947-48. He died July 14, 1974.

PA 562 (S. Reading Ave.) at W. 2nd St., Boyertown. Dedicated June 27, 1991.

29 GOSHENHOPPEN

Re-named Bally for Father Augustin Bally. The third Roman Catholic mission and first Catholic school in the State were established here in 1743 by Father Theodore Schneider.

PA 100 (7th & Main Sts.), Bally. Erected Apr. 30, 1947.

30 HEREFORD FURNACE

Established by Thomas Maybury in 1745 on the west bank of the Perkiomen Creek for the purpose of manufacturing iron. Maybury is credited with producing here in 1767 the first cast-iron cooking-stove in North America.

PA 29 & 100 at junction SR 1010 (former LR 06119), Hereford. Erected May 5, 1967.

Carbon County

B CARBON COUNTY

Formed March 13, 1843 from Northampton and Monroe counties. Carbon is the basic element of this area's rich deposits of anthracite coal. The county seat, incorporated in 1850 as Mauch Chunk, was renamed in 1954 for Jim Thorpe, Indian athlete.

City type: County Courthouse, Broadway & Susquehanna Sts., Jim Thorpe. Dedicated June 13, 1982.

31 WALKING PURCHASE

On Sept. 20, 1737, the two surviving walkers used an Indian path from present-day Northampton to "Pokopoghcunk" Indian Town (now Parryville), then continued by compass. Later in the morning, Yeates became exhausted, leaving Marshall to go on alone.

US 209, 1.5 miles E of Weissport. Erected May 25, 1971 (revised 1948 marker). For background see Walking Purchase below.

32 FORT ALLEN

Built in 1756 by the Province of Pennsylvania. One of a series of frontier defenses erected during the French and Indian War. The site was within present Weissport.

US 209 at Weissport. Erected July 14, 1947.

32 FORT ALLEN WELL

Only remaining part of Fort Allen, which was built by the Province of Pennsylvania, 1756, under the supervision of Benjamin Franklin. The well, now restored, is located directly behind houses opposite.

City type: park opposite 112-116 Franklin St., Weissport. Erected May 25, 1971.

33 GNADENHUETTEN

The Moravian Mission of this name was built in 1746 for Mahikan-Delaware converts and was the first settlement in present-day Carbon County. It was burned on Nov. 24, 1755, by Munsee Indians. Victims of the attack are buried in the cemetery north of here.

PA 443 near junction SR 3002 (former LR 13002) at S end Lehighton. Erected May 25, 1971 (revised 1947 marker).

34 PHILIP GINTER

While hunting, Ginter discovered anthracite on Sharp Mountain here in 1791. He showed it to Col. Jacob Weiss, a prominent area settler. In 1792 Weiss and others formed the Lehigh Coal Mine Co., the first anthracite company and a forerunner of Lehigh Coal & Navigation.

City type: Ludlow Park in Summit Hill. Dedicated May 27, 1991.

35 SWITCHBACK RAILROAD

A gravity railroad was built along this mountain in 1827 to carry coal from the mines near Summit Hill to the Lehigh Canal at Mauch Chunk. A back-track and two planes were added in 1844 for the return trip by gravity. Railroad crossed highway here.

SR 3012 (former LR 13033) 3 miles SW of Jim Thorpe. Erected May 25, 1971 (revised 1951 marker).

36 PACKER MANSION

Standing on the nearby hill is the home of Asa Packer, industrialist, philanthropist, congressman and founder of Lehigh University. The ornate mansion, built in 1860, has been carefully preserved with its original furnishings and is maintained as a memorial.

US 209 at park near railroad station, Jim Thorpe. Erected May 14, 1971.

37 WALKING PURCHASE

Measured 1737, according to a supposed Indian deed of 1686, granting lands extending a day-and-a-half walk. Using picked men to force this measure to its limit, Thomas Penn reversed his father's Indian policy, losing Indian friendship.

PA 903, 2 miles NE of Jim Thorpe. Erected Apr. 22, 1948.

37 WALKING PURCHASE

In the early afternoon of Sept. 20, Edward Marshall, with an official timer, ended the ''Indian Walk,'' having covered some 65 miles in 18 hours' travel. His stopping place is supposed to have been in this general area.

Accompanies marker immediately above. Erected Apr. 22, 1948.

Lehigh County

C LEHIGH COUNTY

Formed March 6, 1812 from part of Northampton County and named for the Lehigh River. Home of George Taylor, signer of Declaration of Independence. County seat of Allentown sheltered the Liberty Bell during occupation of Philadelphia, 1777-1778.

City type: Old Courthouse, Hamilton & 5th Sts., Allentown. Dedicated Oct. 30, 1982.

38 INDIAN JASPER QUARRIES

One of the most famous of Pennsylvania's Indian quarries may be seen in the woods a short distance northwest of here. Articles made from the jasper were carried by the Indians as far as New England.

City type: SR 2027 (former LR 39001) near intersection SR 2023 (former LR 39017), Vera Cruz. Erected Oct. 23, 1952.

39 EMMAUS

Called by the Indians ''Macungie,'' or ''feeding place of the bears.'' Area settlement was begun in the 1730's and Shelter House erected in 1734. Moravians established a ''Gemein-Ort,'' or congregational village, and named it after the biblical town of Emmaus in 1761.

Main St. at library, Emmaus. Erected July 26, 1966.

40 PORTLAND CEMENT

This industry was born in the Lehigh Valley. David O. Saylor first made portland cement at Coplay in 1871. Here also was the first use of the rotary kiln process commercially Nov. 8, 1889. This region has continued to lead in the industry.

Kuhnsville Rd. (old US 22) W of Kuhnsville. Erected Nov. 7, 1947.

41 ABRAHAM BLUMER (1736-1822)
Born in Grabs, Switzerland, Chaplain of the First Battalion, Northampton County Militia, 1781, is buried in this cemetery. He ministered to the Reformed congregations of Jordan, Union, Egypt and Allentown from 1771 to 1801. Lorentz Guth in 1752 presented 53 acres of land to the congregation for church and school purposes. Marked by the Pennsylvania Historical Commission and the Valley Forge Chapter, S. A. R., 1929.
Plaque: on grounds of Jordan United Church of Christ at Walbert, South Whitehall Twp. Dedicated Nov. 28, 1929.

42 ALLENTOWN
Founded 1762 by the noted colonial leader and jurist, William Allen. Known until 1834 as Northampton. Here the Liberty Bell was hidden in 1777, and Revolutionary wounded hospitalized. City incorporation, 1867. Long a textile and cement center.
On main highways leading into city. Erected Sept. 3, 1947.

42 TROUT HALL
Built, 1769-70, by James Allen, son of Allentown's founder, William Allen. Later known as the Livingston Mansion. In 1848 it became Allentown Seminary, and in 1867 part of Muhlenberg College. Now the home of the Lehigh Co. Historical Society.
S. 4th St. near Walnut St., Allentown. Erected Jan. 24, 1967.

42 HARRIET A. BAKER (1829-1913)
This African-American evangelist opened a mission about 1900 at 738 North Penn Street, where she preached until her death. In 1914 her mission became the first home of St. James A.M.E. Zion Church, which built at this location in 1936.
City type: 410 Union St., Allentown. Dedicated May 4, 1990.

43 STEPHEN VINCENT BENET
This talented author was born here July 22, 1898; died in New York March 13, 1943. "John Brown's Body" and his other poems and stories give vivid expression to the best in American spirit and tradition.
City type: NE corner, Ostrum & Bishop Thorpe Sts., Fountain Hill. Dedicated May 7, 1960.

[UNKNOWN SOLDIER]
Plaque: 1st Ave. & W. Market St., Bethlehem (Lehigh County). See Unknown Soldier, Northampton County.

44 GEORGE TAYLOR HOUSE
The home of the signer of the Declaration of Independence is just opposite in the rear of the mill building. Built in 1768. Now owned by the Lehigh County Historical Society.
Lehigh St. (SR 1007, former Spur 153) S of Catasauqua. Erected Sept. 2, 1947.

44 BIERY'S PORT
First structure, a grist mill, was built about 1752. Starting 1801, Frederick Biery developed the area commercially; erected several landmark stone buildings. This is the oldest part of Catasauqua (incorporated 1853) which was an early home to the anthracite iron industry.
City type: corner Race & Lehigh Sts., Catasauqua. Dedicated April 24, 1988.

45 FIRST CEMENT
David O. Saylor was the first to make portland cement in the United States, at Coplay in 1871. First use of the rotary kiln to manufacture cement on a commerical scale was also here, Nov. 8, 1889.
Opposite Coplay Cement office bldg. at Coplay. Erected Sept. 2, 1947.

45 FORT DESHLER
The site of the stone fort built in 1760 by Adam Deshler, Switzerland native, was just opposite. A frontier refuge against marauding Indians, it stood until about 1940.
PA 145 between Coplay & Egypt. Erected Sept. 3, 1947.

46 TROXELL-STECKEL HOUSE
The house built originally in 1756 by John Peter Troxell and acquired by Peter Steckel in 1768 lies one-half mile west. Restored in 1943, the house is now owned and maintained as a museum by the Lehigh County Historical Society.
PA 329 in Egypt. Erected Nov. 2, 1970 (revision of 1947 marker).

46 TROXELL-STECKEL HOUSE
Just west of here is the house built originally by John Peter Troxell in 1756 and acquired by Peter Steckel in 1768. It was restored in 1943 and is now owned and maintained as a museum by the Lehigh County Historical Society.
Church St. near Bridge St., Egypt. Erected Nov. 2, 1970 (revised 1947 marker).

47 SLATE INDUSTRY
Slatington has been one of the centers of the slate industry since about 1845. From here came slate for roofs and old-time school slates and pencils, helping maintain the State as leading slate producer.
PA 873 in Slatington. Erected Nov. 6, 1947.

47 TRUCKER'S MILL
A sawmill, built before 1755, and used as a station for troops at time of the French and Indian War, stood about 200 feet north of here. Known also as Kern's Fort, its position on two pioneer roads gave it much military value.
City type: Main St. (PA 873) near Diamond St., Slatington. Erected Jan. 11, 1952.

48 FORT EVERETT
A blockhouse, erected about 1756, stood 300 feet north of here. It was a place of refuge and defense against raids in French and Indian War days. Troops here guarded the area just south of the Blue Mountain, between the Schuylkill and Lehigh Rivers.
PA 143 E of Lynnport. Erected Aug. 21, 1951.

49 FREDERICK LEASER
Whose homestead is located one mile to the north, in September 1777 with his farm team hauled the Liberty Bell from Philadelphia to Allentown, where it was concealed in Zion Reformed Church. His grandson Jesse Follweiler conveyed on the same wagon the Liberty Pole erected on this spot January 1st, 1833. It bore the legend "Jackson — Liberty — and Against Nullification." Marked by the Pennsylvania Historical Commission and the Valley Forge Chapter, Sons of American Revolution, 1928.
Plaque: Leaser Lake Park off Pa 143 near Jacksonville. Dedicated Nov. 29, 1928 near present site & relocated 1976.

Monroe County

D MONROE COUNTY
Formed April 1, 1836 out of Northampton and Pike counties. Named for President James Monroe. Site of Indian raids, 1755-82, and of a segment of Sullivan's March. Pocono Mountains famed as a resort area. County seat, Stroudsburg, was incorporated in 1815.
City type: County Courthouse, 7th & Monroe Sts., Stroudsburg. Dedicated Jan. 22, 1983.

50 NICHOLAS DEPUY
First known settler in this region, 1727. His home, stockaded and garrisoned, became the Fort Depuy of the French and Indian War, after 1755.
SR 2028 (former LR 45012) .5 mile NE of Shawnee. Erected July 30, 1947.

50 NICHOLAS Du PUY, 1682-1762

The first settler of Shawnee. In 1727 purchased 3000 acres of land including the islands of Shawano and Manwalamink from the Minsi Indians. He was a grandson of Nicholas Du Puy and his wife Catharine De Vos, Huguenot refugees from Artois, France, who with their sons Nicholas, John and Moses arrived in New Amsterdam in 1662. William Allen in 1750 conveyed five acres of land to Nicholas Du Puy and others for a Dutch Reformed congregation, now the Presbyterian Church. Marked by the Pennsylvania Historical Commission, the Huguenot Society of Pennsylvania, the Monroe County Historical Society, 1930.

Plaque: intersection SR 2023 (former LR 461 E) & SR 2028 (former LR 45012) at Shawnee. Erected 1930.

51 DANIEL BRODHEAD

Settled here about 1738. Founder of the town, first called Dansbury. Lived here until 1755. His son Daniel became a Revolutionary War leader and later the State Surveyor General.

At hospital, E. Brown St., East Stroudsburg. Erected Aug. 7, 1947.

Entering Stroudsburg

52 JACOB STROUD (1735-1806)

Colonel in the militia and Revolutionary patriot. He stockaded his home as Fort Penn. Member, state constitutional convention, 1776, and state legislature, 1781-1783. He founded Stroudsburg in 1799; he and his son Daniel then laid out the town.

City type: Municipal Bldg., 7th & Sarah Sts., Stroudsburg. Dedicated Mar. 19, 1991.

52 DANSBURY MISSION

Erected about 1744, by Daniel Brodhead, for use by Moravian missionaries. Destroyed by the Indians in 1755, during the French and Indian War. The site adjoined the present cemetery.

Main St. (US 209), Stroudsburg. Erected June 15, 1947.

52 COLONEL JACOB STROUD

Is buried in this graveyard, originally the cemetery of the mission of Dansbury, begun by the Moravian Brethren in 1743. The chapel destroyed in the Indian uprising of 1755 was erected in 1753 under the leadership of Daniel Brodhead, who settled one-half mile to the east in 1736. The members of the mission in 1747 were Daniel and Esther Brodhead, John and Catharine Hillman, Joseph and Helen Haines, Francis and Rebecca Jones, William and Mary Clark, Edward and Catharine Holley, John and Hannah McMichael, George and Mary Salathe, Daniel Roberts, John Baker. Marked by the Monroe County Historical Society and the Pennsylvania Historical Commission, 1931.

Plaque: cemetery, 200 block Main St. (US 209), Stroudsburg. Erected 1931.

52 FORT PENN

Named for Governor John Penn, and replacing Fort Hamilton, the fort stood nearby. In 1763, it was garrisoned by Provincial troops. Later it served as refuge from attacks following the Battle of Wyoming, July 3, 1778.

City type: Main St. (US 209), Stroudsburg. Erected May 25, 1967 (revision of 1947 marker).

52 THE SULLIVAN EXPEDITION AGAINST THE IROQUOIS INDIANS, 1779

Fort Penn, the home of Col. Jacob Stroud, was located here. Rendezvous for several companies for the Expedition uniting with main army at Learned's Tavern. Marked by the Pennsylvania Historical Commission, the Historical Society of Monroe County, and the Jacob Stroud Chapter, D.A.R., 1929.

Plaque: wall at 522 Main St. (US 209), Stroudsburg. Erected 1929.

52 FORT HAMILTON

Built at direction of Benjamin Franklin. Named after James Hamilton, a member of the Governor's Council. Stood NW of here, garrisoned 1755-57, one of a chain of forts later replaced by Fort Penn. Abandoned in 1757.

City type: 9th & Main Sts. (US 209 & PA 611), Stroudsburg. Erected Oct. 30, 1967 (revised 1947 marker).

52 FORT HAMILTON
One of a chain of frontier forts of the Province of Pennsylvania in the French and Indian War, erected under the direction of Benjamin Franklin, stood hard-by to the rear extending across Ninth Street. Built in January 1756 by Captain Levi Trump and garrisoned by Captain John Craig and 41 men. Later commanded by Captain Nicholas Weatherhold, who on April 2, 1757 was succeeded by Captain John Van Etten, and upon his death in the month of July, Lieutenant James Hyndshaw was placed in command. Marked by the Pennsylvania Historical Commission and the Monroe County Historical Society, 1930.

Plaque: building at NW corner 9th & Main Sts. (US 209 & PA 611), Stroudsburg. Placed 1930.

Leaving Stroudsburg

53 SULLIVAN'S MARCH
Brinker's Mill was the storehouse and advance post for the Sullivan Expedition, which left Easton June 18, 1779, to attack the hostile Iroquois Indians.

Business US 209, Sciota. Erected Aug. 2, 1947.

53 THE SULLIVAN EXPEDITION AGAINST THE IROQUOIS INDIANS, 1779
Brinker's Mill, site of The Sullivan Stores, the advance post of the Expedition. Marked by the Pennsylvania Historical Commission, the George N. Kemp Post, American Legion, and the Valley Forge Chapter, S.A.R., 1929.

Plaque: Business US 209, Sciota. Erected 1929.

54 SULLIVAN'S MARCH
Learned's Tavern marked the end of the second day's march from Easton to Fort Wyoming, at Wilkes-Barre. The army camped here June 19, 1779, after a 16-mile march from Heller's Tavern.

PA 611, Tannersville. Erected Aug. 2, 1947.

54 THE SULLIVAN EXPEDITION AGAINST THE IROQUOIS INDIANS, 1779
Learned's Tavern, the last house on the frontier, the end of the second day's march, June 19, 1779. Distance 16 miles. Marked by the Pennsylvania Historical Commission and the Monroe County Historical Society, 1929.

Plaque: PA 611, Tannersville. Erected 1929.

55 THE SULLIVAN EXPEDITION AGAINST THE IROQUOIS INDIANS, 1779
White Oak Run, site of Chowder Camp where Sullivan dined on trout chowder. End of the third day's march, June 20, 1779. Distance 5 miles. Marked by the Pennsylvania Historical Commission and the Valley Forge Chapter, S.A.R., 1929.

Plaque: Sullivan Trail (SR 4004, formerly LR 45024) 5 miles NW of Tannersville. Original erected 1929; lost ca. 1945. Duplicate placed by the Monroe County Historical Society, 1975.

56 FORT NORRIS
Built in 1756 by the Province of Pennsylvania. One of a series of frontier defenses erected during the French and Indian War. The site was about a mile distant.

US 209, Kresgeville. Erected Aug. 2, 1947.

Northampton County

E NORTHAMPTON COUNTY
Formed March 11, 1752 out of Bucks County. Named for Northamptonshire in England. Easton, county seat, was incorporated in 1789. County is noted as a leading center for the steel industry and for cement and slate production.

City type: Canal Museum, Hugh Moore Park, PA 611, Easton. Dedicated July 8, 1982.

57 PORTLAND CEMENT

This industry was born in the Lehigh Valley. David O. Saylor first made portland cement at Coplay in 1871. Here also was the first use of the rotary kiln process commercially Nov. 8, 1889. This region has continued to lead in the industry.
PA 611 S of Martins Creek. Erected 1947.

57 DAVID BRAINERD

The log house occupied by the Presbyterian missioner to the Indians in 1744 was a short distance away on the side road. It was here the youthful zealot wrote part of his famed journal.
PA 611 S of Martins Creek. Erected Aug. 5, 1947.

58 THE SULLIVAN EXPEDITION AGAINST THE IROQUOIS INDIANS, 1779

Sullivan Road, over which the army began its advance, June 18, 1779. Marked by the Pennsylvania Historical Commission, the Valley Forge Chapter, S.A.R., and the City of Easton, 1929.
Plaque: junction Sullivan Trail & Knox Ave. (following SR 2025, former PA 115) just N of Easton. Erected 1929.

58 SULLIVAN CAMPAIGN

This major expedition of the Revolution aimed at the Indian-Tory alliance in New York, was organized at Easton under Gen. John Sullivan. Over a month's preparations preceded the first day's march, begun near here June 18, 1779.
Knox Ave. (SR 2025, former PA 115) just N of Easton. Erected Aug. 5, 1947.

Entering Easton

59 EASTON

Key center of travel, trade and industry at the Forks of the Delaware since the days of the Indian. Laid out in 1752 by William Parsons. Site of several Indian peace councils. The home of Lafayette College.
On main highways leading into city. Erected Aug. 4, 1947.

59 FIRST REFORMED CHURCH

Congregation organized 1745. This building, enlarged and restored, was erected, 1776. Scene of Indian Treaty, 1777. During the Revolutionary War, it was used as a military hospital.
City type: N. 3rd St. at church, Easton. Erected July 20, 1953.

59 INDIAN PEACE COUNCILS

Held on this Square between 1756 and 1762 to strengthen English friendship with the Delawares and Six Nations; to bring about peace with hostile Indians, drawing those of Ohio away from the French.
City type: NE part of square, Easton. Erected July 20, 1953.

59 SAMUEL PHILLIPPE

Recognized as the inventor of the split-bamboo fishing rod in the U.S. His first rent and glued-up cane rod was made about 1846 in his gunsmith shop that stood on this site.
City type: S. 3rd St. just N. of Pine St., Easton. Erected July 20, 1953.

59 GEORGE TAYLOR

One of the Signers of the Declaration of Independence, member of Continental Congress, ironmaster, lived in this house built in 1757 by William Parsons, Surveyor-General. First occupied by Parsons.
City type: NE corner of 4th & Ferry Sts., Easton. Erected July 20, 1953.

59 DAVID MARTIN'S FERRY

Operated at ''The Forks'' on grants received in 1739 and 1741. It was an important link on a main route to the west until 1806. Transported troops and supplies in the Revolutionary War.
City type: Front & Ferry Sts., at Scott Park, Easton. Erected July 20 1953.

Leaving Easton

60 ## PENNSYLVANIA CANAL
A system of State-built public works to connect Philadelphia, Pittsburgh, Lake Erie. The Delaware Division, Bristol-Easton, begun 1827; operated by the State 1831-58, and by private owners to 1931. A State Park since 1940.
PA 611 S of Raubsville. Erected Apr. 12, 1949.

60 ## DELAWARE CANAL
The canal channel, which parallels the Delaware River, lies just below the highway. Here are locks No. 22 and 23, the last lift locks in the 60 miles of canal from Bristol to the Lehigh River at Easton.
PA 611 S of Raubsville. Erected Apr. 12, 1949.

Hugh Moore Historical Park and Museums, Inc., Easton

Delaware Canal at the Raubsville lock

Entering Bethlehem

61 ## BETHLEHEM
Religious, cultural, and industrial center. Founded 1741 by Moravians, who excelled as missionaries and musicians. Place of refuge during Indian wars. Lehigh Canal, opened 1828, brought industrialization. Home of Bethlehem Steel.
PA 412 entering city from S. Erected July 26, 1948.

61 ## EDWIN L. DRAKE
Drilled first oil well in America in 1859 at Titusville, Pa. Lived at Bethlehem in this house for last seven years of his life, 1873-1880. In 1902 his remains were moved from Bethlehem to memorial monument erected at Titusville.
City type: 331 Wyandotte St. (PA 378), Bethlehem. Dedicated Oct. 21, 1959.

61 ## CROWN INN
A two-story log inn, built here in 1745, was Bethlehem's first public house. Located near the ferry that crossed the Lehigh River, it was visited by famous political and military leaders of the era. A bridge replaced the ferry, 1794, and the inn closed; was razed, 1857.
City type: Riverside Dr. just SE of Lehigh River bridge (PA 378), Bethlehem. Dedicated June 21, 1991.

61 ## OLD WATERWORKS
As early as 1754, water was pumped from a spring to a water tower, that stood east of here, through hollowed trunks of trees. It then flowed by gravity to five cisterns or reservoirs. Original engine house stands about 60 yds. S. W.
City type: Main St. N of Lehigh River bridge, Bethlehem. Erected Oct. 13, 1953.

61 BRETHREN'S HOUSE

Built 1748 by Moravians as house for single men. Early industry center; bell foundry, silkworm culture, other crafts and trades. Military hospital in Revolution. Girls' school from 1815. Now part of Moravian College and a museum.

City type: W. Church St. at site, Bethlehem. Erected Sept. 2, 1964 (revised 1953 marker).

61 MORAVIAN COMMUNITY

Community organized June 25, 1742. The oldest buildings are on West Church Street. Those marked are: Gemeinhaus, Sisters' House, Bell House, Brothers' House, and Old Chapel.

City type: Main St. at Church, Bethlehem. Erected Oct. 13, 1953.

61 OLD CHAPEL

The second place of worship, 1751-1806. Here many noted persons of the American Revolution heard early Moravian music and the Gospel. Prominent clergy were Bishops Nitschmann, Spangenberg, de Watteville, and Ettwein.

City type: Heckewelder St. at site, Bethlehem. Erected Oct. 13, 1953.

61 GEMEINHAUS

Erected in 1741. First place of worship in Bethlehem was on the second floor. Count von Zinzendorf had quarters here, 1742. Place of many notable conferences in the Colonial and Revolutionary periods.

City type: 66 W. Church St., Bethlehem. Erected Oct. 13, 1953.

61 GEMEIN HAUS

Erected in 1741. The first house of worship in Bethlehem. Home for the clergy, among whom were Zinzendorf - Spangenberg - Nitschmann - Ettwein - Seidel. Scene of the Great Wedding, July 15, 1749. Place of the only school for the teaching of Indian languages. The treaty of friendship between the Nanticoke and Shawnee Indians and the Moravian Brethren was made in the Saal in 1752. Many notable conferences both in Colonial and Revolutionary periods were held in the building — now a home for the aged. Marked by the Pennsylvania Historical Commission and the Moravian Union of King's Daughters, 1930.

Plaque: on front of Gemeinhaus, 66 W. Church St., Bethlehem. Dedicated Apr. 4, 1931.

61 BELL HOUSE

As early Germanic type of building; erected in 1745. Used first as the Family House. Girls' School, 1749. Bell, still in use, was cast in Bethlehem. Turret had first town clock, 1746. Weathervane is the church seal in metal.

City type: 56 W. Church St., Bethlehem. Erected Oct. 13, 1953.

61 SISTERS' HOUSE

Built in 1744. Brothers' House until 1748. Here unmarried sisters plied many of the arts and crafts for women. In 1778, Pulaski's banner was made by them.

City type: 50 W. Church St., Bethlehem. Erected Oct. 13, 1953.

61 HILDA DOOLITTLE (H.D.)

The renowned poet was born here on September 10, 1886; died in Zurich, September 27, 1961. H.D. sought the Hellenic spirit and a classic beauty of expression. She is buried in nearby Nisky Hill Cemetery. ''O, give me burning blue.''

City type: 10 E. Church St., City Center Plaza, Bethlehem. Dedicated Sept. 10, 1982.

(61) HECKEWELDER HOUSE
One-half block south, stands the home of John Heckewelder, famed Indian missionary and interpreter, author of works on American Indians. House was erected in 1810.

City type: 67 W. Market St., Bethlehem. Erected Oct. 13, 1953.

(61) MORAVIAN CEMETERY
Used as a burial place, 1742-1910. Site selected and consecrated by Count von Zinzendorf. Only flat gravestones were permitted. Here are the graves of persons of various nationalities and races.

City type: W. Market St. at cemetery, Bethlehem. Erected Oct. 13, 1953.

(61) PULASKI'S BANNER
While Pulaski guarded this area in 1778, the Moravian women made a banner which his cavalry bore until he died at the Siege of Savannah in 1779. The banner was later immortalized in a poem by Longfellow.

City type: W. Market St. at Moravian Cemetery, Bethlehem. Dedicated Oct. 12, 1974.

(61) [FIRST HOUSE OF MORAVIAN SETTLEMENT]
The first house of the Moravian settlement, occupied March 9, 1741, stood on this site. In this house on Christmas Eve 1741, Count Zinzendorf, conducting a love feast, named the place Bethlehem. Marked by the Pennsylvania Historical Commission and the Bethlehem Chapter, D.A.R., 1929.

Plaque: wall of Hotel Bethlehem, 437 Main St., Bethlehem. Dedicated May 8, 1929.

(61) LAFAYETTE
Here stood the George Frederick Beckel house, 1762-1872, famed as the place where General Lafayette convalesced from a leg wound suffered at the Battle of Brandywine, 1777. Beckel was then superintendent of the community farm here in Bethlehem.

City type: 534 Main St., Bethlehem. Dedicated May 16, 1987.

(61) SUN INN
Erection begun, 1758; enlarged and altered in 19th century. Considered one of the best inns of its time. Here many notable patriots and military leaders of the Revolutionary War period were entertained.

City type: 560 Main St., Bethlehem. Erected Oct. 13, 1953.

The following plaque at 1st Ave. & W. Market St. is in a part of Bethlehem — across Monocacy Creek from the historic Moravian section — that is in Lehigh County. It is listed here, however, for ease of reference.

(61) [UNKNOWN SOLDIER]
Within this crypt rest the bones of an unknown soldier in the War for Independence. He was one of more than five hundred men who died in the Continental hospital here at Bethlehem and were buried on this hillside. Marked by the Pennsylvania Historical Commission, the City of Bethlehem, the Valley Forge Chapter, S.A.R., and the Bethlehem Chapter, D.A.R., 1931.

Plaque: 1st Ave. & W. Market St., Bethlehem. Erected 1931.

(61) MORAVIAN ARCHIVES
Repository for a very valuable collection of manuscripts and rare books on Moravian work among the Indians and pioneer settlers, and on original art and music of the Colonial period.

City type: Main St. & Elizabeth Ave., Bethlehem. Erected Oct. 13, 1953.

Leaving Bethlehem

(62) PORTLAND CEMENT
This industry was born in the Lehigh Valley. David O. Saylor first made portland cement at Coplay in 1871. Here also was the first use of the rotary kiln process commercially Nov. 8, 1889. This region has continued to lead in the industry.

PA 329, .5 mile E of Northampton. Erected 1947.

62 **[HOCKENDAUQUA]**

Hockendauqua Indian Town of the noted chiefs Lappawinzo and Tishcohan, who treated with the Penn Proprietors of Pennsylvania in the famous Walking Purchase, was located in the present Northampton upon the east bank of the Lehigh River three fourths of a mile to the northwest of this marker. The fleet-footed youth Edward Marshall and his associates of the walk of a day and a half, September 19-20, 1737, crossed Hockendauqua Creek a half mile below this point on the stream and slept the first night in the woods a half mile from the Indian town. The survey line of the purchase was run later in 1737, 1³/10 miles to the east. Marked by the Pennsylvania Historical Commission and the Northampton County Historical and Genealogical Society, 1925.

Plaque: PA 329 at eastern approach to Hokendauqua Creek bridge, .5 mile E of Northampton. Dedicated Sept. 20, 1925.

63 **[INDIAN WALK]**

The famous Indian Walk of a day and a half from Wrightstown, Bucks County to near the present Mauch Chunk was performed for the Penn Proprietors of Pennsylvania, September 19-20, 1737 by Edward Marshall and his associates, who slept at the end of the first day near Hockendauqua Indian Town, which was 1½ miles to the south, and the next morning passed near this point. The survey line of the Walking Purchase was run later in 1737 a half mile east of this marker by Benjamin Eastburn, Surveyor General of Pennsylvania. Marked by the Pennsylvania Historical Commission and the Northampton County Historical and Genealogical Society, 1925.

Plaque: junction of Indian Trail Rd. (SR 3016) & Kohls Rd., at Hokendauqua Creek .25 mile NW of Kreidersville. Dedicated Sept. 19, 1925. (Mauch Chunk was consolidated with East Mauch Chunk in 1956 to form borough of Jim Thorpe.)

64 **GEORGE WOLF**

Congressman; Governor for two terms, 1829-35, was born on a nearby farm on Aug. 12, 1777. His fame rests on his support of the Free School Act of 1834, foundation of the public school system of the State.

PA 329 SW of Bath. Erected Aug. 6, 1947.

65 **PORTLAND CEMENT**

Same text as Portland Cement above.

PA 248, .2 mile W of Nazareth. Erected 1947.

65 **NAZARETH**

Moravian settlers arrived here in 1740 from a failing colony in Georgia. Bishop August B. Spangenberg led an experiment in communal living, called the "Great Economy," 1754-1765. It was designed to support Christian missionaries to the Indians.

PA 191 (E. Center St.) opposite N. Pine St. at Whitefield House, Nazareth. Erected Nov. 18, 1966.

65 **WHITEFIELD HOUSE**

Planned by George Whitefield in 1740 when he obtained 5000 acres of land for a Negro school and begun by Peter Boehler and several Brethren. Purchased by the Moravians, 1741. Completed for a family home, 1743. Converted into a boarding school for girls, 1745, and into a nursery for children of missionaries three years later. Used as a home for retired mission workers since 1764 except for the years 1855-1858 when it was occupied by the Theological Seminary. Seat of the Moravian Historical Society and Museum since 1871. Marked by the Pennsylvania Historical Commission and the Moravian Historical Society, 1931.

Plaque: PA 191 (E. Center St.) opposite N. Pine St., Nazareth. Erected 1931.

65 **WHITEFIELD HOUSE**

Begun in 1740 at request of Methodist missionary Reverend George Whitefield as a school for Negroes. Completed by the Moravians in 1743. Served as a communal church-home for 32 newly married German couples brought over in 1744.

Off PA 191 (E. Center St.) at S. New St., Nazareth. Erected Nov. 18, 1966.

66 HENRY'S GUN FACTORY
Here rifles and other firearms were made for use in the War of 1812. Built by William Henry, 2nd, about 1800, the famous Henry shotgun was made here as late as 1904. The site is about half a mile away.
SR 1005 (former PA 115 or LR 166), Belfast. Erected Jan. 8, 1974 (revised 1947 marker).

67 SULLIVAN'S MARCH
Heller's Tavern near Wind Gap was the camp site for Sullivan's army at the end of the first day's march from Easton, June 18, 1779. The army was astir at 4 the next morning, crossing the mountains at Wind Gap.
PA 512 just N of SR 1028 (former LR 48110), Wind Gap. Erected Aug. 5, 1947.

67 THE SULLIVAN EXPEDITION AGAINST THE IROQUOIS INDIANS, 1779
Heller's Tavern the end of the first day's march, June 18, 1779. Distance 12 miles. Marked by the Pennsylvania Historical Commission and the Valley Forge Chapter, S.A.R., 1929.
Plaque: PA 512 just N of SR 1028 (former LR 48110), Wind Gap. Erected 1929.

68 SLATE INDUSTRY
Robert M. Jones of Wales, who came here in 1848 as an immigrant, began the slate quarrying industry. The region became a major world center for slate. From here came slate for roofs and old-time school slates and pencils.
PA 512, East Bangor. Erected Aug. 6, 1947.

69 EDWARD MARSHALL
Measurer of the notorious Walking Purchase, 1737, lived in this area, 1755-1759. In the many Indian raids of this time, his wife and his oldest son were killed, 1757, supposedly in revenge. Later he returned to Bucks County.
Corner Hester St. & Delaware Ave., Portland. Erected Aug. 2, 1948.

Schuylkill County

F SCHUYLKILL COUNTY
Formed March 1, 1811 out of Northampton and Berks counties. Parts of Columbia and Luzerne counties added 1818. The name honors the Schuylkill River. County seat, Pottsville, was made a borough in 1828; city in 1911. A center of the anthracite coal industry.
City type: SE corner, Laurel Blvd. & N. 2nd St., Pottsville. Dedicated May 26, 1982.

70 FORT FRANKLIN
Built in 1756 as defense from Indian attacks. Named for Benjamin Franklin, who ordered construction. It was of limited use; abandoned in 1757. The Fort stood a short distance above present highway.
PA 309 SE of Snyder at rest area. Erected March 16, 1955 (revised 1948 marker).

71 FORT LEBANON
One of a line of defenses about 1755 to ward off Indian raids after Braddock's defeat. Called Fort William in 1758. The site is marked on the side road just below here.
PA 895 NE of Auburn. Erected Feb. 21, 1949.

72 UNION CANAL
The Swatara Feeder Branch extended along the creek from Pine Grove to the main line at Water Works. It was navigable from 1832 to 1862. Coal from nearby mines was carried to Reading and Middletown, and to points along the way.
PA 443 just S of Pine Grove. Erected Feb. 17, 1950.

73 TULPEHOCKEN PATH

Along this ridge, between Deep and Pine Creeks, ran the Tulpehocken Path. It connected Shickellamy's capital of Shamokin, now Sunbury, with the Tulpehocken Valley. Travelled by Indian ambassadors and Christian missionaries.

PA 25 between Hegins & Valley View. Erected Feb. 7, 1950.

74 JOHN O'HARA

This was the home, from 1916 to 1928, of one of America's best known novelists and short-story writers. Born at Pottsville in 1905, he used this anthracite region as a setting for several of his major works. O'Hara died at Princeton, N.J., in 1970.

City type: 606 Mahantongo St., Pottsville. Dedicated June 19, 1982.

75 VALLEY FURNACE

First furnace to use only anthracite for fuel, 1836. Built by Dr. F. W. Geissenhainer, who patented the method in 1833. Process in use continuously by the Pottsville or Pioneer Furnace, 1839 and after.

US 209 just E of New Philadelphia. Erected Oct. 20, 1948.

76 ST. MICHAEL'S CHURCH

Founded by Ukrainian immigrants in 1884, St. Michael's was the first church of the Greek Catholic Rite in America. Present church edifice, of the Byzantine style, was erected in 1983.

City type: corner Chestnut & Oak Sts., Shenandoah. Original marker dedicated 1970; 1908 edifice destroyed by fire 1980; new marker erected & church dedicated Nov. 4, 1984.

REGION III

Capital-Area Crossroads

Cumberland, Dauphin, Lebanon and *Perry* counties as a group are divided at the Blue Mountain into the fertile plain of the Cumberland and Lebanon valleys on the south, and the ridges and valleys characteristic of the Appalachian Mountain landscape to the north and west.

Economically, the four counties blend fertile farms with small cities blessed with a diversity of industry. The area was settled early in the eighteenth century by immigrants from the German states, a presence manifest in the churches of the Lutherans and the Reformed (now the United Church of Christ), and by the Scotch-Irish — witness the old meetinghouses and churches of the Presbyterians. Meanwhile, their non-farm cousins, mingling with later immigrants and descendants of southern slaves, worked the iron mines of Lebanon County, notably at Cornwall; the rural iron plantations; the iron and steel industries of Lebanon, Steelton and Harrisburg; the coal mines of northern Dauphin County; and the diverse industries of Chambersburg and other communities.

What was to become Harrisburg in 1785 and the State capital in 1812 began with John Harris's establishment of a trading post and, in 1733, the licensing of his ferry across the Susquehanna River. By the 1750's a once more-peaceful frontier had fallen into conflict between white settlers and Native Americans, and between Great Britain and France. The construction of frontier forts had begun.

Because of the threat, the Carlisle Barracks, the oldest army post in the United States, was established in 1757 to support military operations in western Pennsylvania. The last major mobilization there came in 1794, and was joined by President Washington, who had directed the United States army to suppress the Whiskey Rebellion among farmers of western Pennsylvania.

Carlisle has achieved distinction as both a military and an educational center. It was also for a time the home of a national founder. James Wilson, a Carlisle lawyer, signed the Declaration of Independence in 1776 and played a prominent part in the deliberations of the Constitutional Convention in 1787.

At Harrisburg, government has vied with transportation as the leading enterprise, the city on the Susquehanna having emerged, with its canals, railroads and highways, as a center of transportation. It was because of its importance to military transportation and its proximity to the Confederacy that the Army of Virginia, commanded by General Robert E. Lee, invaded Pennsylvania in 1863 and forced a military showdown at Gettysburg with the Union's Army of the Potomac, commanded by General George Gordon Meade.

Over time the establishment of several military installations has reinforced the region's interest in military preparedness. Indeed, the links that have been forged between politics, industry, defense, agriculture and transportation in this increasingly populous region have remained firm.

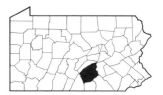

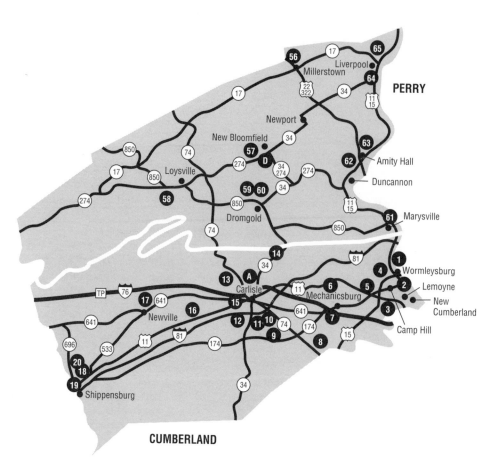

PERRY

56
17
Liverpool
65
Millerstown
64
22
322
34
11
15

17

Newport
34
New Bloomfield
63
57
D
62
Amity Hall
850
74
274
34
274
Duncannon
17
850
Loysville
34
274
274
59
60
34
58
850
11
15
Dromgold
61
Marysville
74
850
14
81
1
34
34
Wormleysburg
13
A
4
Carlisle
6
5
2
Lemoyne
TP
76
11
Mechanicsburg
3
New
17
641
Cumberland
16
15
641
7
Camp Hill
Newville
12
11
10
74
174
641
9
15
11
81
8
533
174
696
20
18
34
19
Shippensburg

CUMBERLAND

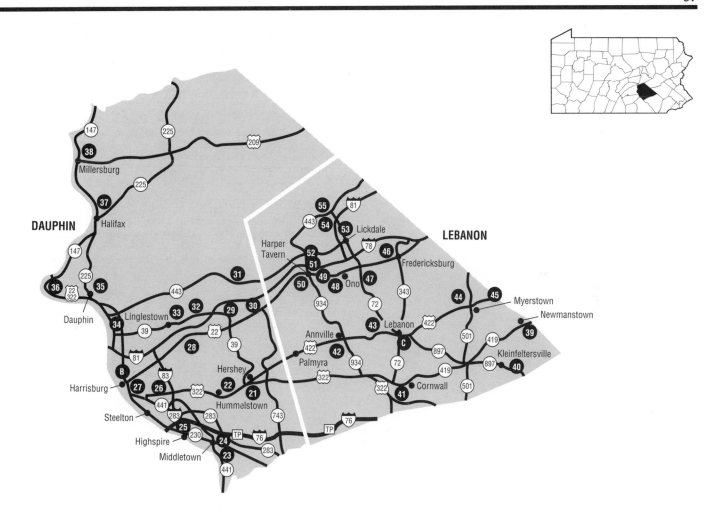

DAUPHIN

LEBANON

147
225
209
38
Millersburg
225
37
Halifax
55
81
443
54
53
Lickdale
147
Harper
Tavern
52
78
46
Fredericksburg
225
51
31
36
35
50
49
48
Ono
47
22
322
443
32
29
30
934
343
44
45
Myerstown
Dauphin
34
Linglestown
33
72
Newmanstown
39
22
43
Lebanon
422
501
419
39
28
39
Annville
42
C
897
Kleinfeltersville
422
897
B
Hershey
Palmyra
934
72
419
40
Harrisburg
27
26
83
322
22
21
322
41
Cornwall
501
Steelton
441
283
743
25
283
76
Highspire
230
24
TP
TP
76
23
Middletown
283
441

Cumberland County

(A) CUMBERLAND COUNTY

Formed January 27, 1750 from Lancaster County. Named for Cumberland County in England, it originally extended to Pennsylvania's western limits. Carlisle, county seat, was founded 1751. Crossed by major roads, county had a key role in westward migration.

City type: Old Courthouse, High & Hanover Sts., Carlisle. Dedicated May 17, 1982.

(1) HARRISBURG

Pennsylvania's capital since 1812. As Harris' Ferry, was settled a century before by John Harris, Sr. Laid out as a town in 1785 by John Harris, Jr. For over 200 years a center of travel, trade, and historic events.

Front St., Wormleysburg, N of Walnut St. Bridge. Erected Aug. 1, 1947.

(2) FORT COUCH

Remains of breastworks, at Eighth and Ohio Streets, built before the battle of Gettysburg, to oppose the expected Southern drive on Harrisburg. June 29, 1863, a few Confederate scouts neared here but withdrew.

8th & Market Sts., Lemoyne. Erected Aug. 10, 1947.

(2) FORT COUCH

Remains of breastworks built in June 1863 to oppose an expected attack on Harrisburg by Confederate troops. Site then known as Hummel's Heights. Fort was named for Gen. Couch, Commander, Eastern Pennsylvania Military Department.

City type: 8th St. & Ohio Ave., Lemoyne. Erected Oct. 13, 1954.

(3) DANIEL DRAWBAUGH

Inventor of a telephone for which he sought a patent in 1880. Claims contested by Bell Telephone, which won the court decision in 1888. Born in this village, July 14, 1827, where he developed his inventions; he removed in 1904 to Camp Hill, where he died November 2, 1911.

SR 2033 (former LR 21023) at Eberlys Mill, 1 mile W of New Cumberland. Dedicated May 1, 1965.

(4) CUMBERLAND RIFLEMEN

Capt. William Hendricks led, from nearby Cumberland County points, a company of riflemen to Quebec, Canada. There they fought, Dec. 31, 1775, at the side of Gen. Richard Montgomery. Hendricks was killed in action.

At park, Market St. between 24th & 25th Sts., Camp Hill. Erected May 25, 1948.

(4) GETTYSBURG CAMPAIGN

Farthest advance of a body of Confederate troops toward Harrisburg. Southern units under General A. G. Jenkins of Ewell's Corps reached Oyster Point on June 28, 1863. On the next day defending militia faced them here in a skirmish in which both sides suffered casualties.

At 3025 Market St., Camp Hill. Dedicated June 28, 1963.

(5) PEACE CHURCH

Present building erected in 1798 by a Reformed congregation. Half-interest obtained in 1806 by a Lutheran congregation; in joint use until 1866. Kept in its original form; used for special services.

PA 641 (Trindle Rd.) at St. John's Rd. W of Camp Hill. Erected Aug. 4, 1947.

(5) PEACE CHURCH

Present building erected in 1798 by a Reformed congregation. Half-interest obtained in 1806 by a Lutheran congregation; in joint use until 1866. Kept in its original form; used annually by St. John's Lutheran. A half-mile away.

Carlisle Pike (SR 1010) at St. John's Rd., 1.2 miles W of Camp Hill. Erected May 25, 1948.

(6) SILVER SPRING PRESBYTERIAN CHURCH

Founded 1734 on land of James Silver by Scotch-Irish Presbyterians, earliest settlers of the Cumberland Valley. Present church built in 1783, restored in 1928 to its original style, and still used for worship.

SR 1011 (former LR 21051) S of US 11 at church. Erected June 1974 (revised 1947 marker).

7 IRVING FEMALE COLLEGE
Site of the College that was chartered in 1857, and named for Washington Irving, a trustee. First women's college in Pennsylvania to grant degrees in arts and sciences. It was closed in 1929.
City type: E. Main St. (PA 641) near Filbert St., Mechanicsburg. Erected Sept. 29, 1954.

7 UNION CHURCH
Oldest public building in Mechanicsburg. Built in 1825 on land given by Martin Rupp. As provided in the charter, it has been used by many religious sects on payment of small fee.
City type: E. Main St. (PA 641) at church, Mechanicsburg. Erected Sept. 29, 1954.

7 SIMPSON FERRY ROAD
Built about 1792. It extended from Michael Simpson's Ferry on the Susquehanna to Carlisle, following, at this point, a course later known as Simpson St. Used by many persons traveling to western part of State.
City type: Simpson St. near Walnut St., Mechanicsburg. Erected Sept. 29, 1954.

8 WILLIAMS GROVE
With its excellent railroad connection, this became the site of the Great Grangers' Interstate Picnic Exhibition, founded 1874 by Robert H. Thomas of the Pennsylvania State Grange. A week's attendance at this annual event was estimated at 100,000 or more by the 1890's. The John Williams House, built about 1799, is nearby.
SR 2011 (former LR 21027) .5 mile S of Williams Grove. Dedicated Oct. 19, 1980.

9 CARLISLE IRON WORKS
Founded about 1762 by John Rigbie and Co. Operated after 1781 by Michael Ege, noted ironmaster of the period. Ruins of the charcoal furnace still stand.
PA 174 just E of Boiling Springs. Erected Aug. 4, 1947.

10 GETTYSBURG CAMPAIGN
Gen. J. E. B. Stuart's Southern cavalry arrived July 1, 1863, by Dover and Dillsburg. Finding Ewell had left the day before, Stuart burned the U.S. Barracks and left for Gettysburg, where the battle had begun.
PA 74 just E of Carlisle near Interstate 81. Erected July 29, 1947.

11 GETTYSBURG CAMPAIGN
June 30, 1863, Gen. Ewell's Southern army, ordered to retire from Carlisle and rejoin Lee's army, marched over this road to Mt. Holly Springs, York Springs, and Heidlersburg, where they camped for the night.
PA 34, .3 mile S of Carlisle near Interstate 81. Erected July 29, 1947.

12 GETTYSBURG CAMPAIGN
June 27, 1863, Gen. Ewell's Confederate army, marching over this road toward Harrisburg, reached Carlisle; Jenkins' cavalry went on to reconnoitre. On June 29, Lee ordered Ewell to join the main army at Cashtown.
SR 3023 (former LR 35) .5 mile SW of Carlisle near I 81. Erected July 29, 1947.

Entering Carlisle

13 CARLISLE
Founded in 1751 as the seat of Cumberland County. Historic old frontier town. Supplied a contingent for the first regiment of the Continental Army in 1775. March against the Whiskey Rebels began here, 1794.
On main highways leading into town. Erected July 30, 1947.

13 DICKINSON SCHOOL OF LAW
Oldest law school in Pennsylvania; founded in 1834 by the Honorable John Reed, eminent jurist, and author of ''Pennsylvania Blackstone.'' Andrew Curtin, Civil War Governor, was one of earliest graduates.
City type: S. College St. at Law School, Carlisle. Erected Oct. 20, 1949.

13 GEORGE WASHINGTON
Here George Washington reviewed militia from Pennsylvania and New Jersey, rendezvoused at Carlisle, October 1794, before marching to the western part of State to quell the Whiskey Rebellion.
City type: W. High St. at Denny Hall, Carlisle. Erected Oct. 20, 1949.

13 DICKINSON COLLEGE
Grammar school founded in 1773. College chartered in 1783, and named for John Dickinson. "Old West," built 1804, was designed by Benjamin H. Latrobe, architect of the national Capitol.
W. High St. at campus in Carlisle. Erected July 1, 1947.

13 THOMAS BUTLER
On this lot Thomas Butler had his home and gunshop about 1764; the latter still stands to the rear. Butler and five sons, all officers, served in the Revolution. Often referred to as the "Fighting Butlers."
City type: W. High St. between West & Pitt Sts., Carlisle. Erected Oct. 21, 1949.

13 JAMES WILSON
Early Carlisle lawyer, and representative to Continental Congress, occupied house that stood on this site. He was a signer of the Declaration of Independence, and one of the framers of the Constitution of U.S.
City type: SW corner, High & Pitt Sts., Carlisle. Erected Oct. 20, 1949.

13 CARLISLE FORT
First fort authorized by Pennsylvania. Laid out by Gov. Morris, July, 1755, "in the middle of this town," on news of Braddock's defeat. Col. John Armstrong's headquarters till 1758. Called "Fort Lowther" by some later writers.
City type: W. High St. between Pitt & Hanover Sts., Carlisle. Erected Nov. 3, 1961 (revised 1949 marker).

13 "MOLLY PITCHER"
Mary (Ludwig) Hays McCauley, known as "Molly Pitcher," heroine at Battle of Monmouth, is buried in Old Graveyard just east of here. In this burial ground are graves of many distinguished citizens.
City type: S. Hanover St. between Walnut & South Sts., Carlisle. Erected Nov. 30, 1949.

13 MAJOR ANDRÉ
For a short time in 1776, Major Andre and Lt. Despard, British prisoners of war, were detained in a tavern that stood on this site. Some years later, after an exchange and recapture, Andre was executed as a spy.
City type: S. Hanover St. between South & Pomfret Sts., Carlisle. Erected Dec. 6, 1949.

13 GREEN TREE INN
In 1753, Benjamin Franklin stayed at inn on this site while he, Richard Peters, and Isaac Norris treated with Indians. Hamilton and Knox, members of Washington's cabinet, lodged here in 1794.
City type: S. Hanover St. between Pomfret & High Sts., Carlisle. Erected Nov. 30, 1949.

13 BLAINE HOUSE
Home of Gen. Ephraim Blaine, Commissary General of Revolutionary Army, stood on this site. George Washington was a guest here, Oct. 4-11, 1794, while mustering an armed force to quell Whiskey Rebellion in Western Pennsylvania.
City type: S. Hanover St. between Pomfret & High Sts., Carlisle. Erected Dec. 6, 1949.

13 FIRST PRESBYTERIAN CHURCH
Oldest public building in Carlisle; erection begun, 1757. Here colonists met in 1774 to declare for independence, and George Washington worshiped, 1794. Congregation organized at Meeting House Springs in 1734.
City type: NW corner, High & Hanover Sts., Carlisle. Erected Oct. 21, 1949.

13 EPISCOPAL SQUARE
This square was set apart by the Penns in 1751 for the Church of England; in continuous use since that time by St. John's Episcopal Church. In 1752, the first church building was erected.

City type: NE corner, High & Hanover Sts., Carlisle. Erected Oct. 21, 1949.

13 JOHN BANNISTER GIBSON
Distinguished jurist and author of legal books, lived in this house from about 1820 until his death, 1853; Chief Justice of the Supreme Court of Pennsylvania for 24 years of his 37 years membership.

City type: E. High St. between Hanover & Bedford Sts. in Carlisle. Erected Nov. 30, 1949.

13 GEN. JOHN ARMSTRONG
"Hero of Kittanning," Revolutionary officer, member of Continental Congress, County Judge, lived in a house on this site. Died at Carlisle, 1795. Buried in Old Graveyard, two blocks south.

City type: NE corner, High & Bedford Sts., Carlisle. Erected Nov. 30, 1949.

13 GEN. WILLIAM IRVINE
Early Carlisle physician, member of Provincial Convention, Revolutionary officer, Commander at Fort Pitt, occupied house that stood on this site before 1800.

City type: SE corner, High & Bedford Sts., Carlisle. Erected Nov. 30, 1949.

13 THOMPSON'S RIFLE BATTALION
The first battalion in the colonies authorized by Congress, June 1775. Totaling nine companies, it was initially led by Col. William Thompson of Carlisle. Later the organization became the First Pennsylvania Continental Regiment.

City type: E. South St. at Old Graveyard (where Thompson is buried), Carlisle. Dedicated Nov. 11, 1986.

13 ST. PATRICK'S CHURCH
In 1779, Father Charles Sewall, S.J., took title to a lot here. Log structure built 1784; brick edifice in 1806. Present church erected 1893 by Father Henry G. Ganss. Adjacent is St. Katherine's Hall, built by Mother Katherine Drexel, 1901, for Catholics at Carlisle Indian School.

City type: 140 E. Pomfret St. at church, Carlisle. Dedicated Oct. 19, 1986.

13 CARLISLE BARRACKS
Established 1757. Oldest Army Post in U.S. A powder magazine built by Hessian prisoners in 1777 survives. Burned by Confederates on July 1, 1863. Indian School, 1879-1918. Army Medical Field Service School, 1920-1946. Army War College since 1951.

US 11 opposite War College, NE end Carlisle. Erected 1982 (revised 1948 marker).

Carlisle Barracks—Deputy Commandant Quarters

Leaving Carlisle

14 **[FARTHEST NORTH OF CONFEDERATES]**
The farthest north attained by any organized body of the Confederate Army of General Robert E. Lee was reached here at the farm of Joseph Miller on the morning of June 28, 1863. Hearing that Sterrett's Gap was occupied by Union troops, these outposts returned to their command at Carlisle. From these hills the tide of Confederate invasion receded, destined never to return. Marked by the Pennsylvania Historical Commission and the Hamilton Library Association.
Plaque: PA 34 (E side) 1 mile N of Carlisle Springs. Dedicated Oct. 26, 1929.

15 **FORBES ROAD** (RAYSTOWN PATH)
To capture Fort Duquesne, General Forbes marched an army, in 1758, from his main base at Carlisle to the Forks of the Ohio. He followed, as closely as he could with army wagons, the Raystown Indian and Traders Path, widened by axemen under Colonel Henry Bouquet.
US 11 just SW of Carlisle. Erected Jan. 7, 1952.

16 **JOSEPH RITNER**
Governor of Pennsylvania, 1835-1839, lies buried in this cemetery. Born, 1780, in Berks County; died, 1869, at Carlisle. He was noted for having put into practical operation the law of 1834, which established the public school systems.
US 11, 6 miles SW of Carlisle. Erected Oct. 11, 1951.

17 **LAUGHLIN MILL**
Grist mill built about 1763 by William Laughlin. Owned by his family until 1896. Preserved by Ethel T. McCarthy. The oldest such structure remaining in this region.
PA 641 at E end of Newville. Erected July 29, 1947.

17 **STATE POLICE SCHOOL**
The Pennsylvania State Police Training School, first of its kind in the nation, was established here in 1920 at the old Big Spring Hotel, which stood nearby. In 1923 the location of the school was transferred to Hershey in Dauphin County.
Walnut St. near Big Spring Ave., Newville. Dedicated July 29, 1970.

17 **BIG SPRING PRESBYTERIAN CHURCH**
Original log meeting house was erected 1737 near the Big Spring. Church was fully organized, October, 1738. Present stone structure was built 1789, and in 1790 the trustees laid out Newville as a town on the church-owned glebe.
S. Corporation St. at church, Newville. Dedicated Aug. 18, 1985.

18 **FORBES ROAD** (RAYSTOWN PATH)
At Shippensburg, the Raystown Path forked; one branch led directly west over three steep mountains to Burnt Cabins; the other, taken by General Forbes to avoid heavy grades, went south round Parnells Knob to Fort Loudon, crossing the Tuscarora Mountain at Cowan Gap.
US 11, 1 mile NE of Shippensburg. Erected Jan. 7, 1952.

Entering Shippensburg

19 **SHIPPENSBURG**
Founded 1730 by Edward Shippen. Second oldest town in the State west of the Susquehanna River. Important community on colonial frontier. Temporary seat of Cumberland Co., whose first courts were held here in 1750-1751.
US 11 at E end of Shippensburg. Erected June 1, 1948.

19 **SHIPPENSBURG**
Settled about 1733. Laid out by and named for Edward Shippen (1703-1781), merchant, mayor and justice of Philadelphia, later a resident of Lancaster, paymaster in the Forbes Expedition, a founder and trustee of Princeton University. Grandson of Edward Shippen (1639-1712) who was the host of William Penn, mayor and merchant of Philadelphia, Speaker of the Assembly, President of the Provincial Council, and Chief Justice of Pennsylvania. Marked by the Pennsylvania Historical Commission and the Colonial Dames of America, Chapter II, Philadelphia, 1925.
Plaque: wall, King & Prince Sts., Shippensburg. Dedicated June 6, 1925.

19 **OLD COURT HOUSE**
"Widow Piper's Tavern," used for Cumberland County court sessions, 1750-1751, until a court house was erected at Carlisle, the county seat. The house is now the home of the Shippensburg Civic Club.
US 11 (E. King St.) at Queen St., Shippensburg. Erected Nov. 18, 1947.

19 FORT MORRIS

Named for Gov. R. H. Morris, and built by local settlers under the supervision of James Burd after Braddock's defeat in July, 1755. Later garrisoned by provincial troops commanded by Hugh Mercer. The fort site, long marked by the soldiers' well, lies a block to the north on Burd Street.

US 11 (King St.) at Queen St., Shippensburg. Erected Nov. 3, 1961 (replaced 1949 Fort Franklin marker).

19 FORT MORRIS

This tablet marks the site of Fort Morris, erected in November 1755 by Col. James Burd and used as one of the chain of forts to protect the frontiers during the period of Indian hostility following the defeat of General Edward Braddock. This site was purchased by the Pennsylvania Historical Commission and the Civic Club of Shippensburg in 1920 and the tablet placed by these organizations in 1921.

Plaque: N side W. King St. (US 11) between Spring & Morris Sts., Shippensburg. Dedicated Oct. 21, 1921.

19 BRADDOCK EXPEDITION

In 1755 supplies for Braddock's army were stored here in Edward Shippen's strong stone house "at the back Run." James Burd, the son-in-law of Shippen, opened a road to carry these supplies to the west. After Braddock's defeat remaining supplies were given to sufferers from Indian attacks.

US 11 (W. King St.), Shippensburg. Erected Nov. 3, 1961 (replaced 1947 Fort Morris marker).

19 ONE-ROOM SCHOOLHOUSE

The Mount Jackson or Potato Point School, originally built in 1865, is an authentically reconstructed one-room schoolhouse. It was relocated here by alumni and friends of Shippensburg State College to preserve part of America's educational heritage.

PA 696 at Shippensburg University. Erected May 29, 1970.

Leaving Shippensburg

20 MIDDLE SPRING CHURCH

Founded 1738 by pioneer Scotch-Irish Presbyterians. Until 1781, the church was at the old cemetery which is about one-tenth mile NW from here. Present church built, 1847; parsonage built, 1855.

SR 4001 (old PA 696) 2.6 miles N of Shippensburg. Erected Nov. 6, 1950 (revised 1947 marker).

Dauphin County

B DAUPHIN COUNTY

Formed March 4, 1785 from part of Lancaster County. The name honors the eldest son of the French King Louis XVI. Harrisburg, the county seat, was laid out in 1785 and chartered a city in 1860. Since 1812 it has been the State capital of Pennsylvania

City type: Courthouse, Front & Market Sts., Harrisburg, Dedicated Dec. 9, 1982.

21 DERRY CHURCH

Founded in 1729; the first pastor, William Bertram, installed in 1732 by Donegal Presbytery. Its grove was patented to it by the sons of William Penn in 1741. The churchyard is the oldest pioneer graveyard in this region.

PA 743 N of US 422 near church, Hershey. Erected Feb. 28, 1948.

21 DERRY CHURCHYARD

Oldest pioneer graveyard in Dauphin County. Here, near Pastors William Bertram and John Roan, lie heroes of the French and Indian Wars and the Revolution; and Colonel John Rodgers, signer of the Hanover Resolves in 1774.

US 422 at E end of Hershey. Erected Feb. 28, 1948.

22 UNION CANAL

At Union Deposit, just to the north, can be seen the remains of the canal. It united the Susquehanna at Middletown with the Schuylkill at Reading. Suggested by William Penn, the canal was surveyed 1762, in use by 1828; abandoned in 1885.

Hanover St. just S of Union Deposit & N of PA 39 (Hersheypark Drive). Erected Mar. 1, 1948 (originally on old US 422 E of Hummelstown).

23 UNION CANAL

This canal was operated from 1828-1884. It connected the Susquehanna at Middletown with the Schuylkill at Reading, following the Swatara and Tulpehocken Creeks. Much coal and iron ore were transported. Course of canal was just west of old mill race.

PA 320 E of Middletown at Swatara Creek. Erected Apr. 1950.

24 "SAINT PETER'S KIERCH"

Cornerstone laid July 13, 1767, and dedicated in 1769 by Henry Melchior Muhlenberg, patriarch of American Lutheranism. Church erected on ground provided by George Fisher, the founder of Middletown, for annual rental of "one grain of wheat."

At church, Spring & High Sts., Middletown. Erected Feb. 28, 1969.

24 CAMP GEORGE GORDON MEADE

Covering three square miles, the former Camp Meade was situated a half mile to the northwest. Named for famed Civil War General, it was opened during the Spanish-American War and visited by President William McKinley on August 27, 1898.

PA 441 at Middletown Area School near Turnpike underpass. Erected Oct. 10, 1966.

24 BURD TOMBS

Col. James Burd of "Tinian," able and gallant officer in the colonial wars, author of the Middletown Resolves for Independence, June, 1774, and wife, Sarah Shippen, lie buried near the entrance of Middletown Cemetery.

PA 441 just N of Middletown. Erected Sept. 23, 1946.

24 MIDDLETOWN

The oldest town in Dauphin County; laid out in 1755 by George Fisher, Quaker. It was an important port at the junction of the Pennsylvania and Union Canals in the 19th century. Site of early flour, lumber, and iron industries.

PA 230 just W of Middletown. Erected Apr. 17, 1952.

25 COL. JAMES BURD

"Tinian," home of Col. Burd, is still standing on the opposite hill. Burd was road-builder of Braddock's expedition. French and Indian War commandant at Fort Augusta. Patriot and a soldier in the Revolution.

PA 230 in Highspire. Erected Sept. 23, 1946.

26 PAXTON CHURCH

A short way from here is early 18th century Paxton Church. The first pastor was installed in 1732. In the churchyard are buried John Harris, Jr., founder of Harrisburg, Senator William Maclay, and many other eminent leaders.

Derry St. near Wilhelm Rd., Paxtang. Erected Dec. 19, 1947.

26 PAXTON CHURCH
Organized as a congregation in 1732 with William Bertram as first pastor. The second pastor was the famed "Fighting Parson," John Elder. In the churchyard are buried John Harris, Jr., William Maclay and other notables of this region.
At church on Paxtang Ave., Paxtang. Erected Dec. 3, 1947.

Entering Harrisburg

27 HARRISBURG
Pennsylvania's capital since 1812. As Harris' Ferry, was settled a century before by John Harris Sr. Laid out as a town in 1785 by John Harris Jr. For over 200 years a center of travel, trade, and historic events.
On older main highways leading into city. Erected Sept. 23, 1946.

27 HARRISBURG CEMETERY
This 35-acre cemetery, chartered by the Commonwealth and opened in 1845, is the oldest and largest in the capital city. It is noted for its ornate statuary, original caretaker's house designed by A.J. Downing, and late Victorian landscape architecture. More than 30,000 persons are interred here, including Revolutionary War dead, Pennsylvania Governors, and others of local, State and national renown.
NE corner, 13th & State Sts., Harrisburg. Dedicated Sept. 30, 1990.

27 OLD SALEM CHURCH
Standing on land granted for religious purposes in 1785 by John Harris, this church was erected, 1822. It replaced one built of logs in 1787, the first church structure in present-day Harrisburg.
City type: Chestnut St. between 2nd & 3rd Sts., Harrisburg. Erected June 11, 1968.

27 EXECUTIVE MANSION
The first official Governor's mansion stood at this site. Purchased in 1858, it housed only two governors, Packer and Curtin. It was sold in 1864 when the second mansion, "Keystone Hall," was acquired.
City type: at former 111 S. 2nd St., Harrisburg. Erected Nov. 24, 1970.

27 ABRAHAM LINCOLN
On February 22, 1861, while journeying to Washington for his Inauguration, Lincoln stopped at the Jones House, on this site. From the portico of the hotel, he addressed a large crowd gathered in Market Square.
City type: S. Market Sq. (E side), Harrisburg. Erected Apr. 9, 1953.

27 MARKET SQUARE
For over a century, farm produce was sold here in market sheds and from wagons at the curbs. The first sheds were built soon after the city was laid out in 1785; the last were removed in 1889. Many inns faced the Square.
City type: S. Market Sq. (E side), Harrisburg. Erected Mar. 25, 1953.

27 EAGLE HOTEL
A three-story brick hotel, maintained by the Buehler family, 1811-64, stood on this site. Many State officials and legislators of the time took quarters here. Charles Dickens, a guest in 1842, praised his host in "American Notes."
City type: at former 21 N. 2nd St., Harrisburg. Erected Mar. 25, 1953.

27 OLD COURTHOUSES
Two Dauphin County Courthouses occupied this site. The first, built 1792-99, served as the State House for the Pennsylvania Legislature from 1812 to 1821. It was removed in 1860. The second stood here from 1860 to 1948.
City type: Market St. between 2nd & 3rd Sts., Harrisburg. Erected Apr. 10, 1953.

27 T. MORRIS CHESTER
Journalist, educator, lawyer. Born here, 1834. Taught in Liberia, 1857-61. Recruited Black soldiers in Civil War; noted as war correspondent. In Europe for freedmen's aid; was admitted to the English bar in 1870. Held major posts in Louisiana, 1873-83. Died nearby, 1892.
City type: Market Sq. near 3rd St., Harrisburg. Dedicated Dec. 3, 1986; erected 1990.

27 PRESIDENTIAL CONVENTION
The Whig Convention of Dec. 1839 met in this church and nominated Wm. Henry Harrison for president, John Tyler for vice-president. Popularized as "Tippecanoe and Tyler Too," they were elected 1840.
City type: 15 S. 4th St., Zion Lutheran Church, Harrisburg. Erected Aug. 11, 1953.

27 PENNSYLVANIA CANAL
A State-owned canal system, built 1826-34, to connect Philadelphia, Pittsburgh, Lake Erie. The first lock on the canal to be dedicated, March 13, 1827, was "Penn Lock," 150 yards east. It was replaced in 1859 by Locks No. 10 and 11.
City type: Walnut St. at Forum Bldg., Harrisburg. Erected Aug. 10, 1953.

27 JOHN HARRIS' GIFT
In 1785, the founder of Harrisburg set aside a four-acre lot, now this section of Capitol Park, to be held in trust for the use of the State. The Legislature accepted the gift, 1810, when it voted to make this city the capital.
City type: Capitol Park, 3rd & Walnut Sts., Harrisburg. Erected Aug. 10, 1953.

27 STATE CAPITOL
This building, which replaced the old brick capitol, was designed by Joseph M. Huston, and erected, 1902-1906. It was dedicated on October 4, 1906, in the term of Governor Samuel W. Pennypacker.
City type: main entrance Capitol (S of steps), Harrisburg. Erected Aug. 11, 1953.

27 OLD BRICK CAPITOL
The first State Capitol on this site was designed and built by Stephen Hills, 1819-1821. It was first occupied by the Legislature on January 2, 1822, and was used until destroyed by fire, February 2, 1897.
City type: main entrance Capitol (N of steps), Harrisburg. Erected Aug. 11, 1953.

27 GRACE METHODIST CHURCH
After the state capitol was destroyed by fire on February 2, 1897, this church building became the temporary quarters of the state legislature while the new capitol was being constructed.
City type: State St. between 2nd & 3rd Sts., Harrisburg. Erected June 10, 1968.

27 EXECUTIVE MANSION
The present residence of the Governor of Pennsylvania was completed in 1968. It is the third official executive mansion to have been located in Harrisburg.
City type: at Governor's Home, N. 2nd St. near Maclay St., Harrisburg. Erected Dec. 10, 1970.

27 EXECUTIVE MANSION
Opposite is the present residence of the Governor of Pennsylvania. Of Georgian-style architecture, it was completed in 1968 and is the third executive mansion to be located in Harrisburg. "Keystone Hall," earlier residence of the governors, was razed in 1960 after being in use for 96 years.
Riverfront Park, Front & Maclay Sts., Harrisburg. Erected Dec. 10, 1970.

27 PAXTANG MANOR
A tract of 1272 acres, now this part of Harrisburg, was first surveyed in 1732 for Thomas Penn, and was known as Paxtang Manor. It was sold, 1760, to three colonial settlers: Thomas Simpson, Thomas Forster, Thomas McKee.
City type: Riverfront Park, Front & Calder Sts., Harrisburg. Erected Aug. 1953.

27 WILLIAM MACLAY
In the stone house opposite lived William Maclay, who as a member of the first U.S. Senate, wrote a famous journal of its debates. A critic of Washington and Hamilton. Pioneer leader of Jeffersonian Democracy.
Riverfront Park, Front & South Sts., Harrisburg. Erected Sept. 23, 1946.

27 EXECUTIVE MANSION
The second official Governor's residence occupied a site across this street. Originally a private home acquired in 1864, it was altered and enlarged by many of its occupants. In the 1880's it was referred to as "Keystone Hall." After 96 years of use, it was demolished in 1960.
Park opposite former 311-313 N. Front St., Harrisburg. Erected Mar. 3, 1966.

27 CAMEL BACK BRIDGE
Covered wooden bridge, designed by Theodore Burr, was built here in 1813-17; called "Camel Back" because of its unique arch design. The structure, partly rebuilt in 1847 and 1867, was replaced after severe flood damage in 1902.
City type: Riverfront Park, Front & Market Sts., Harrisburg. Erected Oct. 19, 1953.

JOHN HARRIS MANSION
Built by John Harris, Jr., founder of Harrisburg, in 1764-66. It was Simon Cameron's home, 1863-89, and many famous people visited there. It is now home of The Dauphin County Historical Society.

S. Front St. at mansion in Harrisburg. Erected Sept. 23, 1946.

HARRIS' FERRY
The landing of the historic ferry first licensed in 1733 to John Harris, Sr., was on the river bank here. For over half a century it was a leading crossing for pioneers going West. Nearby is Harris' grave.

Riverfront Park opposite John Harris Mansion, S. Front St., Harrisburg. Erected Nov. 23, 1970 (revised 1946 marker).

[HARRIS' FERRY]
On the river bank, a short distance west of this stone, was the landing place of Harris' Ferry, the most historic crossing place on the Susquehanna. A great part of the early migration into western Pennsylvania and the Ohio Valley passed this way. The ferry-right was first granted to John Harris, father of the founder of Harrisburg, in December, 1733. For over half a century the site of Harrisburg was known as Harris' Ferry. Erected by the Pennsylvania Historical Commission, September 24, 1915.

Plaque: Riverfront Park opposite John Harris Mansion, S. Front St., Harrisburg. Dedicated on above date.

PENNSYLVANIA FARM SHOW
First held in January 1917, the Farm Show took place each year at various Harrisburg locations until 1931, when it moved to the new Main Exhibition Building here. The Large Arena first opened for the 1939 show. From modest beginnings, the Farm Show ultimately grew into one of the world's largest indoor gatherings devoted to the celebration and promotion of agriculture.

Maclay St., front of Farm Show Complex, Harrisburg. Dedicated Jan. 7, 1991.

HARRISBURG STATE HOSPITAL
The first State mental hospital in Pennsylvania. Opened in 1851, a result of efforts by the noted humanitarian, Dorothea Lynde Dix, to improve this State's treatment of the mentally ill. The hospital is on the wooded hills east of this marker, overlooking the city.

N. Cameron St. (US 22) beside hospital. Dedicated Oct. 7, 1987.

Leaving Harrisburg

PAXTON RIFLEMEN
Under Capt. Matthew Smith and Lt. Michael Simpson, a company of riflemen from Paxton Township marched to Quebec, Canada, to serve with Montgomery in the attack on that city on December 31, 1775.

US 22, 5.7 miles NE of Harrisburg. Erected Dec. 24, 1947.

UNION CANAL
At Union Deposit, five miles south, can be seen remains of this canal. It connected the Susquehanna at Middletown with the Schuylkill at Reading. Suggested by William Penn, the canal was surveyed in 1762. Completed in 1828; abandoned in 1885.

US 22, 9.3 miles NE of Harrisburg. Erected Mar. 1, 1948.

HANOVER CHURCH
About two miles north is the site of this pioneer Presbyterian church founded in 1736. First pastor was Richard Sankey. In the graveyard are buried many first settlers and veterans of frontier wars and the American Revolution.

US 22, 13.4 miles NE of Harrisburg, intersection PA 743. Erected Dec. 10, 1947.

HANOVER RESOLVES
The earliest resolves for independence in the State. Drawn June 4, 1774, by Col. Timothy Green and eight Hanover Township patriots. They committed their cause to "Heaven and our Rifles."

US 22, 14 miles NE of Harrisburg, E of junction Pa. 743. Erected Sept. 23, 1946.

31 FORT MANADA

In this vicinity stood James Brown's log house-fort, named Fort Manada when garrisoned as an outpost of Fort Swatara from January, 1756, to May, 1757. Its usual complement consisted of 21 officers and men. No description of the fort has survived.

PA 443 near Manada Gap. Erected Nov. 19, 1970 (replaced 1946, 1948 markers).

32 BARNETT'S FORT

North at the head of Beaver Creek, Joseph Barnett's log house was a frontier refuge in 1756-63 against Indians raiding the frontier. His son William was stolen by Indians in 1756 and not recovered until 1763 by Col. Henry Bouquet.

PA 39, 1.3 miles E of Linglestown. Erected Dec. 22, 1947.

33 PATTON'S FORT

Nearby stood Patton's Fort, a station of the Paxton Rangers, who defended the gaps and farmsteads along the Blue Mountains from the Susquehanna River to Swatara Creek, near Indiantown, against Indian raids from 1756 to 1763.

PA 39, 1.4 miles W of Linglestown. Erected Dec. 22, 1947.

34 FORT HUNTER

Stockaded blockhouse, built 1755-56, on site of present Fort Hunter Museum. Used to protect the frontier and as a supply base in building Fort Augusta. Abandoned and fell into ruins after 1763.

N. Front St. (old US 22 & 322) .5 mile N of Rockville Bridge at entrance to county park. Erected July 3, 1947.

34 [FORT HUNTER]

A short distance west of this stone stood Fort Hunter, otherwise known as the fort at Hunter's Mill. This fort, consisting of a block house surrounded by a stockade, was built during the winter of 1755-56. It was used as a base of supplies and as a rendezvous for troops during the period of the Indian Wars. All traces of this fort were removed when the present building was erected in 1814. Erected by the Pennsylvania Historical Commission, 1916.

Plaque: N. Front St. (W side) opposite Fort Hunter Rd. N of Rockville. Dedicated Nov. 9, 1916.

35 COL. TIMOTHY GREEN

In the graveyard to the south rests Timothy Green, officer in the French and Indian War; signer of the Hanover Independence Resolves in June, 1774; an outstanding leader of this region in the Revolution.

PA 225, .2 mile N of Dauphin. Erected Feb. 24, 1948.

36 PENNSYLVANIA CANAL (EASTERN DIVISION)

This Division was built, 1826-33; operated until 1901. Here, at old Clark's Ferry Towpath Bridge, the State's great inland canal traffic in iron, coal, and lumber crossed the Susquehanna. Lykens Valley coal trade, by way of Wiconisco Canal, joined it on the east bank.

US 22 & 322 just S of Clarks Ferry Bridge. Erected July 2, 1952.

PENNSYLVANIA CANAL
PENNSYLVANIA CANAL (JUNIATA DIVISION)

US 11 & 15 SW of Amity Hall. See Perry County.

37 FORT HALIFAX

Just west of this point stood Fort Halifax. It was built in 1756 by Col. William Clapham, and was one of the chain of frontier forts built to protect settlers in this region during French and Indian War days.

PA 147, .5 mile N of Halifax. Erected Sept. 23, 1946.

37 FORT HALIFAX

One of the chain of frontier defenses of the Province of Pennsylvania in the French and Indian Wars stood 500 feet to the west. Built 1756 by its commander, Colonel William Clapham. Marked by the Pennsylvania Historical Commission and the Society of Pennsylvania Women in New York, 1926.

Plaque: PA 157 (W side) .5 mile N of Halifax. Dedicated May 15, 1926.

38 MILLERSBURG FERRY

The only surviving ferry service across the Susquehanna began as early as 1825. Boats were poled by manpower until 1873, when the first paddlewheeler was acquired. In the 1920's, gasoline engines replaced steam power, and the paddlewheels were shifted from the side to the stern. The ferry landing is a short distance west.

PA 147 at Market & North Sts., Millersburg. Dedicated Oct. 22, 1972.

The Millersburg Ferry

Upper Dauphin Sentinel, Lon Zeiders

Lebanon County

C LEBANON COUNTY

Formed on February 16, 1813, from Dauphin and Lancaster counties. Named for old Lebanon Township, originally created 1729. Lebanon, county seat, is dated from 1740. Early settlers began the building of a rich agricultural and religious heritage.

City type: County-Municipal Bldg., 400 S. 8th St., Lebanon. Dedicated Oct. 6, 1982.

39 FORT ZELLER

The State's oldest existing fort is half a mile to the north. Pioneers who came to the Tulpehocken from the Schoharie valley built it in 1723, rebuilt it in 1745. It was used as a place of refuge during Indian wars.

PA 419 (Main St.) at Mill Creek Ave., Newmanstown. Erected Mar. 21, 1947.

40 JACOB ALBRIGHT

The son of German immigrants, Jacob Albright (1759-1808) founded the Evangelical Association, preached to poor farmers, and rose to become Bishop in the Methodist Church. His grave is nearby at Albright Memorial Church.

City type: PA 897 near Main & Shad Sts., Kleinfeltersville. Erected June 7, 1967.

41 GRUBB'S FIRST FORGE

Peter Grubb (c. 1700-54) carried on his initial efforts at iron making in 1735 just slightly to the north. He used the Catalan-type forge which had originated in Spain sometime during the tenth century.

City type: Boyd St. & Gold Rd., Miners' Village, Cornwall. Erected June 7, 1967.

41 CORNWALL BANKS

One of world's greatest iron mines, oldest operated continuously in the New World. It has been mined for more than two centuries, and is still the greatest iron ore deposit east of Lake Superior.

Boyd St., Cornwall, at now abandoned mine. Erected Mar. 1947.

41 CORNWALL FURNACE
Charcoal iron furnace built by Peter Grubb, operated 1742-1883. Best surviving example of the early Pennsylvania ironworks. Now a State historical shrine, gift of Mrs. Margaret Coleman Buckingham, heir of its famous owner, Robert Coleman.
Boyd St. in Cornwall. Erected Aug. 1948.

41 CORNWALL FURNACE
Built by Peter Grubb. Operated from 1742 to 1883. Administered by the Pennsylvania Historical and Museum Commission.
Rexmont Rd. at site in Cornwall. Erected 1948.

42 CORNWALL FURNACE
The oldest fully preserved example of the early iron furnaces of Pennsylvania is a few miles away at Cornwall. In blast from 1742 to 1883, the works are now a State historical shrine. Nearby ore banks have been mined since 1756.
US 422 at W end Annville. Erected Sept. 10, 1948.

43 UNION CANAL TUNNEL
Monument to first canal tunnel in America stands not far up this road. Built in 1823, the tunnel under the ridge may be reached by a short walk down the hill on either side. Union Canal was opened in 1827, and operated until 1884.
At site on SR 4001 (former LR 38025) just W of Lebanon. Erected Mar. 21, 1947.

44 UNION CANAL
This canal was in use from 1828-1884. About .3 mile to the south, at the Tulpehocken, are remains of one of the locks by which boats descended from the summit level north of Lebanon to the Schuylkill at Reading.
US 422, 1 mile W of Myerstown. Erected Jan. 6, 1950.

45 TULPEHOCKEN EVANGELICAL AND REFORMED CHURCH
Organized in 1727 by Tulpehocken settlers. Since 1745, one red rose has been paid annually by the Church to the heirs of Caspar Wistar as rental for the land granted by him for erection of the second place of worship. Since 1902, a white rose, a token of appreciation, has been given to Wistar's descendants.
US 422, 3 miles E of Myerstown. Erected Aug. 27, 1954.

45 ONE RED ROSE
Is annually paid by Trinity Reformed Church to the heirs of Caspar Wistar of Philadelphia who in 1738 gave 100 acres of land for church and school purposes. The congregation was formed by Reformed families among the Tulpehocken settlers. The first communion service was conducted by Reverend John Philip Boehm, October 18, 1727. Marked by the Pennsylvania Historical Commission, 1930.
Plaque: old US 422 between SR 2019 (former LR 38105) & Berks County line. Erected 1930.

46 JAMES LICK
The California financier and philanthropist, donor of the Lick Observatory, was born in Fredericksburg, Aug. 21, 1796. The Lick family monuments may be seen in the local cemetery.
US 22 near junction PA 343 just S of Fredericksburg. Erected Mar. 1947.

47 UNION CANAL
At Water Works, 3.7 miles SW, water was raised from Swatara Creek by water wheels and steam pumps, and carried by a Feeder Tube to the summit level near Lebanon. From that point the canal descended east to Reading, and west to Middletown.
PA 72, 5 miles NW of Lebanon. Erected Apr. 1950.

48 JOHN WALTER

Co-laborer of Jacob Albright in founding of Evangelical Church, born 1791, died 1818, is buried in this cemetery. An effective preacher and hymn writer, he published the first songbook for his church.

Old US 22 W of Ono at cemetery. Erected Mar. 1947.

49 REED'S FORT

Just south of this point stood the house of Adam Reed, Esq. In 1755 it was turned into a fort. Here, with Rangers from Hanover Township, Reed protected the people of the countryside against Indian raids.

US 22, 19.2 miles NE of Harrisburg. Erected Dec. 6, 1949.

50 "INDIANTOWN"

A native village from which, in turn, the Creek, Gap, and great Military Reservation derived their names, formerly stood nearby. The Delaware Indians took this route to Shamokin, upon their removal from the Schuylkill region.

Intersection PA 934 & old US 22, Harper Tavern. Erected Mar. 1947.

50 LINDLEY MURRAY

Famous grammarian, author of the English Grammar, was born, June 7, 1745, in a house near this point. Robert Murray, his father, owned a mill here from 1745 to 1746.

Intersection PA 934 & old US 22, Harper Tavern. Erected Mar. 1947.

51 LINDLEY MURRAY

Same text as above.

US 22, 18 miles NE of Harrisburg, E of junction PA 934. Erected Mar. 1947.

51 INDIANTOWN GAP MILITARY RESERVATION

Authorized in 1929, first land bought in 1931, and first used by the National Guard in 1932. In 1940 it was leased to the Federal government as an Army cantonment. Total area now more than 16,000 acres.

US 22 S of Fort Indiantown Gap, junction PA 934. Erected Mar. 1947.

51 LINDLEY MURRAY

Famous grammarian, author of the English Grammar, was born, June 7, 1745, in a house on Indiantown Creek near this point. Robert Murray, his father, owned a mill here from 1745 to 1746.

PA 934, .2 mile N of US 22. Erected Mar. 21, 1947.

52 INDIANTOWN GAP MILITARY RESERVATION

Same text as Indiantown Gap Military Reservation above.

SR 4019 (former LR 38001) 1.3 miles N of US 22 approaching Fort Indiantown Gap. Erected Mar. 1947.

53 SWATARA GAP

This gap in the Blue Mountain, named for Swatara Creek, a pass through which enemy Indians raided frontier settlements during the French and Indian War. Fort Swatara was built nearby to guard it.

SR 1001 (former LR 140) 2 miles N of Lickdale. Erected Mar. 1947.

54 UNION CANAL

Following the Swatara Creek from Pine Grove to main line of the Canal at Water Works was a Feeder Branch. It was in use from 1832-1862. A portion of the Big Dam, a guard lock, and several lift locks remain on the other side of the Swatara.

SR 1001 (former LR 140) 4 miles NW of Lickdale, just S of junction PA 443. Erected Sept. 28, 1950.

55 SATTAZAHN LUTHERAN CHURCH

Founded by German immigrants who settled as early as 1729. Initially served by traveling missionaries including John Caspar Stoever, Jr., first Lutheran pastor to visit regularly. A log structure was built about 1756; this church erected 1872. Named in honor of Peter Sattazahn, Revolutionary soldier buried here.

At church on Green Point School Rd., N of PA 443 near Murray. Dedicated Oct. 12, 1980.

Perry County

(D) PERRY COUNTY
Formed March 22, 1820 from Cumberland County. Named for Oliver Hazard
Perry, War of 1812 hero. Birthplace of two governors of Pennsylvania, one of
California, and one of Minnesota. The county seat, Bloomfield (P.O., New
Bloomfield) was incorporated 1831.
City type: County Courthouse, on Square, New Bloomfield. Dedicated Oct. 21,
1982.

(56) JAMES A. BEAVER
Civil War hero; Governor of Pennsylvania, 1887-91; a Superior Court judge,
1895-1914, was born in Millerstown, Oct. 21, 1837. Site is marked by a plaque.
His adult life was spent at Bellefonte, where he died on Janury 31, 1914.
US 22 & 322 just NW of Millerstown. Erected Apr. 19, 1948.

(57) CARSON LONG MILITARY INSTITUTE
A military school since 1919, it is the oldest in Pennsylvania. Originally
Bloomfield Academy, founded in 1837. Owned 1914-21 by Theodore K. Long
and renamed as a memorial to his son, William Carson Long. First building,
''The Maples,'' was completed in 1840.
N. Carlisle St. at school, 1 block from Square, New Bloomfield. Dedicated May 9,
1987.

(58) FORT ROBINSON
Pioneers' stronghold built 1755 on land of George Robinson; in use for several
years as refuge from Indian attacks. The site was about a mile away on the side
road.
Junction PA 274 & 850, 2.1 miles W of Loysville. Erected Apr. 28, 1947.

(59) JOHN BANNISTER GIBSON
Born Nov. 8, 1780, in a house near here. Chief Justice of Pennsylvania, 1827-51.
This was also the birthplace of William Bigler, who was Governor of
Pennsylvania, 1852-55; and U.S. Senator, 1856-61.
PA 850, 1.2 miles W of Dromgold. Erected July 25, 1947.

(59) JOHN BANNISTER GIBSON
Chief Justice of Pennsylvania, 1827-1851. Born November 8, 1780, in the home of
his parents, Colonel George Gibson and Ann West Gibson, 124 feet northwest of
this marker. His fame was unequalled. Marked by the Pennsylvania Historical
Commission and the Perry County Historical Society, 1929.
Plaque: PA 850 at Mill Rd., 1 mile W of Dromgold. Dedicated Sept. 27, 1929.

(60) WILLIAM BIGLER
Governor of Pennsylvania, 1852-55; birthplace, about one mile west of here. In
office he opposed the chartering of wildcat banks and passage of ''omnibus''
bills. U.S. Senator, 1856-1861. A brother, John, also born here, was Governor of
California, 1852-56.
Junction PA 34 & 850, Dromgold. Erected July 3, 1951.

(61) ROCKVILLE BRIDGE
The longest stone masonry arch railroad bridge in the world, one mile to the
south, was built 1900-02. With forty-eight arches, it has a length of 3,820 feet.
This was the third bridge constructed here by the Pennsylvania Railroad. A
wooden structure had been built 1847-49, followed by an iron bridge in 1877.
US 11 & 15 at N end Marysville. Dedicated Sept. 21, 1986.

*The triangular area between the Juniata and Susquehanna rivers and south of Amity Hall
— seemingly in Perry County — is part of Dauphin County. The two markers
immediately below are listed under Perry County, however, for ease of reference.*

62 PENNSYLVANIA CANAL

This State-owned artificial waterway system, built 1826-1834, was designed to connect points like Philadelphia, Pittsburgh and Erie in a vast inland trade. It embraced six chief canal divisions and two railroads. Here the Susquehanna, Juniata and Eastern Divisions joined in a canal basin.

US 11 & 15 (W side) SW of Amity Hall. Erected June 12, 1952.

62 PENNSYLVANIA CANAL (JUNIATA DIVISION)

This Division was built in 1828-33. It extended to the eastern end of the Allegheny Portage Railroad at Hollidaysburg, a distance of 127 miles. Just west of here, the Canal crossed the Juniata by an aqueduct which was used until 1901. Abutment and piers remain.

US 11 & 15 (E side) SW of Amity Hall. Erected June 12, 1952.

63 PENNSYLVANIA CANAL (SUSQUEHANNA DIVISION)

Built 1828-31; operated until 1901. It extended from Duncan's Island to Northumberland. In its 41-mile course, the Division embraced 13 locks, 7 aqueducts, old Shamokin Dam, and West Branch Towpath Bridge. Traces of the canal can be seen at points along this road.

US 11 & 15 just N of Amity Hall. Erected June 12, 1952.

64 MILLERSBURG FERRY

The only surviving ferry service across the Susquehanna began as early as 1825. Boats were poled by manpower until 1873, when the first paddlewheeler was acquired. In the 1920's, gasoline engines replaced steam power, and the paddlewheels were shifted from the side to the stern. The ferry landing is a short distance east.

US 11 & 15 S of Liverpool, near junction PA 34. Dedicated May 20, 1973.

65 DR. REIFSNYDER

Dr. Elizabeth Reifsnyder, M.D., a pioneer medical missionary to China for more than thirty years, lived in this house both before and after her work abroad. Born 1858 she died here in 1922.

US 11 & 15, Liverpool. Erected July 30, 1947.

65 PENNSYLVANIA CANAL (SUSQUEHANNA DIVISION)

Here is Lift-Lock No. 5 of this Division. Through it thousands of canal boats, bearing products from various points along the North and West Branches of the Susquehanna, passed annually until 1901, with their destination Philadelphia, New York, and Baltimore.

US 11 & 15 just N of Liverpool. Erected June 12, 1952.

REGION IV

Breadbasket of the East

With an invitation from William Penn to secure the greater opportunities and breathe the freer air of his benevolent Commonwealth, the early immigrants of Britain, Germany and other countries began their settlement on the fertile land of southeastern Pennsylvania.

Many of them were families who lacked sufficient opportunity in Europe, and who often lived under the cloud of war, religious conflict or economic distress. Armed with farming know-how and other skills, the Germans, Scotch-Irish and others made the rich limestone soil of this region the most productive in the British colonies of North America.

Three of these counties, having similarities in heritage, are *Adams, Lancaster* and *York.* They are situated on the once-disputed Maryland boundary, the location of which was resolved only by the famous survey, 1763 to 1767, of Charles Mason and Jeremiah Dixon.

Lancaster County was first settled in 1709 by immigrants from Switzerland and France, and by peasants from the German lowlands by the Rhine River. Their history is marked conspicuously by their churches, schools and colleges, by their neat farms and orderly towns, and by the way of life of the "Plain People" among them. In the midst of their eighteenth-century settlements, displaced Indians took refuge.

Wheat, cattle, milk and tobacco have been the agricultural mainstays of Lancaster County. Its craftsmen established its reputation for manufacture with the Pennsylvania rifle, Stiegel glassware and the Conestoga wagon, the main cargo carrier before the opening of canals. The Susquehanna River canals gave the region direct commercial access to the Chesapeake Bay and Baltimore.

Prominent among Lancaster County citizens were James Buchanan, pre-Civil War President; Thaddeus Stevens, post-Civil War Reconstruction Congressman and public-school champion; and Robert Fulton, steamboat inventor. Lancaster, the market town, was Pennsylvania's capital from 1799 to 1812.

York County was also settled by German farmers and families, by Scotch-Irish and by others. Iron furnaces have been replaced by other manufactures, making York city and its region an important industrial community. During the Revolution the Continental Congress removed to the city of York when, in September, 1777, the British occupied Philadelphia. From York it guided the war and the new nation under the Articles of Confederation until the British departed Philadelphia in June, 1778.

Adams County shares in the productivity of the region. Even more so than York County, it is a major grower of fruit. Its pastoral calm, however, was interrupted in 1863 by the Confederate attempt to turn the tide of the Civil War. The showdown came at Gettysburg on three days in July, and the Southern advance was repelled. Events connected with this historic battle, involving 160,000 men, are marked for posterity by numerous battlefield monuments.

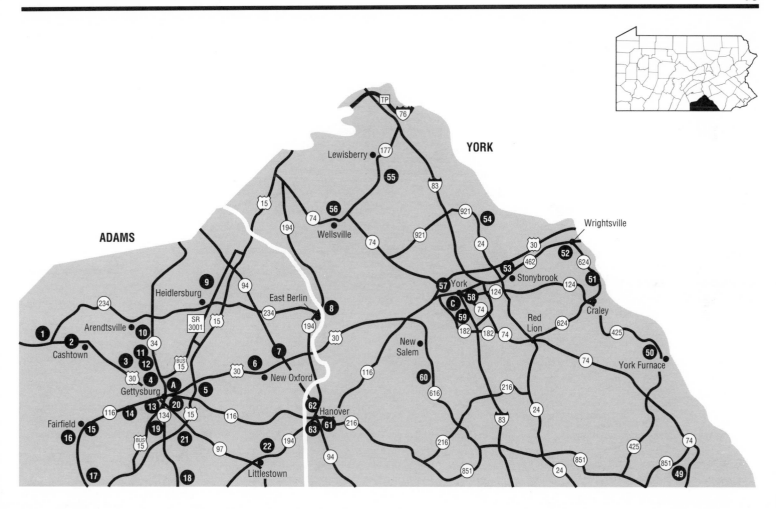

ADAMS

YORK

TP
76

Lewisberry ● 177

55

15

194

74 56

Wellsville

921

54

921

24

30

Wrightsville

462 52

53 624

Stonybrook 51

124

57 York

58 124

C 59 74

182 182 74

Red Lion 624

Craley

425

74 50

York Furnace

9

Heidlersburg ●

94

234

East Berlin

8

234

194

30

116

New Salem ●

60

616

234

SR 3001

15

1

2

Arendtsville ●

Cashtown

10

34

11

3 12

BUS 15

4 30

A

Gettysburg

13 20

134

19

15

116 14

Fairfield ●

15

16

BUS 15

21

17

18

6

30

New Oxford ●

5

116

116

97

22 194

Littlestown

62

Hanover

63 61 216

94

216

851

216

83

24

851

24

851

425

74

851

49

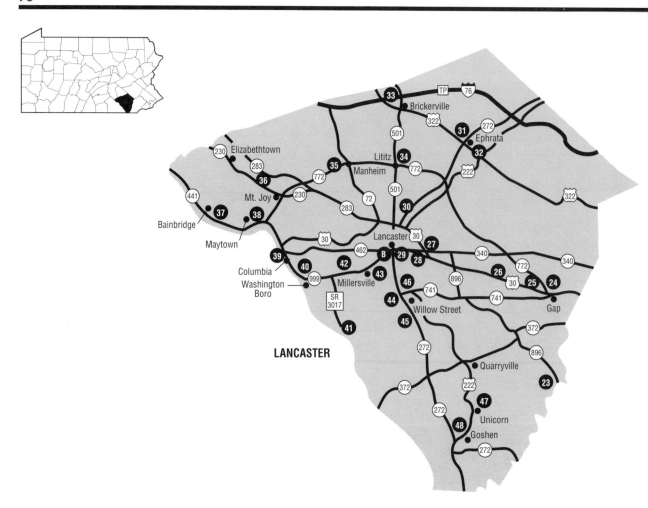

Brickerville

Ephrata

Elizabethtown

Lititz

Manheim

Mt. Joy

Bainbridge

Maytown

Lancaster

Columbia

Washington
Boro

Millersville

Willow Street

Gap

LANCASTER

Quarryville

Unicorn

Goshen

Adams County

(A) ADAMS COUNTY

Formed January 22, 1800 out of York County. The name honors President John Adams. Important center for fruit growing industry. County seat of Gettysburg, incorporated 1806, was site in 1863 of key Civil War battle and President Abraham Lincoln's great address.

City type: Old Courthouse, Baltimore & W. Middle Sts. (Business US 15 & PA 116) in Gettysburg. Dedicated Nov. 6, 1982.

(1) MARY JEMISON

The monument marking the home of the ''White Squaw of the Genessee'' prior to her capture by the French and Indians is 3 miles north. The remainder of Mary Jemison's life was spent as an Indian.

US 30 at junction PA 234, 4 miles W of Cashtown. Erected Dec. 12, 1947.

(2) GETTYSBURG CAMPAIGN

Crossing South Mountain from Chambersburg, Gen. Hill's Corps of Lee's army assembled here on June 29-30, 1863. On July 1, his advance guard moved up from near Marsh Creek and met Union troops west of Gettysburg.

Old US 30 just W of SR 3011, Cashtown. Erected Dec. 12, 1947.

(3) MANOR OF MASKE

Surveyed in 1766. Named for an estate in England. The Manor was about 6 miles wide and 12 miles long with the southern boundary at present Mason-Dixon Line. It was the second largest reserved estate of the Penns in Pennsylvania. The western boundary line of the Manor was near this point.

US 30 W of Seven Stars. Erected Aug. 11, 1954.

(4) GETTYSBURG CAMPAIGN

The Battle of Gettysburg began here the morning of July 1, 1863, when Union cavalry scouts under Gen. Buford met Gen. Hill's army advancing from the west. Arrival of Gen. Ewell's army that afternoon drove Union troops to south of the town.

US 30 at W approach to Gettysburg. Erected Dec. 12, 1947.

(4) DOBBIN HOUSE

Built in 1776 by the Rev. Alexander Dobbin. In use for some 25 years as one of the first classical schools west of the Susquehanna River. It is now refurnished in keeping with the early period.

Business US 15 (Steinwehr Ave.) near PA 134, Gettysburg. Erected Dec. 12, 1947.

(4) THADDEUS STEVENS

Lawyer, congressman, abolitionist, ironmaster, and defender of free public schools in Pennsylvania, lived in a house that stood on this site. He moved from here in 1842.

City type: 51 Chambersburg St., Gettysburg. Erected Sept. 1, 1954.

(4) OLD COURTHOUSE

First courthouse for Adams County stood in old Center Square from 1804 to 1859. The land for the Square was given by James Gettys.

City type: SW section of Square, Gettysburg. Erected Sept. 1, 1954.

(4) WILLS HOUSE

Abraham Lincoln was a guest of David Wills in this house, Nov. 18 and 19, 1863. Here he met Governor Curtin and others, greeted the public, and completed his Gettysburg Address.

City type: SE section of Square, Gettysburg. Erected Nov. 19, 1949.

4 GETTYS CROSSROADS AND TAVERN
Here the Shippensburg-Baltimore and the Philadelphia-Pittsburgh Roads crossed. Near the crossroads, stood the tavern of Samuel Gettys. In 1775, troops gathered here for Continental service.
City type: 44 York St., Gettysburg. Erected Sept. 1, 1954.

4 DANIEL ALEXANDER PAYNE (1811-1893)
Born a free African-American. He taught the colored people at this college, 1837, while a student at the Lutheran Seminary. A historian, he was elected bishop of the A.M.E. Church, 1852, and was president of Wilberforce University, 1863-76.
City type: 239 N. Washington St. at Gettysburg College. Dedicated Mar. 10, 1991.

4 MANOR OF MASKE
Surveyed in 1766. Named for an estate in England. The Manor was about 6 miles wide and 12 miles long with the southern boundary at present Mason-Dixon Line. It was the second largest reserved estate of the Penns in Pennsylvania. The eastern boundary line of the Manor was near this point.
US 30 at E end of Gettysburg. Erected Aug. 11, 1954.

Leaving Gettysburg

Other markers in the immediate Gettysburg area will be found at 13, 19, 20 & 21 below.

5 GETTYSBURG CAMPAIGN
Gen. J. E. B. Stuart's cavalry moved from north of Gettysburg, July 3, 1863, to attack the Union rear in time with Pickett's Charge. Met by Union cavalry a mile south of here, they were driven back again.
US 30, 2 miles E of Gettysburg. Erected Dec. 12, 1947.

6 CONEWAGO CHAPEL
Four miles south of New Oxford. Original Jesuit chapel built 1787 still in use and one of oldest in the United States. The mission was founded 1730. First Sacred Heart church in Pennsylvania.
US 30 W of New Oxford. Erected Dec. 12, 1947.

7 GETTYSBURG CAMPAIGN
Part of Gen. Early's Confederate army, under Gen. J. B. Gordon, passed here June 27, 1863, to York. Early's main force followed a parallel route through Hampton and East Berlin. Both entered York the following day.
US 30 E & W of junction PA 94, E of New Oxford. 2 markers, erected 1947 & 1948.

8 STUDEBAKER HOME
Built ca. 1790 by David Studebaker, carpenter, farmer and minister. He was related to the family that later built wagons and automobiles. The house is privately maintained as a museum.
City type: 200 W. King St. (PA 234 W of PA 194) in East Berlin. Dedicated Aug. 15, 1970.

9 ROCK CHAPEL
This is the oldest Methodist place of worship in this region. Built originally in 1773. Rebuilt in 1849, the second building is still standing about a mile north of this point on the side road.
SR 3001 (old US 15) at junction with SR 1016 N of Heidlersburg. Erected Dec. 12, 1947, altered slightly Apr. 1954.

9 GETTYSBURG CAMPAIGN
Gen. Rodes' Confederate troops, returning from Carlisle to join Lee's army, camped here the night of June 30. The next morning, July 1, they marched west toward Biglerville, then known as Middletown.
SR 3001 (old US 15) just N of Heidlersburg. Erected Dec. 12, 1947.

9 GETTYSBURG CAMPAIGN
Gen. Early's Confederate troops, marching from York to join Lee's army, camped, June 30, three miles to the east. Arriving here next morning, they turned south toward Gettysburg, on orders of Gen. Ewell.
SR 3001 (old US 15) .2 mile S of PA 234, Heidlersburg. Erected Dec. 12, 1947.

9 JOHN STUDEBAKER
Had his wagon works 2.5 miles SE of here, 1830 to 1836, when he moved west. In 1852 his sons formed the Studebaker Company, the world's largest maker of horse-drawn vehicles and, in 1897, a pioneer in the automobile industry.
SR 3001 (old US 15) just S of Heidlersburg. Erected Dec. 6, 1948.

10 RUSSELL TAVERN
The original building in which George Washington lodged in October, 1794, while engaged in quelling the Whiskey Rebellion is standing just west within view of this point.
PA 34 at Goldenville Rd., 4 miles N of Gettysburg. Erected Dec. 12, 1947.

11 GETTYSBURG CAMPAIGN
Gen. Rodes' Confederate troops marched down this road July 1, 1863, on their way from Carlisle. At this point they turned right along the ridge to Oak Hill, to attack the Union flank.
PA 34, 3 miles N of Gettysburg. Erected Dec. 12, 1947.

12 RURAL ELECTRIFICATION
In 1936 seventy-five percent of Pennsylvania farms had no electric service. During the next five years, with Federal support, 14 consumer-owned cooperatives were formed in this Commonwealth. Adams Electric Cooperative at Gettysburg, serving members in south-central Pennsylvania, was incorporated on August 21, 1940.
PA 34, 1.7 miles N of Gettysburg. Dedicated Aug. 21, 1990.

13 GETTYSBURG CAMPAIGN
The Confederate Army, the afternoon of July 4, 1863, began an orderly retreat by this road to the Potomac, which they crossed the night of July 13, after delay caused by high water.
PA 116 W of Gettysburg. Erected Dec. 12, 1947.

14 LOWER MARSH CREEK CHURCH
Present building erected 1790 by a Presbyterian congregation dating from 1748. Later remodeled, its exterior preserves much of the old-style design.
PA 116 at SR 3013 (former LR 01002), 4 miles W of Gettysburg. Erected July 15, 1948.

15 FIELD HOSPITAL
Wounded of the Sixth U.S. Cavalry and Sixth Virginia Cavalry C. S. A. were cared for in this church building after a severe engagement that took place two miles north of here on July 3, 1863.
City type: PA 116 (Main St.) at St. John Lutheran Church, Fairfield. Erected Sept. 1951.

16 "TAPEWORM RAILROAD"
Begun in 1836 by the State of Pennsylvania, largely through the efforts of Thaddeus Stevens. The meandering railroad's nickname was provided by its opponents. It was put up for sale in 1842. Just west of here [2.8 miles] stands its granite stone viaduct.
PA 116 at SR 3014 (former LR 01021) SW of Fairfield. Erected May 2, 1967.

17 CAPTAIN JOHN HANSON STEELMAN (1655-1749)
Indian trader and interpreter of Maryland and Pennsylvania, first permanent white settler in Pennsylvania west of Susquehanna River, lived in this valley on Paxton Indian trail or road leading from present Harrisburg. Born of Swedish parents at what is now Grays Ferry Bridge in the city of Philadelphia. Largest contributor toward erection of Old Swedes Lutheran Church, Wilmington, Delaware, 1698. Guest and correspondent, 1700-1, of William Penn. Deponent in chancery suit of the Penn heirs versus Lord Baltimore, 1740. Marked by the Pennsylvania Historical Commission, the Swedish Colonial Society, and Citizens of Adams County, 1924.
Plaque: intersection of Crum Rd. with Topper & Pecher Rds., just E of junction PA 16 & 116 at Zora. Plaque with above text dedicated Nov. 29, 1924; missing about 1950. New plaque with modified text dedicated by Fairfield Area Bicentennial Committee & Liberty Township Supervisors, July 24, 1977.

18 GETTYSBURG CAMPAIGN

Gen. George G. Meade, who had replaced Hooker as Union commander, June 28, 1863, traveled this road from Taneytown to Gettysburg the night of July 1. He made his headquarters just south of Gettysburg.

PA 134, .7 mile N of State line. Erected Dec. 12, 1947.

Gettysburg National Military Park

19 GETTYSBURG ADDRESS

Nearby, Nov. 19, 1863, in dedicating the National Cemetery, Abraham Lincoln gave the address which he had written in Washington and revised after his arrival at Gettysburg the evening of November 18.

PA 134 at entrance to National Cemetery. Erected Dec. 12, 1947.

20 GETTYSBURG ADDRESS

Same text as above.

Baltimore Pike (former US 140) at entrance to National Cemetery. Erected Dec. 12, 1947.

21 GETTYSBURG CAMPAIGN

The Union Army 12th Corps arrived here the afternoon of July 1, 1863; and later moved into battle line on Culp's Hill. On July 2, the 6th Corps arrived by this same road, and the 5th Corps by the Hanover Road.

Baltimore Pike, 2 miles SE of Gettysburg near junction US 15 & PA 97. Erected Dec. 12, 1947.

22 CHRIST REFORMED CHURCH

Known as "Mother of Reformed Churches" of this region. Congregation organized, May 1747, marking settlement of German pioneers in southern part of Conewago Valley. Section of present building erected, 1798. Many notable persons lie buried in the old churchyard.

PA 194 at SR 2023 (former LR 01029) 1.1 miles NE of Littlestown. Erected Feb. 21, 1950.

Lancaster County

B LANCASTER COUNTY

Formed on May 10, 1729 out of Chester County. Named for Lancashire in England. County seat, Lancaster, was chartered a borough in 1742; a city in 1818. It was the State capital, 1799-1812. County is noted for its rich farmland and ethnic diversity.

City type: Old Courthouse, N. Duke St., Lancaster. Dedicated June 12, 1982.

23 WILLIAM C. SPROUL

Governor of Pennsylvania, 1919-23, was born .4 mile SW, in 1870. The house is marked. His term is noted for road building, the Edmonds Act improving the public school system, and the creation of the Department of Welfare. He died near Chester in 1928.

PA 896 at Octoraro Creek, just W of county line. Erected Jan. 3, 1951.

24 GREAT MINQUAS PATH

An Indian trail, which was later the original Conestoga Road, passed through Gap, half a mile south of here. Over it, in the 17th century, Minquas (Conestoga) Indians carried quantities of beaver skins from the Susquehanna Valley to trading posts near Philadelphia.

US 30 just N of Gap. Erected Aug. 23, 1951.

25 SLAYMAKERTOWN

Once known as Salisburyville, the village was planned by Amos Slaymaker before the completion of the Lancaster-Philadelphia Turnpike and is noted for a few of its original buildings. ''White Chimneys,'' a residence enlarged through the years, was begun about 1720. Lafayette was entertained here July 28, 1825.

US 30 between Gap & Kinzer. Erected Aug. 21, 1968.

26 FIRST SETTLEMENT

On September 10, 1712, a patent for 2000 acres of land surrounding this spot was granted by William Penn, Proprietor of Pennsylvania, to Daniel Fiere and Isaac Lefever. The patentees were from France and were Huguenots. Here they, with their mother, Madam Mary Fiere, and her family settled. These were the first white settlers in this part of Lancaster County. On account of an error in measurement, the original patent was surrendered, and a new patent for 2300 acres was granted on October 29, 1734. Within sight of this marker, Daniel Lefever, the son of Isaac Lefever and Catharine Fiere, his wife, was born. He was the first white child in the settlement. Erected by the Pennsylvania Historical Commission and the Lancaster County Historical Society, 1918.

Plaque: US 30 at Bethany Ave., E end of Paradise. Erected 1918.

27 WITMER'S TAVERN

One of the best surviving structures of its type. Original east end built about 1725 by Benjamin Witmer, agent for the London Land Company. Passed on to his son, tavern-keeper John Witmer. Enlarged by Henry Witmer, 1773. Family was prominent in many early enterprises, including the Philadelphia-Lancaster Turnpike (1792), bridge over the Conestoga (1800), and first Columbia-Wrightsville bridge (1812).

PA 340 (2014 Old Philadelphia Pike) just E of junction US 30. Dedicated Sept. 26, 1988.

28 CONESTOGA WAGON

Product of this Conestoga Valley. Developed here in mid-18th century by local wagon makers, this vehicle of empire was the freight carrier of frontier days, and was the ancestor of the prairie schooner.

PA 462 (old US 30) .8 mile E of Lancaster. Erected Mar. 17, 1947.

28 PENNSYLVANIA RIFLE

Misnamed Kentucky Rifle, this famous weapon of the frontier was developed in the 1700's at Lancaster, which was the center for its manufacture.

PA 462 (old US 30) .8 mile E of Lancaster. Erected Mar. 19, 1947.

Entering Lancaster

29 ROCK FORD

Name of Colonial mansion of Edward Hand, Adjutant General of the Continental Army, and notable Lancaster physician. George Washington was entertained here in 1791. The old mansion is about a half mile to the southeast.

S. Duke St. extended, Lancaster at Conestoga River. Erected June 29, 1951.

29 JAMES BUCHANAN

Lawyer, statesman, diplomat, and fifteenth President of United States, lies buried in this cemetery, about 350 yards southeast. His home, Wheatland, located on Marietta Avenue, is marked with a bronze tablet.

City type: S. Queen St., Lancaster at Woodward Hill Cemetery. Erected Mar. 24, 1950.

29 HOLY TRINITY LUTHERAN CHURCH

Founded in 1730. A session for an Indian treaty was held in the original church building in 1762. The present edifice was dedicated in 1766. Here are interred the remains of Thomas Wharton (1778) and Gov. Thomas Mifflin (1800).

31 S. Duke St., Lancaster. Dedicated June 15, 1975.

29 JAMES BUCHANAN

Fifteenth President of the United States, lies buried at Woodward Hill Cemetery located five blocks to the south on Queen Street.

City type: SE section of Square, Lancaster. Erected June 11, 1951.

29 LANCASTER COUNTY COURTHOUSE
Old courthouse stood in the center of this square, 1739-1853. Here Continental Congress met for a day, Sept. 27, 1777, thus making Lancaster one of the capitals of the United States.
City type: SW section of Square, Lancaster. Erected June 11, 1951.

29 REYNOLDS HOUSE
Birthplace and residence of Major General John F. Reynolds of the Army of the Potomac. Killed on the morning of the first day of the Battle of Gettysburg, July 1, 1863, his body lies buried in Lancaster Cemetery.
City type: 42 W. King St., Lancaster. Erected May 14, 1971 (revised 1950 marker).

29 BAILEY'S PRINTSHOP
Francis Bailey, official printer to both the U.S. Congress and the Commonwealth, operated a printing office on this site from 1773 to 1780. Here, he produced many historic imprints including Thomas Paine's "Crisis No. 4."
City type: 14 W. King St., Lancaster. Erected May 14, 1971.

29 CHARLES DEMUTH
Born in Lancaster, Nov. 8, 1883. Demuth achieved international fame for his precise, modernist paintings including "My Egypt" and "I Saw the Figure 5 in Gold." He traveled in the U.S. and abroad but resided after 1889 in this house. Here he died in 1935.
City type: 118 E. King St., Lancaster. Dedicated Nov. 8, 1983.

29 GEORGE ROSS
Soldier, ardent patriot, jurist, and a Signer of the Declaration of Independence; settled at Lancaster about 1751. Site of his country house, now marked by monument, is on Ross Street, nine blocks north. Died, 1779.
City type: SW corner, King & Lime Sts., Lancaster. Erected Mar. 13, 1950.

29 COLONIAL MANSION
This house, of true Georgian style, was built before 1760. The ground was purchased by Thomas Poultney, merchant, in 1749. John Passmore, first mayor of Lancaster, occupied the house at one time.
City type: NW corner, Orange & Shippen Sts., Lancaster. Erected Mar. 14, 1950.

29 SHIPPEN HOUSE
Site of house occupied, 1751-1781, by Edward Shippen; lawyer, judge, Chairman Committee of Observation, and grandfather of Peggy Shippen Arnold. An earlier occupant was Thomas Cookson, first Burgess of Lancaster Borough.
City type: NW corner, Orange & Lime Sts., Lancaster. Erected Mar. 30, 1950.

29 FIRST PRESBYTERIAN CHURCH
Congregation traces its origin to 1742. The first regular pastor was Rev. John D. Woodhull, Revolutionary patriot. First building completed here in 1770; present edifice dedicated 1851. James Buchanan, 15th President of the U.S., was a member.
City type: 140 E. Orange St., Lancaster. Dedicated June 17, 1984.

29 MILITARY STABLES AND BARRACKS
This long building was used as military stables during the Revolution. On opposite side of street, stood the Barracks where British and Hessians were imprisoned during that period.
City type: 307 N. Duke St., Lancaster. Erected Mar. 24, 1950.

29 ST. JAMES' CHURCH (EPISCOPAL)
Founded 1744. Original structure built 1746-53; this building begun 1820. George Ross, signer of the Declaration of Independence, was vestryman. Buried here are the patriots Edward Shippen, William Atlee, Edward Hand, and Jasper Yeates.
City type: 119 N. Duke St., Lancaster. Dedicated June 15, 1980.

29 SIMON SNYDER
Born, 1759, on this site. Governor of Pennsylvania for three terms, 1808-17. His strong appeal for a call to arms, and defense of sound currency, during War of 1812, are noteworthy. Died in 1819 at Selinsgrove.
City type: N. Queen St. between Chestnut & Walnut Sts., Lancaster. Erected Mar. 24, 1950.

29 FULTON OPERA HOUSE

Built in 1852 and named Fulton Hall in honor of Robert Fulton. It is considered an excellent example of the 19th century "Opera House." For more than 75 years, every major star of the American theatre appeared on its stage.

City type: N. Prince St. between King & Orange Sts., Lancaster. Erected Oct. 11, 1952.

29 EARLY ARCHITECTURE

This one and a half story house is typical of the architecture during the period of early settlement of Lancaster, dating from 1730. Most of the local houses in 1800 were of this style.

City type: 28 N. Water St., Lancaster. Erected 1950, relocated 1980.

29 THADDEUS STEVENS

Lawyer, congressman, defender of free public schools, abolitionist, lies buried in the rear of this cemetery. He believed in the "Equality of man before his Creator." Resided in Lancaster from 1842 until his death, 1868.

City type: W. Chestnut St., Shreiner's Cemetery, Lancaster. Erected Mar. 24, 1950.

29 FRANKLIN AND MARSHALL COLLEGE

Third oldest college in the State. Franklin College, 1787, named for its patron and benefactor, Benjamin Franklin, was united with Marshall College in 1853. Campus site selected by James Buchanan, President Board of Trustees.

Harrisburg Pike at entrance to college, Lancaster. Erected Nov. 28, 1950.

29 WHEATLAND

The home of James Buchanan, statesman, diplomat and the fifteenth President of the United States (1857-61), is located on Marietta Avenue, seven blocks south. Buchanan maintained Wheatland as his home from 1848 until he died there on June 1, 1868.

N. President Ave. near Harrisburg Pike, Lancaster. Erected May 14, 1971 (revised 1947 marker).

29 PENNSYLVANIA RIFLE

Misnamed Kentucky Rifle, this famous weapon of the frontier was developed in the 1700's at Lancaster, which was the center for its manufacture.

PA 23 (Marietta Ave.) near W end of Lancaster. Erected Mar. 19, 1947.

29 WHEATLAND

Home of President James Buchanan from 1849 to his death is a few blocks away. Statesman and diplomat, Member of Congress, U.S. Senator, Secretary of State, and Minister to England. Elected President in 1856.

PA 462 (Columbia Ave.) near President Ave. just W of Lancaster. Erected Mar. 17, 1947.

James Buchanan Foundation for the Preservation of Wheatland

Wheatland, James Buchanan's home, Lancaster

Leaving Lancaster

30 ISAAC LONG BARN

The United Brethren in Christ, and the Evangelical United Brethren Church, trace their origin to the joint efforts of Rev. Philip W. Otterbein of the German Reformed Church and Martin Boehm, a Mennonite preacher, at a revival held here about 1767. The barn stands a mile and a half to the north.

Off PA 272 (Oregon Pike) at Landis Valley Museum. Dedicated June 16, 1960.

31 EPHRATA CLOISTER

Surviving buildings of the famous Ephrata community of Seventh Day Baptists, founded by Conrad Beissel, 1732. Turn to the right here to see this State historic shrine.

PA 272 N & S of US 322 underpass, Ephrata. 2 markers, erected Mar. 18, 1947.

32 EPHRATA CLOISTER

Surviving restored buildings of the Seventh Day Baptist community founded by Conrad Beissel. Original buildings erected between 1735 and 1749. Administered by the Pennsylvania Historical and Museum Commission.

At the site on US 322, Ephrata. Erected 1948.

33 HOPEWELL FORGE MANSION

Built c. 1740 by Peter Grubb, pioneer ironmaster at nearby Cornwall Furnace, and named for the Upper and Lower Hopewell Forges located on Hammer Creek near the house. Remnants of the forge dams may still be seen in the creek.

US 322, 2 miles W of Brickerville. Dedicated July 11, 1959.

34 LITITZ

Settled during 1740's, Moravians established here a ''Land Gemeine,'' or country congregation in 1756. It was named by Count Zinzendorf after a Bohemian town which sheltered persecuted Moravians in 1456.

City type: PA 501 at Lititz Spring Park, Lititz. Erected 1967.

34 JOHN A. SUTTER

In the cemetery opposite is buried the California pioneer. Founder of Sacramento, 1839. Gold was discovered on his lands, 1848. Ruined by the gold rush, he made Lititz his home from 1871 until death, 1880.

PA 501 (S. Broad St.) at Lemon St., Lititz. Erected Mar. 5, 1948.

34 LINDEN HALL

Oldest girls' resident school in the United States. Founded in 1746 by the Moravian Church. Originally a day school, it has since 1794 drawn boarding students from a wide area. The school was chartered under its present name in 1863.

City type: PA 772 (E. Main St.) at school in Lititz. Erected Apr. 8, 1980 (revised 1947 marker).

34 MORAVIAN GEMEINHAUS

Built in 1746 by the Moravians as Church, Parsonage, and School. It stood 125 yards to the north, on the elevation on this side of Carter's Run.

City type: NE corner, Main (PA 772) & Elm Sts., Lititz. Erected March 1953.

35 HEINTZELMAN HOUSE

Birthplace of Maj. Gen. Samuel P. Heintzelman, September 30, 1805. A veteran of the Mexican War and the Civil War, he died May 1, 1880, at Washington, D.C., and was buried at Buffalo, N.Y.

City type: 24 S. Main St. (PA 72), Manheim. Dedicated May 13, 1962.

35 BARON STIEGEL

The famed glassmaker and ironmaster of colonial days founded Manheim in 1762, and set up his glassworks in 1764. He gave land for the Lutheran Church which still pays his heirs one red rose a year.

PA 72 at Square in Manheim. Erected Mar. 19, 1947.

35 STIEGEL MANSION

Built in 1763; home of ''Baron'' Henry William Stiegel, the renowned glass manufacturer and ironmaster, 1763-1774. Also the residence, 1777-1778, of Robert Morris, Revolutionary War financier.

City type: 1 N. Main St. (PA 72), Manheim. Dedicated May 13, 1962.

35 STIEGEL GLASS MANUFACTORY

On this site, from 1763 to 1774, ''Baron'' Henry William Stiegel made the glass for which he is famous. Erected in 1763, the building was torn down in 1813.

City type: 102 W. Stiegel St., Manheim. Dedicated May 13, 1962.

36 DONEGAL CHURCH

A few miles west is the early Presbyterian church, organized 1714. Present structure built about 1740. In 1777, the congregation met at the Witness Tree in front of the Church to avow their patriotism.

PA 230, 3.5 miles SE of Elizabethtown. Erected Mar. 18, 1947.

36 EARLY TELEGRAPH

First commercial telegraph line in the U.S. ran along this railroad right-of-way. Completed from Lancaster to Harrisburg, 1845. The first message, ''Why don't you write, you rascals?'', was received Jan. 8, 1846.

PA 230, 3.1 miles SE of Elizabethtown. Erected Mar. 18, 1947.

37 CONOY INDIAN TOWN

From about 1718-1743, the Conoy Indian Tribe had its settlement slightly to the west of here. Closely related to the Nanticoke Tribe, with whom they eventually merged, the Conoy Indians gradually migrated into Pennsylvania from the area of Chesapeake Bay.

PA 441, 1 mile S of Bainbridge. Erected 1967.

37 SAMUEL S. HALDEMAN (1812-1880)

The internationally known scientist and philologist was born one-quarter mile south, in the mansion at Locust Grove. Built 1811 by his grandfather, John B. Haldeman, this was the younger man's home until he moved to Chickies, seven miles south, in 1835. Author of over 150 books and scientific papers, Haldeman taught and lectured widely.

PA 441 S of Bainbridge at Locust Grove Rd. Dedicated Sept. 7, 1991.

38 SIMON CAMERON

Noted leader in state and national politics, statesman, diplomat, member of Lincoln's cabinet, U. S. Senator. Was born, 1799, in a log house that stood on this site. Died 1889 at Donegal Springs.

City type: W. High St. near square, Maytown. Erected June 9, 1951.

39 COLUMBIA

Originally Wright's Ferry, founded by John Wright in 1726. An early center for turnpike, canal, and railroad activity, at an important Susquehanna River crossing. First bridge built in 1812.

PA 462 (old US 30) at E end of Columbia. Erected Mar. 19, 1947.

40 MARTIN CHARTIER

Died 1718. Noted Indian trader and interpreter in early Pennsylvania and Maryland. Frenchman from Canada who resided at Fort St. Louis of the Sieur de la Salle in present Illinois, 1684-1690. A leader thence of the Shawnee Indians to Maryland, 1692, and to Susquehanna River at Pequea Creek, now Lancaster County, Pennsylvania, 1697. Agent in William Penn's treaties with the Indians of the Susquehanna. Settler here in later years at the site of Washington Borough on a 300 acre tract granted to him by Penn. Father by his Shawnee wife of Peter Chartier, the Indian trader and interpreter. Marked by the Pennsylvania Historical Commission and the Lancaster County Historical Society, 1925.

Plaque: PA 441 (River Rd.) at Charlestown Rd., Washington Boro. Dedicated Sept. 26, 1925.

41 CONESTOGA INDIAN TOWN

The Conestoga Indians, in origin largely the survivors of the defeated ancient Susquehannas [Susquehannocks] or Minquas of Iroquoian stock, located their village variously on these lands in the Penn Proprietary Manor of Conestoga chiefly west of this point. They were visited here in 1701 by William Penn, who made treaties with them. The tribe was exterminated by the Paxton Boys in 1763. Marked by the Pennsylvania Historical Commission and the Lancaster County Historical Society, 1924.

Plaque: SR 3017 (Safe Harbor Rd.) at Indian Marker Rd. near Letort, 4 miles SW of Millersville. Dedicated Sept. 13, 1924.

42 CONESTOGA INDIAN TOWN

About one mile eastwards stood the Conestoga Indian Town. Its peaceful Iroquoian inhabitants were visited by William Penn in 1701 who made treaties with them. In 1763 they were ruthlessly massacred by a frontier mob called the ''Paxtang Boys.''

PA 999 between Washington Boro & Millersville, 200 ft. W of SR 3017. Erected 1967.

43 MILLERSVILLE UNIVERSITY
Founded 1855 as the Lancaster County Normal School, it was named the first Pennsylvania State Normal School, 1859. Fully Commonwealth-owned after 1917, Millersville became a State Teachers College in 1928, and a State College for liberal arts and education, 1960. Since 1983 it has been Millersville University of Pennsylvania of the State System of Higher Education.

On N George St. at campus, Millersville. Erected 1989 (revised 1947 marker, first revised 1968).

44 MARTIN MEYLIN'S GUNSHOP
Old gunshop, built in 1719, is located about one mile northeast. Here, before 1745, the earliest known Pennsylvania Rifle, misnamed Kentucky Rifle, was made. Building is marked with a tablet.

US 222 at junction PA 272 northbound near Willow Street. Erected Nov. 21, 1950.

45 BOEHM'S CHAPEL
Built 1791, this "Temple of Limestone" is the oldest existing structure designed for Methodist use in Pennsylvania, and one of the oldest in the U.S. Erected on land formerly owned by Bishop Martin Boehm, co-founder of the United Bethren in Christ, it was frequently visited by Bishop Francis Asbury, "Father of American Methodism."

PA 272 northbound at Boehm's Rd., 1 mile S of Willow Street. Dedicated Apr. 29, 1984.

46 HERR HOUSE
Three-quarters of a mile south on the side road is the stone house built in 1719 by Christian Herr, son of Hans Herr, founder, in 1710, of the first Mennonite community in this area. It is the oldest building this far west in Pennsylvania.

US 222 at Hans Herr Dr., West Lampeter Twp. Erected May 14, 1971.

47 [DRUMORE CELEBRATION]
This marker perpetuates the memories of four illustrious Americans who were identified with this part of Drumore Township. Erected by the Historical Commission of Pennsylvania and the Lancaster County Historical Society, 1921.

Plaque: US 222 (E side) at Unicorn, S of Quarryville. Dedicated Sept. 17, 1921. The inscription above is at base of monument. On its sides are 4 plaques, which see below.

47 DR. DAVID RAMSAY
Historian-surgeon-poet. Born one mile southwest, 1749. Continental Army surgeon, friend of Washington, constructive leader in Congress, talented man in letters, the father of American history. He is best known for his History of the American Revolution, Life of Washington, History of America, and Universal History Americanized. Practiced medicine and died 1815 in Charleston, S.C.

Plaque: one of 4 accompanying the above. Dedicated Sept. 17, 1921.

47 GENERAL JOHN STEELE
Born three miles north, 1753. Resident of this farm. Volunteered at 18, Captain at 19, Colonel on Washington's staff at 21, wounded at Brandywine and at Germantown. Pennsylvania legislature (House), 1801. Speaker of Senate, 1806. Collector of Port of Philadelphia, 1808-1825. As commissioner to treat with warring tribes, to him was addressed the famous speech of Logan, the Indian Chief. Died, 1827.

Plaque: one of 4 accompanying the above. Dedicated Sept. 17, 1921.

47 COLONEL THOMAS PORTER
Born three miles north, 1738. A pioneer spirit of American independence. Committee of Sixty, 1774. Organizer of ten Lancaster County companies when failing health prevented his leading into the field. Died, 1777.

Plaque: one of 4 accompanying the above. Dedicated Sept. 17, 1921.

47 COLONEL ARCHIBALD STEELE
Born three miles north, 1742. Picturesque in his ruggedness and ardor. Walked to Boston at the call of Bunker Hill. Leading six picked men, he broke the trail for the Montgomery Expedition against Quebec, where he fought with distinction. Traveling on an overcrowded boat on the retreat, he contracted a chronic illness in the icy St. Lawrence. Thereafter commissary and finally head of the Philadelphia Arsenal. Died, 1832.

Plaque: one of 4 accompanying the above. Dedicated Sept. 17, 1921.

48 ROBERT FULTON BIRTHPLACE
The inventor and painter was born here Nov. 14, 1765. Famous for his steamboat "Clermont," he also invented canal machinery, a "diving boat," and torpedoes. Administered by the Pennsylvania Historical and Museum Commission.

At site US 222 N of Goshen. Erected 1978 (revised 1947 marker, first revised 1968).

York County

ⓒ YORK COUNTY
Formed August 19, 1749 from Lancaster County, it was Pennsylvania's fifth to be established. York, the county seat, was laid out in 1741. Continental Congress met in York, 1777-78. Here it adopted Articles of Confederation; ratified treaties with France.

City type: Colonial Courthouse, 205 W. Market St., York. Dedicated Aug. 19, 1982.

49 MASON-DIXON LINE
The historic boundary between Pennsylvania and Maryland was surveyed, 1763-1767, by Charles Mason and Jeremiah Dixon to settle border disputes between the two Provinces. This section of the Mason-Dixon Line was first surveyed June 26, 1765.

PA 74 (Maryland 165) on State line. Erected May 27, 1970.

50 SUSQUEHANNA AND TIDEWATER CANAL
Chartered by Pennsylvania, 1835; run by the canal company, 1840-1872, and the Reading Railroad until 1894. Followed the river for 45 miles below Columbia.

PA 425 at York Furnace. Erected Apr. 2, 1948.

50 SUSQUEHANNA CANAL
Now housing the Tucquan Club, the nearby stone building was originally a warehouse for deposit and shipping on the canal. Masonry fragments and a portion of the canal-bed may be seen nearby.

Accompanies marker above. Erected Apr. 5, 1948.

51 SUSQUEHANNA AND TIDEWATER CANAL
Same text as Susquehanna and Tidewater Canal above.

PA 624, 1.8 miles NE of Craley. Erected Apr. 2, 1948.

51 SUSQUEHANNA CANAL
Masonry visible beside the river remains from a lock of the canal which carried goods southward from Columbia, and provided an outlet for trade from Pennsylvania to Baltimore.

Accompanies marker above. Erected Apr. 5, 1948.

51 CAPTAIN THOMAS CRESAP, 1703-1790
A Marylander. Settled on these Indian lands of Conejohela in 1730 and held them for Lord Baltimore against the Penn Proprietors until 1736, when in the Border War he was burned out of his log house or fort near this marker toward the river — on his plantation "Pleasant Garden" — and carried prisoner to Philadelphia. Marked by the Pennsylvania Historical Commission and the Historical Society of York County, 1924.

Plaque: PA 624 at Bank Hill Rd., 2.4 miles NE of Craley. Dedicated Sept. 27, 1924.

51 CRESAP'S FORT
Thomas Cresap settled here about 1730 on lands claimed by Lord Baltimore of Maryland. Forcibly evicted in 1736 by Penn agents who burned his "fort," Cresap moved to western Maryland where he continued active in frontier affairs and died about 1790.

PA 624, 2.4 miles NE of Craley. Erected June 6, 1960 (revised 1947 marker).

52 SUSQUEHANNA AND TIDEWATER CANAL
Same text as Susquehanna and Tidewater Canal above.

PA 624, .1 mile SE of Wrightsville. Erected Apr. 2, 1948.

52 SUSQUEHANNA CANAL
Lock masonry, just below the bridge, and part of the old channel mark the north end of the canal which met the State-owned canal at Columbia. Until 1863, the river-bridge had a towpath for mules; later, tugboats pulled canal craft across.

Accompanies marker above. Erected Apr. 2, 1948.

52 GETTYSBURG CAMPAIGN

Confederate troops, sent from York by Gen. Early to cross the river and march on Harrisburg, reached here June 28, 1863. U.S. militia withdrew, firing the bridge and barring any Southern advance beyond the river.

PA 462 (old US 30) at Susquehanna River bridge, Wrightsville. Erected Nov. 12, 1947.

52 SPRINGETSBURY MANOR

Established by warrant of June, 1722; resurveyed in 1768. Extending from the Susquehanna to about 18 mi. west, and about 3 mi. on each side of this highway, it was largest reserved estate of the Penns in Pennsylvania.

PA 462 (old US 30) in Wrightsville. Erected Nov. 20, 1950.

52 AMERICA'S FIRST IRON STEAMBOAT

The "Cordorus," built in York by John Elgar, was launched at present-day Accomac, on the Susquehanna River, Nov. 22, 1825. The site is about two miles distant.

PA 462 (old US 30) .3 mile W of Wrightsville. Erected Oct. 23, 1947.

53 CAMP SECURITY

Stockade, built in 1781 by Col. Jas. Wood on land of Daniel Brubaker. British troops of Burgoyne's army imprisoned here, guarded by York County militia. The camp was about a mile to the south.

PA 462 (old US 30) 3 miles E of York at Stonybrook. Erected July 17, 1947.

54 CODORUS FURNACE

Erected in 1765 by William Bennet. Operated by James Smith, a signer of the Declaration of Independence, during the Revolutionary War. It is the oldest remaining landmark of the iron industry in York County. The old Furnace, now restored, is 2.5 miles NE of here.

PA 24 at SR 1008 (former LR 66040), Starview. Erected Aug. 12, 1954.

55 FIRST PINCHOT ROAD

To "get the farmer out of the mud" was the road from here to Rossville. Gov. Gifford Pinchot broke ground here, July 23, 1931, to inaugurate the rural road improvement program of the Pennsylvania Department of Highways under the Act of June 22, 1931.

PA 177, 1.5 miles S of Lewisberry. Dedicated May 25, 1963.

56 WARRINGTON MEETING HOUSE

Site of Friends' meeting house since 1745. Preserved building erected 1769, enlarged 1782. Preserved in its early state, and used for regular meetings.

PA 74, .2 mile E of Wellsville. Erected July 17, 1947.

57 GETTYSBURG CAMPAIGN

June 28, 1863, Confederate Gen. Gordon's brigade of Early's division followed this route through York to Wrightsville. Early's main force remained here until June 30, when it left to rejoin Lee's army.

PA 462 (old US 30) W of York, .3 mile W of PA 234. Erected Oct. 8, 1947.

Entering York

58 YORK

Laid out in 1741, by order of the Proprietors; the first Pennsylvania town west of the Susquehanna River. Seat of the Continental Congress, 1777-78; birthplace of the Articles of Confederation.

On main highways leading into city. Erected July 17, 1947.

58 YORK INTER-STATE FAIR

Recognized as America's oldest agricultural fair, dating its origin from a charter issued by the Penns in 1765. Discontinued after 1815, the fair has been conducted annually since 1853 by the York County Agricultural Society. The present ground has been used since 1888.

PA 462 (W. Market St.) at fairgrounds, near W end of York. Dedicated Sept. 10, 1978.

58 PHINEAS DAVIS

Site of shop where, in 1831, Davis designed and built first coal-burning locomotive steam engine in United States, called "The York." Here, also, was built "The Codorus," first iron steamboat made in America.

City type: NW corner, King & Newberry Sts., York. Dec. 6, 1949.

58 GOLDEN PLOUGH TAVERN

Possibly the oldest surviving building in York. Built, c. 1741, by Martin Eichelberger, native of the German Black Forest. Its massive hewn half-timbers reflect a style, almost unknown today, of medieval architecture.

City type: W. Market St. (PA 74 & 462 eastbound) just E of Pershing Ave., York. Erected June 23, 1967.

58 GEN. HORATIO GATES

This building was the residence of Gen. Gates in 1778. At that time he was President of Board of War. It is said that the "Conway Cabal" was thwarted here by Lafayette's loyalty to Washington.

City type: W. Market St. between Pershing Ave. & Beaver St., York. Erected Dec. 14, 1949.

58 MAJOR JOHN CLARK

Revolutionary officer, aide-de-camp to General Greene, Auditor of the Continental Army, lived on this site.

City type: S. Beaver St. near W. Market St., York. Erected Dec. 6, 1949.

58 HALL & SELLERS PRESS

First printing press west of Susquehanna River was set up on this site. Here, government publications and continental currency were printed while Congress met in York, Sept. 1777 to June 1778.

City type: SW corner, Market & Beaver Sts., York. Erected Dec. 14, 1949.

58 GEN. WAYNE HEADQUARTERS

Building erected in Colonial Period was headquarters of Gen. Anthony Wayne while his command was in York, Feb.-May, 1781, awaiting orders to join Lafayette in the Yorktown Campaign.

City type: NW corner, Market & Beaver Sts., York. Erected Dec. 14, 1949.

58 COLONEL THOMAS HARTLEY

On this site was the house of Col. Thomas Hartley, first congressman from York County. In 1777, he was prominent in the defense of Philadelphia; led an expedition to avenge the Wyoming Massacre in 1778.

City type: W. Market St. between Beaver & George Sts., York. Erected Dec. 14, 1949.

58 BLACK HORSE TAVERN

Old tavern stood on this site, which was the lot granted to Baltzer Spengler by the sons of William Penn for services in the laying out of York in 1741.

City type: NW section of Square, York. Erected Dec. 15, 1949.

58 GLOBE INN

Many distinguished persons stayed at old inn located on this site. Here, in 1825, Lafayette was given a reception. His toast "To the Town of York" is memorable.

City type: SW section of Square, York. Erected Dec. 15, 1949.

58 PROVINCIAL COURTHOUSE

Continental Congress held its session, Sept. 30, 1777-June 28, 1778 in Courthouse which stood in the center of this square. Here, treaties with France and Articles of Confederation were adopted.

City type: SE section of Square, York. Erected Dec. 15, 1949.

58 McCLEAN HOUSE

On this site stood the house of Archibald McClean; surveyor for the Penns, county officer, and ardent patriot. Traditionally the Treasury of U.S., 1777-1778, while York was national capital.

City type: NE section of Square, York. Erected Dec. 15, 1949.

58 JAMES SMITH

A Signer of the Declaration of Independence, delegate to Continental Congress, Colonel of Associators, lawyer, and ironmaster, lies buried in this churchyard.

City type: E. Market St., First Presbyterian churchyard, York. Erected Dec. 14, 1949.

58 "YORK HOUSE"

Built in 1860 by Charles Billmeyer, railroad car manufacturer. Noted for its hand-painted ceiling and exquisite interior ornamentation, building is outstanding example of mansion-type Victorian architecture.

City type: 225 E. Market St., York. Erected July 25, 1967.

58 WILLIAM C. GOODRIDGE

Here lived an ex-slave, born 1805, who became a prominent York businessman, 1824-1863. Tanner, newpaper distributor, barber. Erected York's first five-story building. His 13 rail cars operated commercially and were used in his work for the Underground Railroad.

City type: 123 E. Philadelphia St. (PA 74 & 462 westbound), York. Dedicated Dec. 16, 1987.

58 YORK MEETING

A center for Friends' activities since 1766. It is the oldest existing house of worship in York. The eastern part of the building was erected in 1766; the western part about 1783.

City type: W. Philadelphia St. at meetinghouse, York. Erected Oct. 3, 1953.

58 YORK LIBERTY BELL

Old bell originally hung in Provincial Courthouse; now in the vestibule of this church. Announced the signing of Declaration of Independence and sessions of Congress when it met in York.

City type: N. Beaver St. in Episcopal churchyard, York. Erected Dec. 6, 1949.

58 PHILIP LIVINGSTON

One of the Signers of the Declaration of Independence; died in June, 1778, while attending Continental Congress as delegate from New York. His grave is about 300 feet west of here.

City type: N. George St. (Business I 83) at Prospect Hill Cemetery. Erected Dec. 14, 1949.

58 YORK COUNTY PRISON

The old county prison stood on this site from about 1750-1855. In early years of the Revolution, prominent British prisoners of war were held here.

City type: NE corner, King & George Sts., York. Erected Dec. 6, 1949.

58 PENN COMMON

Set aside in 1805 by the heirs of William Penn as a common for the inhabitants of York.

City type: College Ave. at Penn Common, York. Erected Dec. 6, 1949.

Leaving York

59 YORK IMPERIAL APPLE

Here at a nursery located on Springwood Farms, a new variety of apple was propagated by Jonathan Jessop in 1820. In 1855 it was named the "York Imperial." It became a leading variety which was widely grown in the U.S.

S. George St. (SR 3001, old US 111) 2 miles S of York. Erected Apr. 5, 1948.

60 HANOVER JUNCTION

Here, Nov. 18, 1863, a special train carrying Abraham Lincoln and party to Gettysburg for dedication of National Cemetery changed railroads. Earlier in that year, wounded soldiers were transported from Gettysburg battlefield to this Junction, thence to distant hospitals. It was a chief point on the Military Telegraph line, 1863.

PA 616, 4 miles S of New Salem at Hanover Junction. Dedicated May 31, 1953.

61 GETTYSBURG CAMPAIGN

Men of Gen. Early's Confederate army, detached by Gen. Gordon to destroy a bridge at Hanover Junction, passed through Hanover by this route, June 27, 1863. This work done, the detachment rejoined Gen. Gordon west of York.

PA 116 near junction PA 216 just E of Hanover. Erected Nov. 11, 1947.

Entering Hanover

62 McALLISTER TAVERN

Here, along the Monacacy Road, Richard McAllister erected a two-story log building and opened a store and tavern. In 1755, Benjamin Franklin was a guest at the Tavern. Old building was razed in 1950.

City type: Baltimore (PA 94) & Middle Sts., Hanover. Erected Oct. 6, 1954.

62 BATTLE OF HANOVER
On the morning of June 30, 1863, Confederate Cavalry under General Stuart attacked the rear of Union Cavalry SE of here and, for a while, had possession of the town. The attack repulsed, Stuart withdrew in the evening.
City type: SW section of Square, Hanover. Erected Sept. 14, 1954.

62 KILPATRICK HEADQUARTERS
On June 30, 1863, Gen. Kilpatrick, commanding the Third Division of the Union Cavalry, took headquarters in this building after part of his forces had been attacked by Confederate Cavalry SE of town.
City type: NW section of Square, Hanover. Erected Sept. 14, 1954.

62 MARKET HOUSE
Stood in this square from 1815 to 1872. Under the Market, at one end, was the jail. Equipment for fighting fires was kept here. Fairs and other public events were held under its roof.
City type: NE section of Square, Hanover. Erected Sept. 14, 1954.

62 ABRAHAM LINCOLN
One-half block east of here, on Nov. 18, 1863, Abraham Lincoln spoke briefly to townspeople from his special train. The President was traveling to Gettysburg for the dedication of the National Cemetery.
City type: Carlisle St. (PA 94) & Park Ave., Hanover. Erected Sept. 14, 1954.

Leaving Hanover

63 GETTYSBURG CAMPAIGN
On June 30, 1863, General J. Kilpatrick's Union Cavalry, hunting Gen. J. E. B. Stuart's cavalry, were attacked here by Stuart. Repulsed, Stuart tried to join Early; finding him gone, he marched to Carlisle, failing to reach Gettysburg until July 2.
PA 194 just SW of Hanover. Erected Nov. 11, 1947.

REGION V

The Trans-Allegheny West

Though the counties of *Bedford, Blair, Cambria, Franklin, Fulton, Huntingdon* and *Somerset* lie at a distance from the great urban centers of Pennsylvania, their history and character owe as much to the concentration there of basic industry as they do to the moderate productivity of their farms. On their western side are the rugged contours of the Allegheny Plateau, which is productive of coal and iron and where ruins of iron furnaces dot the landscape; on their eastern side are the valleys and ridges that shelter many of the family farms; and on the mountainsides are the forests that yield timber and pulp.

A sustained immigration of settlers, their roots in northern Europe, began midway in the eighteenth century. President James Buchanan, who presided over the last attempts to peacefully resolve the slavery crisis, was among their descendants as were three governors and other notables. After them, immigrants came from middle and southern Europe and from the American South to work the steelmills, coal mines and railroads.

Access to the region was facilitated by a road blazed in 1755 by Colonel James Burd, and carved by the British government, alarmed both by the occupation of the west by the French and by the growing number of their Native American allies. The fear that was aroused, in fact, is attested by the number of forts that were built to repel possible armed assault. Finally, in 1758, with General John Forbes's road having been extended across this region almost to Fort Duquesne, the French occupation was abandoned.

The transportation progress that began with the Forbes Road was continued intermittently — in 1818 with the National Road, in 1832 by the Pennsylvania Canal, and in 1834 with the Allegheny Portage Railroad. By 1852 the Pennsylvania Railroad was ready to speed passengers and goods, uninterrupted, as far west as Pittsburgh. What began in 1883 as William Vanderbilt's South Penn Railroad, but which was never completed, was utilized in part — roadbed and tunnels — to construct through the region the first link of the Pennsylvania Turnpike, opened in 1940.

The conclusion of the French and Indian War in 1763, however, did not end the conflict and violence — there were the casualties of a 1780 Revolutionary skirmish, preparations to supress the Whiskey Rebellion in 1794, preliminaries to John Brown's bloody raid on Harper's Ferry in 1859, the Altoona conference of the Union's Civil War governors convened by President Lincoln in 1862, Confederate invasions in 1863 and 1864, and in nature's realm three floods — the first in 1889 — that devastated the city of Johnstown.

Nineteenth-century Johnstown grew rapidly as a manufacturer of steel, fueled with the bituminous coal of nearby mines. Altoona, the region's second industrial city, was founded by the Pennsylvania Railroad in 1849 both to maintain the locomotives that pushed its trains over the Allegheny Front and to build freight and passenger cars. Both cities have declined with the industries from which they prospered. Other manufactures, however, have eased the economic misfortune. Meanwhile, the resort and vacation business, which began at Bedford Springs sometime after 1796, continues to attract visitors to the pleasant landscapes of the region.

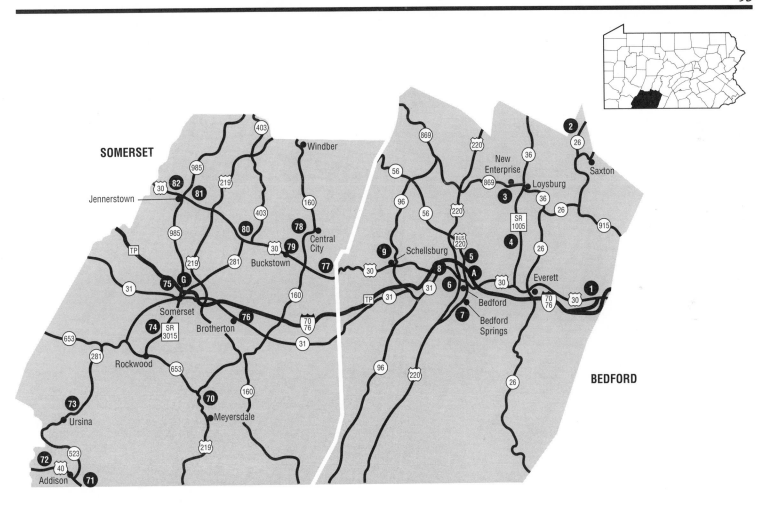

SOMERSET

BEDFORD

Windber

Jennerstown

Central
City

Buckstown

Somerset

Brotherton

Rockwood

Meyersdale

Ursina

Addison

New
Enterprise

Loysburg

Saxton

Schellsburg

Everett

Bedford

Bedford
Springs

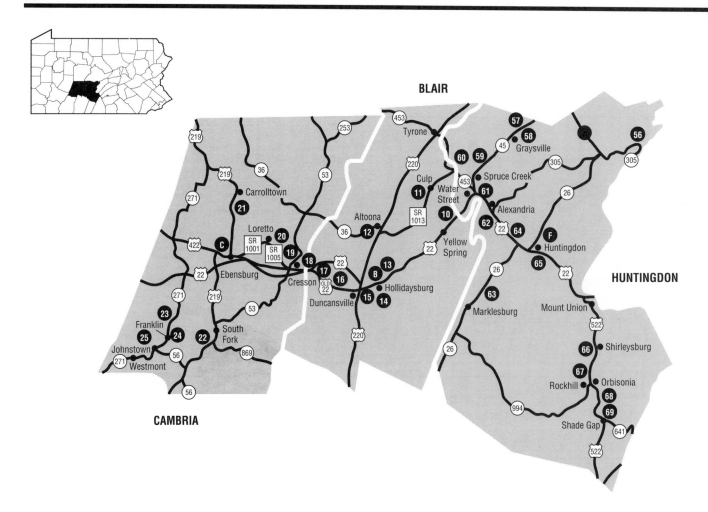

BLAIR

CAMBRIA

HUNTINGDON

219
453
Tyrone
57
56
219
253
58
Graysville
305
36
45
60
59
Spruce Creek
Carrolltown
53
220
305
271
26
Culp
11
453
21
Water
61
Street
Alexandria
Loretto
20
Altoona
SR
10
422
C
SR
1001
12
1013
62
F
Ebensburg
19
64
Huntingdon
SR
1005
22
22
18
65
Cresson
17
Yellow
22
271
219
16
B
13
Spring
22
OLD
26
HUNTINGDON
22
53
Duncansville
15
14
Hollidaysburg
26
23
63
Mount Union
Franklin
Marklesburg
522
25
24
22
South
220
56
Fork
66
Shirleysburg
Johnstown
271
869
67
Westmont
56
Orbisonia
Rockhill
68
994
69
56
Shade Gap
641
522

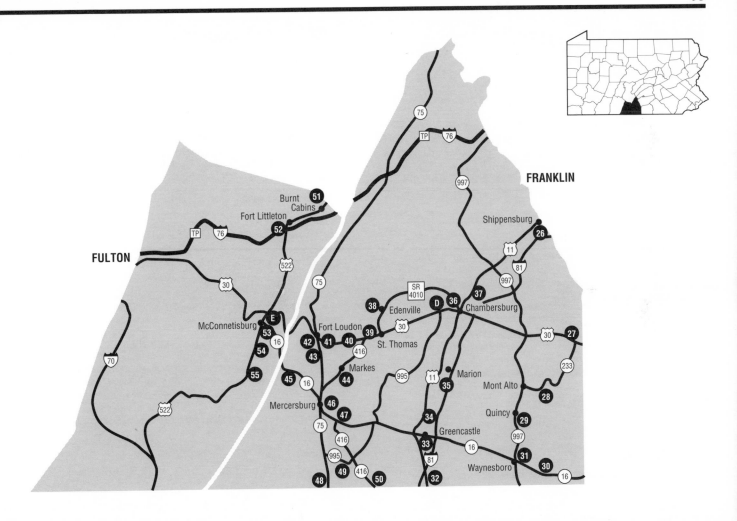

FRANKLIN

FULTON

Burnt
Cabins **51**

Fort Littleton **52**

TP 76

522

30

75

SR
4010

Edenville **D** **36**

38

Fort Loudon **39**

St. Thomas

E

McConnetisburg **53**

54

16

42 **41** **40**

416

43

55

45

16

Markes **44**

995

11

Marion

35

Mont Alto

Mercersburg **46**

47

75

416

995

48 **49** **416** **50**

34

Greencastle

33

81

32

16

Waynesboro

31 **30**

16

Quincy **29**

997

28

233

27

30

Shippensburg **26**

11

81

997

997

75

70

522

Bedford County

A BEDFORD COUNTY

Formed on March 9, 1771 from Cumberland County, it first embraced most of western Pennsylvania. Named for its county seat (formerly Raystown) incorporated 1795. In 1758, Fort Bedford was erected here, and Forbes Road — to become a major highway west — was built.

City type: Courthouse, S. Juliana & Penn Sts., Bedford. Dedicated Oct. 17, 1982.

1 FORBES ROAD (FORT JUNIATA)

At the Juniata Crossings, half a mile north of here, General Forbes erected a small stockade in 1758 to protect the communications of his army moving west to attack Fort Duquesne.

US 30, 6.2 miles E of Everett. Erected Jan. 9, 1952.

2 PHILLIPS' RANGERS

Capt. William Phillips and 11 men of his militia company were captured near this point by Indians, July 16, 1780. Ten men were killed here and were buried later by a search party. Capt. Phillips and son Elijah, taken prisoner, were freed by British at end of Revolution.

PA 26, 2 miles NW of Saxton. Erected Mar. 25, 1966.

2 CAPT. PHILLIPS' RANGERS MEMORIAL

Graves of ten of Capt. Phillips' militia killed by Indians, July 16, 1780. Administered by the Pennsylvania Historical and Museum Commission.

At site, PA 26, 2 miles NW of Saxton. Erected Sept. 2, 1964.

3 RURAL ELECTRIFICATION

In 1936 seventy-five percent of Pennsylvania farms had no electric service. Over the next five years, in response to their needs, 14 consumer-owned cooperatives were formed in this State. Serving users in Bedford, Fulton and Huntingdon counties, New Enterprise Rural Electric Cooperative was incorporated November 18, 1938.

PA 869 at New Enterprise. Erected March 1989.

4 GETTYSBURG CAMPAIGN

Entrenchments still visible by the roadsides were prepared in June, 1863, by militia under Col. J. C. Higgins against threatened Confederate attack toward the railroad at Altoona. The march of troops toward Gettysburg on June 30-July 1 ended the danger and the need for these defenses.

SR 1005 (former PA 36 & LR 286) 5 miles S of Loysburg. Dedicated June 29, 1963.

5 PENNSYLVANIA TURNPIKE

This is one of the original service plazas for the nation's first long-distance superhighway. On October 1, 1940, the Turnpike opened, stretching 160 miles from Irwin to Carlisle. The Turnpike Commission had been created in 1937; construction utilized the old South Pennsylvania Railroad's right-of-way and tunnels. By 1957 the Turnpike spanned 360 miles across the State and extended 110 miles north to Scranton.

South Midway Service Plaza (serving eastbound traffic) just W of Turnpike exit 11. Dedicated 1990.

5 PENNSYLVANIA TURNPIKE

Same text as preceding marker except for inversion of ''Carlisle'' and ''Irwin'' in second sentence.

North Midway Service Plaza (serving westbound traffic) just W of Turnpike exit 11. Dedicated 1990.

6 RURAL ELECTRIFICATION

In 1936 seventy-five percent of Pennsylvania farms had no electric service. During the next five years, with Federal support, 14 consumer-owned cooperatives were formed in this State. Bedford Rural Electric Cooperative, which serves members in Bedford, Fulton and Somerset counties, was incorporated on June 2, 1939.

SR 4010 (old US 30) one-half mile E of Bedford. Dedicated June 2, 1989.

Entering Bedford

FORT BEDFORD
First known as Raystown and built during the summer of 1758 by the forces of Col. Henry Bouquet, the fort was the rendezvous from which the expedition of Gen. Forbes advanced to occupy Fort Duquesne (Pittsburgh). Museum stands on the original site.
US 30 near site in Bedford. Erected Oct. 6, 1972.

BEDFORD VILLAGE
Settled about 1750, known then as Raystown. Site of an early trade post and Fort Bedford, 1758. Base for Forbes, Bouquet expeditions. In 1794 Washington here reviewed forces in Whiskey Rebellion.
Old main highways leading into town. Erected 1947 & 1948.

FRASER TAVERN
Site of lots on which John Fraser and his wife established an inn and trading post in 1758. Fraser had been a guide and interpreter for Colonel Washington. The inn provided meals for army officers at Fort Raystown (Bedford).
City type: NE corner E. Pitt & Richard Sts., Bedford. Erected Mar. 1952.

ANDERSON HOUSE
Built in 1815. East room housed the first bank in Bedford, known as the Allegheny Bank of Pennsylvania, from 1815 to 1832. Original vault can still be seen. Since 1924, used as public library and community center.
City type: E. Pitt St. between Juliana & Richard Sts., Bedford. Erected June 25, 1951.

ESPY HOUSE
Built about 1771. It was the headquarters of George Washington in October, 1794, when he came to Bedford to review troops assembled here to quell Whiskey Rebellion in western part of the State.
City type: E. Pitt St. between Juliana & Richard Sts., Bedford. Erected June 25, 1951.

"KING'S HOUSE"
A log structure, built prior to 1761, stood on this site. Known, also, as the Commandant's House; later as "Rising Sun Inn." Occupied by British officers until close of French and Indian War. Destroyed by fire, Dec. 14, 1885.
City type: E. Pitt St. between Juliana & Richard Sts., Bedford. Erected Mar. 1952.

FORBES ROAD, 1758. FORT BEDFORD TO FORT DUQUESNE
Fort Bedford — Raystown. Depot of supplies, assembling place of an army of nearly eight thousand men, and starting point of General John Forbes' Expedition for the possession of Fort Duquesne. The road leads westward to the Forks. Erected by the Pennsylvania Historical Commission, 1930.
Plaque: on wall at NW corner Pitt & Juliana Sts., Bedford. Erected 1930.

THE SQUARES
Set aside, at the time of Manor survey in 1761, by the family of William Penn, as property of the town of Bedford.
City type: S. Juliana St., Bedford, SE corner of Square. Erected June 25, 1951.

RUSSELL HOUSE
This house, built in 1816 by the Hon. James Russell, first burgess of Bedford, is considered a fine example of Georgian style of the Post-Colonial period.
City type: 203 S. Juliana St., Bedford. Erected June 25, 1951.

Leaving Bedford

BEDFORD SPRINGS
Medicinal values of these springs discovered about 1796. It soon became a leading resort visited by numerous notables. James Buchanan used the Springs as his summer White House while President.
Business US 220, Bedford Springs. Erected June 4, 1947.

The Bedford Springs Hotel

9 OLD LOG CHURCH
On land granted by John Schell for the purpose of erecting a union church, construction of this primitive log church building was begun in 1806 by the Reformed and Lutheran Congregations of this area.
US 30 just W of Schellsburg. Erected Sept. 1974.

9 SHAWNEE CABINS
A village site nearby on the Raystown Path. Named for a group of Shawnee Indians who halted here on their retreat from the Potomac to the lower Allegheny valley in the early 18th century.
US 30 W of Schellsburg. Erected Nov. 17, 1947.

9 FORBES CAMP
Near here was located Shawnee Cabins camp. Used by Gen. Forbes' army in the campaign of 1758 against the French at Fort Duquesne in present Pittsburgh.
US 30 W of Schellsburg. Erected Nov. 17, 1947.

8 FORBES ROAD
This intersection marks the point where Forbes Road of 1758 diverged from the path cut by Col. Burd in 1755. The Forbes Road led through the wilderness west toward Ligonier from this point.
Junction US 30 & PA 31, 4 miles W of Bedford. Erected Nov. 17, 1947.

8 FORBES ROAD, 1758. FORT BEDFORD TO FORT DUQUESNE
The Forks. The road cut by Colonel James Burd in 1755 and the Forbes Road diverge here, Forbes Road leading southwestward to Shawnee Cabins Encampment, 4½ miles from Fort Bedford. Erected by the Pennsylvania Historical Commission, 1930.
Plaque: junction US 30 & PA 31, 4 miles W of Bedford. Erected 1930.

9 FORBES ROAD, 1758. FORT BEDFORD TO FORT DUQUESNE
Shawnee Cabins Encampment. At this point the Forbes Road leads southwestward to the eastern slope of the Allegheny Mountains, 8½ miles from Fort Bedford. Erected by the Pennsylvania Historical Commission, 1930.
Plaque: US 30 at W edge Schellsburg. Erected 1930.

Blair County

B BLAIR COUNTY
Formed on February 26, 1846 from Bedford and Huntingdon counties. Named for the Hon. John Blair, a prominent citizen who died in 1832. Hollidaysburg, county seat, was incorporated 1836. City of Altoona, founded 1849, became a major railroad center.
City type: Courthouse, 423 Allegheny St., Hollidaysburg. Dedicated Apr. 13, 1982.

10 ETNA FURNACE

Built in 1809 by the firm of Canan, Stewart and Moore, and operated until 1877, the furnace produced some of the Juniata iron for which the region was famous. The furnace stack and some of the stone buildings may be seen about one mile to the eastward on the side road.

US 22, .6 mile E of Yellow Spring. Erected Aug. 1, 1961.

11 FORT ROBERDEAU

Site of the Revolutionary fort, 1778, to protect the Sinking Valley lead mines. Named for General Daniel Roberdeau who operated the mines and built the fort. The mines supplied lead for the Continental armies during the Revolution.

Kettle Rd. (SR 1013, former LR 07053) 1 mile S of Culp. Erected Apr. 1947.

Entering Altoona

12 FORT ROBERDEAU

The Revolutionary fort site is located a few miles from here. Built 1778 by Daniel Roberdeau to protect lead mines in Sinking Valley which supplied the Continental army.

Intersection Kettle Rd. & US 220 (Pleasant Valley Blvd.), NE Altoona. Erected Apr. 1947.

12 ALTOONA

Founded 1849 as a terminal for westward expansion of the Pennsylvania Railroad. It soon became a major railroad center of the nation. Scene of the War Governors' Conference, 1862.

Logan Blvd. just W of Plank Rd. (old US 220) leading into city. Erected Apr. 1947.

12 LOGAN HOUSE

At the famous railroad hotel on this site was held the Conference of Northern War Governors, Sept. 24-26, 1862. Governor Andrew Curtin of Pennsylvania called the meeting which united forces behind Lincoln and the Emancipation Proclamation.

On 11th Ave. at 13th St., Altoona. Erected Apr. 1947.

12 ALLEGHENY FURNACE

Opposite are remains of furnace built in 1811, the second in this section. It was operated until 1884. The stone store building built in 1837 is the oldest in the city of Altoona.

PA 36 (Union Ave.) S of 31st St., Altoona. Erected Apr. 1947.

12 BAKER MANSION

This fine example of Greek Revival architecture was the home of Elias Baker, a leading ironmaster of the region. Built in 1846, it is now the museum and home of the Blair County Historical Society. Located on the hill opposite this point.

PA 36 (Union Ave.) at Mansion Blvd., Altoona. Erected Apr. 1947.

Leaving Altoona

13 LOWRY HOMESTEAD

Oldest stone house in Blair County. Erected by Lazarus Lowry in 1785. Located on the Kittanning Path, Indian route between Allegheny and Susquehanna rivers.

US 22, 1.1 miles E of Hollidaysburg. Erected Apr. 1947.

13 FRANKSTOWN

The site, prior to 1748, of a Delaware-Shawnee village called Assunepachla. Here the trader, Frank Stevens, had a fur post as early as 1734. The Kittanning Path led through here.

US 22, .6 mile E of Hollidaysburg. Erected Apr. 1947.

14 DANIEL HALE WILLIAMS (1856-1931)

Here was boyhood home of the Black physician who pioneered successful heart surgery, 1893. Founded Provident Hospital, Chicago, 1891. Chief surgeon at Freedmen's Hospital, Washington, D.C., 1894-98. Charter member, College of Surgeons, 1913.

City type: US 22 eastbound (Blair St., 300 block), Hollidaysburg. Dedicated May 6, 1989.

14 CANAL BASIN

Here at Hollidaysburg the 127-mile Juniata Division of the Pennsylvania Canal met the Allegheny Portage Railroad, which extended 36 miles west over the mountain to Johnstown. The Juniata Division was opened in 1832, the railroad in March 1834. Regarded as an engineering marvel, the railroad climbed 1398 feet in ten miles.

US 22 at Canal Basin Park, W end Hollidaysburg. Dedicated May 31, 1982.

15 ALTOONA CONFERENCE

On Sept. 24-26, 1862, the loyal war governors of the Northern states met at the call of Governor Curtin of Pennsylvania in Altoona. Out of the meeting at the Logan House came new unity and support for Lincoln, and emancipation of the slaves.

US 22 between Hollidaysburg & Duncansville. Erected May 28, 1948.

16 BLAIR HOMESTEAD

Opposite here on the side road is the stone house of Thomas Blair, erected 1785. It was also the home of his son, John Blair, leading citizen of the region for whom Blair County was named in 1846.

SR 3012 (old US 22) 1.4 miles W of Duncansville. Erected May 28, 1948.

16 BLAIR HOMESTEAD

Erected 1785 by Thomas Blair. Residence of his son, John Blair, for whom Blair County was named in 1846. John Blair was a member of the General Assembly and until his death, 1832, a leading citizen of the region.

Twp. road (old William Penn Hwy.) 1.6 miles W of Duncansville. Erected Apr. 1947.

16 JUNIATA IRON

Along the streams of this region are ruins of many charcoal iron furnaces and forges built between 1790-1850. Juniata iron was the best in America. Its reign ended with the rise of coal and coke iron making.

SR 3012 (old US 22) 2 miles W of Duncansville. Erected Apr. 1947.

17 GALLITZIN SPRING

The spring opposite here was a favorite stopping place of Prince Gallitzin, famous Catholic missionary and founder of the Loretto settlement. He was also known as Father Smith.

SR 3012 eastbound (old US 22) 1 mile E of Cresson. Erected Apr. 1947.

17 GALLITZIN SPRING

The spring opposite here was a favorite stopping place of Prince Gallitzin, noted prince-priest and missionary who founded the settlement at Loretto in 1792. He was also known as Father Smith. Buried at Loretto, site of his chapel.

SR 3012 westbound (old US 22) 1 mile E of Cresson. Erected May 28, 1948.

17 PORTAGE RAILROAD

Here was No. 6 of the ten inclined planes used to carry canal boats by rail, Hollidaysburg to Johnstown. This unique engineering feat was completed in 1834. The road was 36 miles long.

SR 3012 east & westbound (old US 22) just E of Cambria County line. Erected Apr. 1947.

Allegheny Portage Railroad National Historic Site

National Park Service, Richard Frear

Cambria County

C CAMBRIA COUNTY
Formed March 26, 1804 out of Huntingdon and Somerset counties. Its name, dating from Roman Britain, means "Wales." County seat, Ebensburg, was incorporated 1825. Famed Portage Railroad extended west to Johnstown. Birthplace of Rear Admiral Robert E. Peary.
City type: County Courthouse, Center St., Ebensburg. Dedicated May 25, 1982.

18 PORTAGE RAILROAD
Here was No. 5 of the ten inclined planes used to carry canal boats by rail, Hollidaysburg to Johnstown. The road to Lilly follows closely the route of the Portage Railroad over the mountain to Johnstown.
SR 2014 (old US 22) just E of Cresson. Erected Aug. 19, 1947.

18 ROBERT E. PEARY
This monument was placed in honor of the Arctic explorer, discoverer of the North Pole April 6, 1909. Peary was born in Cresson, May 6, 1856, the family moving to Maine in 1859.
SR 2014 (old US 22) just W of Cresson. Erected Aug. 19, 1947.

19 ADMIRAL PEARY PARK
Rear Admiral Robert E. Peary was born near Cresson on May 6, 1856. This Park and monument commemorate his birth and achievements. Administered by the Pennsylvania Historical and Museum Commission.
At site on SR 1005 (former LR 276) just N of junction with SR 2014 (old US 22) W of Cresson. Erected [1948].

20 DEMETRIUS GALLITZIN
Here is the tomb of the Russian prince-priest who gave up a life of ease for a frontier mission. Founder of Loretto, Catholic colony, 1799. St. Michael's is on the site of his chapel. He died here May 6, 1840.
SR 1005 (former LR 276), Loretto. Erected Aug. 19, 1947.

20 LORETTO
Founded 1799 by the prince-priest, Demetrius Gallitzin. Here he began in 1800 the first school in the area, a forerunner of Saint Francis College, chartered in 1858. Catholic cultural center. Charles M. Schwab, steel king, had his home here.
SR 1005 (former LR 53), Loretto. Erected June 29, 1948.

20 CHARLES M. SCHWAB
The steel king, of whom Carnegie said he "knew more about steel that any man in the world," had his estate here. The grounds and buildings are owned by St. Francis College.
SR 1001 (former LR 53), Loretto. Erected Aug. 18, 1947.

21 DR. LAWRENCE F. FLICK
Pioneer in antitubercular campaign and among first to recognize this disease was communicable. Organized first American tuberculosis society, 1892. Founded White Haven Sanatorium, 1901. Birthplace 400 yards east of highway.
US 219, 1 mile S of Carrolltown. Erected May 11, 1959.

22 JOHNSTOWN FLOOD
The breast of South Fork Dam which broke the night of May 31, 1889, to cause the historic flood is a short distance away. The remains of the dam can be observed.
Junction US 219 & PA 869, 1 mile S of South Fork. Erected Aug. 18, 1947.

23 STAPLE BEND TUNNEL
First railroad tunnel built in the U.S. and a part of the Portage Railroad. The masonry is intact and a unique engineering feat of the times. Can be visited a few miles east of here, via Mineral Point.
PA 271, 5 miles N of Johnstown. Erected Aug. 19, 1947.

24 SGT. MICHAEL STRANK
A Marine, he was the oldest and highest ranking of the six men who took part in the famous raising of the U.S. flag on Iwo Jima, Feb. 23, 1945. This scene, photographed by Joe Rosenthal of the Associated Press, was later used in the Marine Corps War Memorial at Arlington. Born Nov. 10, 1919, in Czechoslovakia, Strank grew up in Franklin Borough. Killed in action March 1, 1945, he was reinterred 1949 in Arlington Cemetery.
125 Main St. (PA 271), Franklin Borough. Dedicated May 17, 1986.

25 JOHNSTOWN
Named for Joseph Johns, the pioneer settler in 1793. Pennsylvania Canal-Portage R. R. terminal opened 1834. Birthplace of steel industry in U. S. William Kelly developed the converter type blast furnace in 1857-58. Steel rails rolled in 1867.
William Penn Ave. at N city line. Erected Oct. 1, 1947.

Franklin County

D FRANKLIN COUNTY
Formed on September 9, 1784 from Cumberland County and named for Benjamin Franklin. Site of Falling Spring, noted limestone trout stream. Birthplace of James Buchanan, 15th President of the United States. Chambersburg, county seat, was laid out 1764.
City type: County Courthouse, Memorial Sq. (N. Main St., corner US 11 & 30), Chambersburg. Erected May 15, 1982.

26 SHIPPENSBURG
Founded 1730 by Edward Shippen. Second oldest town in the State west of the Susquehanna River. Important community on colonial frontier. Temporary seat of Cumberland Co. whose first courts were held here in 1750-1751.
US 11 at W end Shippensburg. Erected June 1, 1948.

27 CALEDONIA FURNACE
Erected in 1837 by Thaddeus Stevens and James D. Paxton. Stevens' anti-slavery stand led to its destruction by Gen. Jubal Early, June 26, 1863, on his way to York during the early Gettysburg campaign.
Junction US 30 & PA 233, Caledonia State Park. Erected Aug. 25, 1947.

28 JOHN BROWN RAID
Captain John Cooke, one of Brown's followers, was captured near here on October 25, 1859, nine days after the raid on Harper's Ferry. He was hanged December 16, two weeks after John Brown.
PA 233, 1 mile E of Mont Alto. Erected June 11, 1947.

29 SNOW HILL CLOISTER
An offshoot of Ephrata Cloister in Lancaster County, deriving its name from the Snowberger family active in its foundation. Composed of widows, widowers, and single persons, with goods held in common, it prospered from 1814 until the Civil War.
PA 997 just S of Quincy. Erected Dec. 21, 1966.

30 DR. HENRY HARBAUGH
Pennsylvania-German author, theologian, and educator, 1817-1867, was born one and one-half miles distant. The house is marked by a monument.
PA 16, 2 miles SE of Waynesboro. Erected Dec. 5, 1947.

31 GETTYSBURG CAMPAIGN
Gen. Jubal Early's Confederate troops occupied Waynesboro June 23, 1863. Next day they marched by Mont Alto to Greenwood, or Black Gap, where, June 25, they were ordered by Gen. Ewell to march to York.
PA 16 at Roadside Ave., E of Square, Waynesboro. Erected Dec. 5, 1947.

31 OLD LOG BUILDING
The one-and-a-half story structure that stands about 100 yards north of here is one of the oldest buildings in Waynesboro. Built for a schoolhouse and church between 1770 and 1780, by John Bourns. Later used as dwelling.
City type: E. Main St. & Roadside Ave., Waynesboro. Erected June 27, 1955.

31 JOHN WALLACE, JR.

Laid out the present town in 1797 and named it Waynesburg in honor of General Anthony Wayne. In 1831, name changed to Waynesboro. Stone portion of the Wallace house still stands about 200 yards southeast of here.

City type: E. Main & Enterprise Sts., Waynesboro. Erected June 27, 1955.

32 GETTYSBURG CAMPAIGN

Over this route Confederate General R. S. Ewell's 2d Army Corps led Lee's invading forces on June 22, 1863. Next day Gen. Jubal Early, under Ewell's command, entered the State to the east, near Waynesboro.

US 11, 1 mile N of State line. Erected Dec. 5, 1947.

33 CAPTAIN ULRIC DAHLGREN

Commanded a detachment of Union cavalry that made a surprise attack on a larger force of Confederate cavalry on this square, July 2, 1863. Important papers for General Lee were taken from the men who were captured.

City type: SE section of Square, Greencastle. Erected June 21, 1954.

34 GETTYSBURG CAMPAIGN

Here on June 22, 1863, the First N. Y. Cavalry attacked the Southern advance force of cavalry under Gen. A. G. Jenkins. Here died the first Union soldier killed in action in Pennsylvania, Corporal William H. Rihl of Philadelphia, serving in a Pennsylvania unit assigned to the New York regiment.

US 11 just N of Greencastle. Erected Nov. 2, 1964.

35 BROWN'S MILL SCHOOL

Built in 1836. Used until 1921 as one-room elementary school. Administered by the Pennsylvania Historical and Museum Commission.

At site SR 2016 (former LR 28032), Kauffman Station SE of Marion. Erected Apr. 20, 1966.

Entering Chambersburg

36 CHAMBERSBURG

Settled 1734 by Benjamin Chambers, who laid out "Chambers Town" in 1764. Seat of Franklin County since 1784. Scene of Civil War events: Raided by "Jeb" Stuart, 1862; occupied by Confederates in 1863; and burned by them in 1864.

On main highways leading into town. Erected 1948.

36 GETTYSBURG CAMPAIGN

Gen. A. G. Jenkins' Southern cavalry raided Chambersburg June 15-17, 1863, prior to the main invasion; and later led the invading army, June 22-24. Gen. R. E. Lee entered Chambersburg on June 26.

US 11 at S end of Chambersburg. Erected Dec. 5, 1947.

36 GETTYSBURG CAMPAIGN

Gen. Robert E. Lee reached Chambersburg June 26, 1863. Hearing, June 28, that Union troops under Gen. Joseph Hooker had crossed the Potomac to Frederick, he decided to unite his forces at Cashtown; and left the city by this road.

US 30 at E end Chambersburg. Erected Jan. 10, 1948.

36 MESSERSMITH'S WOODS

Name of grove selected by Gen. R. E. Lee for his headquarters, June 26-30, 1863. Here he issued the order for the concentration of troops near Gettysburg. Site of woods is just south of this point.

City type: US 30 (Lincoln Way E.) near Colebrook Ave., Chambersburg. Erected Aug. 20, 1953.

36 JOHN BROWN

Boarded in this house for a while in the summer of 1859 under the name of "Smith." While in Chambersburg, he secretly received firearms and ammunition. Later in 1859, Brown led a raid on the arsenal at Harper's Ferry.

City type: 225 E. King St., Chambersburg. Erected [1953].

36 MASONIC TEMPLE

Built 1823-1824. Oldest Pennsylvania building erected solely for Masonic use and now used exclusively for that purpose. Spared when Confederates burned town on July 30, 1864.

City type: S. 2nd St. (US 11 northbound) near E. Queen St., Chambersburg. Dedicated July 30, 1964.

36 MORROW TAVERN

A two-story stone house occupied as a tavern by William Morrow stood on this site. George Washington, with staff, lodged here, Oct. 12, 1794, when traveling west to review troops assembled at Bedford to suppress the Whiskey Rebellion.

City type: 35 S. Main St., Chambersburg. Erected Aug. 1953.

36 SUESSEROTT HOUSE
Built around 1807. Later, it was the home of Dr. Jacob Suesserott, a prominent physician, dentist and surgeon. The fire started by Confederate cavalry on July 30, 1864, was arrested at this point.
City type: SW corner Main & Washington Sts., Chambersburg. Erected May 1969 (revised 1954 marker).

36 CONFEDERATE CONFERENCE
On June 26, 1863, Gen. Robert E. Lee, and staff, entered this square. After conferring with Gen. A. P. Hill, near the middle of the ''Diamond,'' Lee turned eastward and made headquarters at the edge of town.
City type: SW section of Square, Chambersburg. Erected Aug. 10, 1953.

36 FORT CHAMBERS
Erected in 1756 by Col. Benjamin Chambers, pioneer landowner and founder of the town, who fortified his house and mill with stockade and cannon against Indians.
W. King St. (1 block W of US 11 southbound), Chambersburg. Erected June 3, 1947.

36 FIRST LUTHERAN CHURCH
This church, the third building, stands on the site of a log church built in 1780 by the Lutheran and Reformed and used jointly by the congregations till 1808. The land was donated by Benjamin Chambers.
City type: W. Washington St. at church, Chambersburg. Erected Aug. 10, 1953.

36 PHILIP BERLIN
Recognized as the inventor of the first sleeping car in U.S. for use of travelers. The car, ''Chambersburg,'' was operated as early as 1838 between Harrisburg and Chambersburg. He lies buried in graveyard at rear of church.
City type: W. Washington St. at First Lutheran Church, Chambersburg. Erected Aug. 10, 1953.

36 BURNING OF CHAMBERSBURG
Occupied the morning of July 30, 1864, by cavalry of Confederate Gen. John McCausland. Failing to obtain ransom, he burned the town in reprisal for ruin in the Shenandoah Valley by Gen. David Hunter.
US 30, W end Chambersburg. Erected Dec. 5, 1947.

36 OLD FRANKLIN COUNTY JAIL
Of Georgian design, this jail was built in 1818 and was in continuous use for 152 years. The third oldest building in the borough, it survived the burning of Chambersburg by Confederate forces during the Civil War.
N. 2nd St. (US 11 northbound) at E. King St., Chambersburg. Erected May 9, 1975.

36 FALLING SPRING CHURCH
Founded 1734; main part of present church built 1803. One of the Presbyterian churches marking the first great settlement of Scotch-Irish pioneers west of the Susquehanna.
US 11 at church, 2 blocks N of Square, Chambersburg. Erected May 10, 1948.

36 WILSON COLLEGE
Founded in 1869, and named for Sarah Wilson, its benefactor. One of the oldest colleges for women in the U.S. Opened, 1870, in ''Norland,'' former home of Col. A. K. McClure, close friend of Abraham Lincoln.
City type: Edgar near Ramsey Ave. off US 11 at campus. Erected Oct. 10, 1952.

36 GETTYSBURG CAMPAIGN
On June 26, 1863, Gen. R. S. Ewell, with orders to take Harrisburg, marched his army by this road toward Carlisle, which he reached next day. On June 29, he was ordered to rejoin Lee's army at Cashtown.
US 11 at N end Chambersburg. Erected Dec. 5, 1947.

Leaving Chambersburg

37 MARGARET COCHRAN CORBIN
Heroine of the Revolution; born Nov. 12, 1751, near Rocky Spring, 1½ miles to NE. Accompanied her husband to war, Manned a cannon, Fort Washington, N.Y., Nov. 16, 1776, when he was killed. She was wounded, pensioned, and assigned to Invalid Regt. Died Jan. 16, 1800; buried at West Point, N.Y.
US 11, 1.5 miles N of Chambersburg. Dedicated Oct. 1, 1961.

38 **[FORT McCORD]**

The site of Fort McCord where twenty-seven pioneer settlers, men, women, and children, were massacred by Indian savages or carried into captivity, April 1st, 1756 was a few rods south east of this spot. In the list of victims were Mary McCord, Mrs. John Thorn and babe, Mrs. Anne McCord, wife of John McCord and two daughters, Martha Thorn, a young mother with unborn babe, and a young girl. Names of Provincial soldiers killed in pursuit of the Indians at Sideling Hill: Captain Alexander Culbertson, John Reynolds (ensign), William Chambers, William Kerr, Daniel McCoy, James Blair, James Robertson (tailor), John Layson, James Robertson (weaver), William Denny, James Peace, Francis Scott, John Blair, William Boyd, Henry Jones, Jacob Paynter, John McCarty, Jacob Jones, John Kelly, Robert Kerr, James Lowder. Wounded: Lieutenant Jamieson, Abraham Jones, John McDonald. Francis Campbell, Isaac Miller, William Reynolds, William Hunter, John Barnet, Matthias Ganshorn, Benjamin Blyth, William Swailes. Erected by joint action of Enoch Brown Association and Penna. Historical Commission, 1914.

Plaque: NE of Edenville, ca. 7 miles W of Chambersburg, on road leading S from SR 4008 (intersection former LR 28039 & 28055). Dedicated Oct. 29, 1914.

38 **JOSEPH ARMSTRONG**

Settled here on land applied for in 1737 and warranted 1752. Member of the Assembly 1750-55. Captain of militia 1755 and in Pennsylvania Regiment 1756-57. Died 1761. Home used in 1757 as a ranging station for troops in the French and Indian War and during Pontiac's War in 1763-64.

SR 4010 (former LR 28005) at Coble Rd. near Edenville. Dedicated May 14, 1960.

39 **FORT WADDELL**

One of a line of forts built by settlers in this region for refuge from Indian attacks following Braddock's defeat in 1755. It stood just to the north.

US 30 near junction PA 416, 1 mile W of St. Thomas. Erected May 27, 1947.

39 **FORT WADDELL, 1754**

One of the forts for the defense of the frontier of Cumberland County from Fort Davis to Shippensburg, stood near this marker on the plantation then owned by Thomas Waddell. Marked by the Pennsylvania Historical Commission and the Franklin County Chapter of the Daughters of the American Revolution, 1930.

Plaque: US 30 (N side) near junction PA 416, 1 mile W of St. Thomas. Erected 1930.

40 **FORT McCORD**

Built by the settlers; named for John McCord. Burned April 1, 1756, by Indians, who killed or carried into captivity 27 persons. The site is about nine miles away.

US 30, 2 miles W of St. Thomas. Erected Aug. 8, 1947.

41 **FORT LOUDON**

Built 1756 by Provincial government. Start of Forbes' expedition to take Ft. Duquesne, 1758. In 1765 colonists under James Smith forced the withdrawal of a British garrison from the fort.

US 30, 1 mile E of Fort Loudon. Erected May 27, 1947.

42 **FORT LOUDON**

Erected by Col. John Armstrong in the winter of 1756 by the order of the Province of Pennsylvania, was situated a mile south-east of this spot. The fort was built for the protection of the frontiers against the Indians and took the place of the fort at McDowell's Mill, which was situated at Bridgeport. Fort Loudon was the scene of many thrilling events during the Indian raids into this region. During the expedition of Gen. John Forbes, in 1758, and that of Col. Henry Bouquet, in 1763-4, this fort was used as a rendezvous for troops and as a base of supplies. It was the scene of the exploits of Capt. James Smith and his "Black Boys" in 1765. Before the building of the State Road to Pittsburgh, it was the point of departure of great trains of pack-horses, laden with goods for the west and south. Erected by the Pennsylvania Historical Commission, the Enoch Brown Association and the citizens of this place, 1915.

Plaque: center Fort Loudon, old Lincoln Hwy. (SR 4002). Dedicated Oct. 20, 1915.

43 **WIDOW BARR PLACE**

The buildings seen just west of here are on the site of the Widow Barr house. Here the settlers fought the Indians who made raids in 1755 and 1756. James Brown, a colonist, was wounded by British soldiers at this place in 1765.

PA 75, 1.4 miles S of Fort Loudon. Erected June 20, 1955.

44 **FORT McDOWELL**

John McDowell's mill, stockaded in 1755 by local settlers. Used by Provincial authorities until building of Fort Loudon, 1756. Starting point of Col. Burd's road to the West, 1755.

PA 416 at Markes. Erected Sept. 10, 1947.

44 [FORT McDOWELL]
This stone marks the site of the fort at McDowell's Mill, erected by John McDowell before 1754. It was used as a base of supplies and as a magazine until the erection of Fort Loudon in 1756. The military road from Pennsylvania, connecting with the Braddock Road at Turkey Foot, was built from this point in 1755 under the supervision of Col. James Burd. During the period of Indian hostility the fort at McDowell's Mill was the scene of many thrilling events. Erected by the Pennsylvania Historical Commission, the Enoch Brown Association, the descendents of John McDowell and the citizens of this region, 1916.
Plaque: intersection PA 416 & SR 3007 (former LR 28002) at Markes. Dedicated Oct. 5, 1916.

45 JAMES BUCHANAN
President 1857-1861. Was born April 23, 1791, a half-mile from here. The cabin itself was moved to Mercersburg, 1850, and in 1925 to Chambersburg. In 1953, it was removed to The Mercersburg Academy campus where it may be seen.
PA 416, 3.3 miles NW of Mercersburg. Erected Jan. 1955.

Entering Mercersburg

46 WILLIAM FINDLAY
Governor of Pennsylvania, 1817-20; born on this site, June 20, 1768. First candidate for governor nominated by convention. Advocate of State internal improvements; U.S. Senator, 1821-27. Died, Nov. 12, 1846, at Harrisburg.
City type: N. Main St. (PA 16, 75, 416) & Mill Rd., Mercersburg. Erected Apr. 10, 1950.

46 BUCHANAN HOUSE
Boyhood home of James Buchanan, lawyer, statesman, diplomat, fifteenth President of the United States. Buchanan family moved from Stony Batter to Mercersburg in 1796. From here, James entered Dickinson College in 1807.
City type: 17 N. Main St., Mercersburg. Erected July 2, 1953.

46 LANE HOUSE
Built by Thomas Lane. Was later occupied by the family of Elliott Lane, a brother. Here, Harriet Lane, a niece of James Buchanan, and mistress of the White House during his Presidency, was born.
City type: 16 N. Main St., Mercersburg. Erected July 2, 1953.

46 REFORMED THEOLOGICAL SEMINARY
Was situated on this campus, 1837-71. Here, Drs. Frederick A. Rauch, John W. Nevin, Philip Schaff, taught and wrote. Their works on theology, philosophy, and church history were influential in the U.S and Europe.
City type: at entrance Mercersburg Academy. Erected May 1953.

46 MARSHALL COLLEGE
Used the Theological Seminary building. Was chartered, 1836; removed to Lancaster, 1853, and united with Franklin College. First president was Dr. Frederick A. Rauch, famed scholar and educator; author of textbook on psychology.
City type: at entrance Mercersburg Academy. Erected May 1953.

Leaving Mercersburg

47 REV. STEEL'S FORT
The Rev. John Steel, pastor of Upper West Conococheague, was made militia captain; and his church, stockaded in 1755, provided protection from hostile Indians. The site is at Church Hill.
PA 16, 2.3 miles SE of Mercersburg. Erected June 3, 1947.

48 STUART'S RAID
Confederate cavalry under Gen. J. E. B. Stuart entered this State Oct. 10, 1862. Unable to burn the iron bridge at Chambersburg, they reentered Maryland near Emmitsburg, Oct. 11, circling the Union army.
PA 75 just N of State line. Erected Dec. 5, 1947.

49 FORT DAVIS
Was located near this marker on the plantation of Philip Davis: Welshman, patriot, collector of taxes, member of the presbytery of New Castle who built the fort about 1754 as a protection against the Indians. Marked by the Pennsylvania Historical Commission and the Franklin County Chapter, Daughters of the American Revolution, 1931.
Plaque: W side of road 1.3 miles S of PA 995 at Welsh Run. Dedicated July 11, 1931.

50 BURNING OF CHAMBERSBURG
Over this road Gen. John McCausland's Confederate cavalry marched north on July 29, 1864. By way of Mercersburg, they reached and burned Chambersburg next morning, and were at McConnellsburg next night.
PA 416 200 yards N of State line. Erected Dec. 5, 1947.

Fulton County

E FULTON COUNTY
Formed April 19, 1850 out of Bedford County. Named for steamboat inventor Robert Fulton. Scene of Confederacy's first casualties in the Gettysburg Campaign, and its last campsite (1864) in Pennsylvania. McConnellsburg, county seat, incorporated 1814.
City type: County Courthouse, N. 2nd & Market Sts., McConnellsburg. Erected Dec. 5, 1982.

51 BURNT CABINS
Early settlers' cabins in this vicinity were burned by Provincial forces, 1750, to satisfy Indian protests against white trespassers on their lands. The name is a relic of troubled days on the Pennsylvania frontier.
US 522, .2 mile S of Burnt Cabins, county line. Erected June 4, 1947.

51 FORBES ROAD (RAYSTOWN PATH)
Just east of here is the junction of the two branches of the Raystown Path: a mountain shortcut by way of Fannettsburg, and Gen. Forbes road through Cowan Gap. From here Forbes route is marked by towns named for his forts: Littleton, Bedford, Ligonier, Pittsburgh.
US 522, .2 mile SW of Burnt Cabins. Erected Feb. 21, 1952.

52 FORT LITTLETON
One of Pennsylvania's defenses against the French and Indians stood on this knoll, built 1756 by Governor Robert Hunter Morris. Marked by the Pennsylvania Historical Commission and the Fulton County Historical Society, 1924.
Plaque: US 522, .5 mile E of Fort Littleton. Dedicated July 26, 1924. (See below.)

52 FORT LYTTELTON
Begun in 1755 by George Croghan, named by Governor Morris after Sir George Lyttelton, then the Chancellor of the Exchequer. Garrisoned variously by Provincial and regular troops, as well as local volunteers in 1763. By 1764 it was reported in ruins.
US 522 at Fort Littleton. Erected June 30, 1967 (revised 1947 marker).

53 GETTYSBURG CAMPAIGN
Three times occupied by Southern invaders, chiefly cavalry: June 19, 1863, by Gen. A. G. Jenkins; June 24-26, by Gen. G. H. Steuart; and June 29, after a brief clash with Union troops, by Gen. J. D. Imboden.
PA 16 (old US 30) at E end McConnellsburg. Erected Oct. 23, 1947.

53 CONFEDERATE DEAD
Two Confederate soldiers, killed June 29, 1863, in a skirmish with Union troops, were buried here by local residents. The monument in their honor was erected by Daughters of the Confederacy.
PA 16, .4 mile SE of McConnellsburg. Erected Feb. 10, 1948.

53 LAST CONFEDERATE BIVOUAC
A Confederate force under General Bradley T. Johnson camped here July 30, 1864, after raiding and burning Chambersburg. They were the last Confederates to camp on Pennsylvania soil.
US 522, .6 mile S of McConnellsville. Erected June 4, 1947.

53 [LAST CONFEDERATE BIVOUAC]
General Bradley T. Johnson of the Confederate Army encamped 20 rods west of this marker at the Patterson home, July 31[30], 1864. After the burning of Chambersburg this was the last Confederate bivouac north of the Mason and Dixon Line. Erected by the Pennsylvania Historical Commission and the Fulton County Historical Society and dedicated by the Pittsburgh Chapter, United Daughters of the Confederacy, 1930.
Plaque: US 522 (W side) .6 mile S of McConnellsburg. Dedicated July 31, 1930.

54 BIG SPRING GRAVEYARD
Among those buried here are victims of the Great Cove Massacre of Nov. 1, 1755, at present McConnellsburg. The raid was conducted by Delawares and Shawnees led by Shingas the Delaware ''king.'' Houses were burned, and about 50 settlers were killed or captured. Its revelation at a meeting of Pennsylvania's Provincial Council, Nov. 5, 1755, led Gov. R. H. Morris to ask the Assembly for increased frontier protection.
US 522, 2.8 miles S of McConnellsburg. Dedicated Nov. 6, 1989.

55 HUNTER MILL
This pioneer grist mill was built in 1812 by William Hunter. It has been in use continuously since that date. It is powered by a water wheel and uses much of the old-style machinery in its present operation.
US 522, 5.3 miles S of McConnellsburg at Webster Mills. Erected Oct. 23, 1947.

Huntingdon County

F HUNTINGDON COUNTY
Formed on September 20, 1787 out of Bedford County. Named for the Countess of Huntingdon to honor her support of the University of Pennsylvania. Hungtingdon, the county seat, incorporated 1796. County noted for fertile land, iron, timber, water power, roads.
City type: County Courthouse, Penn St. (PA 26), Huntingdon. Dedicated Sept. 20, 1982.

56 GREENWOOD FURNACE
Built about 1837 to supply iron to Freedom Forge near Lewistown. Restored stack, the Church, Big House, and store common to ironmaking communities remain. Works closed 1904, the last to operate in this region.
PA 305 at Greenwood Furnace State Park. Erected Apr. 30, 1947.

57 PENNSYLVANIA FURNACE
The remaining buildings here were part of the iron works established about 1810. Operating first as a charcoal iron manufactory, the furnace later used coke. Iron was made here as late as 1888.
PA 45 at Pennsylvania Furnace. Erected Apr. 30, 1947.

58 SPRUCE CREEK CHURCH
Present church built 1858 by a Presbyterian congregation organized in 1798. Their first house of worship, a log church built in 1805, was within old Graysville Cemetery on the hilltop opposite.
PA 45 just NE of Graysville, opposite church. Erected Apr. 21, 1949.

59 COLERAINE FORGES
Nearby are sites of two forges, built in 1805 and 1809 by Samuel Marshall. Juniata iron became famous as the best of the charcoal iron made 1790-1850. Spruce Creek was noted for its ironworks.
PA 45, 1.6 miles NE of Spruce Creek. Erected Apr. 30, 1947.

60 FORT ROBERDEAU

The Revolutionary fort site is located a few miles from here. Built 1778 by Daniel Roberdeau to protect lead mines in Sinking Valley which supplied the Continental army.

PA 453 & Truck PA 45 just S of Union Furnace. Erected Apr. 30, 1947.

61 JUNIATA IRON

Along the streams of this region are ruins of many charcoal iron furnaces and forges built between 1790-1850. Juniata iron was the best in America. Its reign ended with the rise of coal and coke iron making.

US 22 just E of Water Street. Erected Apr. 29, 1947.

61 FRANKSTOWN PATH

The path turned south, up the Frankstown Branch of Juniata. The Warriors Path from Great Island came in at Water Street, so named because the river bed was used as a passage through Tusseys Mountain.

US 22 just E of Water Street. Erected Mar. 16, 1949.

62 HART'S LOG

The Frankstown Path, highway of early traders to the West, passed through Hart's Log, now Alexandria, across the river. It was named after John Hart, a trader, who hollowed a log here as a feeding trough for his pack horses.

Junction US 22 & PA 305 just S of Alexandria. Erected Mar. 16, 1949.

63 MARTIN G. BRUMBAUGH

Governor of the State, 1915-19, outstanding educator, was born near here April 14, 1862. Superintendent county schools, 1884-90. Juniata College president, 1895-1906; 1924-30. Died March 14, 1930. Buried in Valley View Cemetery.

PA 26, 1.3 miles NE of Marklesburg. Erected July 23, 1948.

64 MARTIN G. BRUMBAUGH

World War I Governor from 1915-19, one of the most prominent educators of the State, was born a few miles SW, April 14, 1862. Buried in Valley View Cemetery in the same neighborhood. In 1895-1906; 1924-30, he was President Juniata College.

Junction US 22 & PA 26 W of Huntingdon. Erected July 1, 1949.

Entering Huntingdon

65 DAVID R. PORTER

Ironmaster and Governor of the State, 1839-45, lived in this house. A leader in local affairs, he was called "our own Davy R." His son Horace, soldier and diplomat, was born here, 1837.

City type: 3rd & Penn Sts., Huntingdon. Erected Oct. 15, 1955.

65 McMURTRIE MANSION

David McMurtrie built this house in 1817. A pioneer family; leaders in local political and business affairs. Now houses the Historical Society and the Library of Huntingdon County.

City type: 4th & Penn Sts., Huntingdon. Erected Oct. 15, 1955.

65 FORT STANDING STONE

Built to protect the settlers against Indian raids. In July, 1778, Continental troops and Militia were ordered here as part of plan of defense against Indian attacks. Old Fort stood 200 yards south, at Stone Creek and the Juniata.

City type: Penn St. (PA 26) near Front St., Huntingdon. Erected Oct. 15, 1955.

65 RURAL ELECTRIFICATION

In 1936 seventy-five percent of Pennsylvania farms had no electric service. During the next five years, with Federal support, 14 consumer-owned cooperatives were formed in this State. Valley Rural Electric Cooperative, serving seven counties from headquarters at Huntingdon, was incorporated November 1, 1938.

PA 26 at N end of Huntingdon. Dedicated July 18, 1990.

Leaving Huntingdon

66 FORT SHIRLEY

Built 1755-56 by George Croghan. First a stockade and then a major link in the frontier fort chain west of the Susquehanna. Base for the Armstrong expedition, 1756. Site on opposite knoll.

US 522 at N end Shirleysburg. Erected Apr. 25, 1947.

66 FORT SHIRLEY

One of the chain of frontier defenses of the Province of Pennsylvania in the French and Indian Wars stood on this knoll, built 1756 by its commander, the noted Indian trader and agent George Croghan. Here in 1753 at the site of Aughwick Indian Town he had located his trading post and here, September 3-6, 1754, Conrad Weiser, the noted Indian interpreter and agent, had held a conference with the great Iroquoian half king Tanacharison and other chiefs of the Shawnee and Delaware Indians. Marked by the Pennsylvania Historical Commission and the Society of Pennsylvania Women in New York, 1926.

Plaque: US 522 (W side) near Aughwick Creek, Shirleysburg. Dedicated May 29, 1926.

67 ADMIRAL WM. SIMS

Commander of the American naval forces in European waters in the first World War, naval writer and critic, entered the U. S. Naval Academy from this community in 1876. From 1883 to 1902, Sims family occupied the house opposite.

PA 994 in Rockhill W of US 522. Erected Apr. 23, 1950.

68 JUNIATA IRON

Same text as Juniata Iron above.

US 522, 1 mile S of Orbisonia. Erected Oct. 25, 1948.

68 BEDFORD FURNACE

First iron furnace in the Juniata region, famous as a center for making quality charcoal iron. Located on Black Log Creek below its junction with Shade Creek. Completed about 1788.

US 522, 1 mile S of Orbisonia. Erected Apr. 28, 1947.

69 "SHADOW OF DEATH"

The name applied to this locality by Conrad Weiser and other travellers on the Frankstown Path in the mid-18th century. Its local significance is now unknown.

US 522 N of Shade Gap. Erected Apr. 28, 1947.

Somerset County

G SOMERSET COUNTY

Formed April 17, 1795 out of Bedford County and named for Somersetshire, England. County seat of Somerset was incorporated in 1804. Settlement followed the course of Forbes Road, opened 1758. This farm county is noted for production of maple syrup.

City type: County Courthouse, N Center Ave. at Union St., Somerset. Dedicated Oct. 22, 1982.

70 FLORA BLACK (1870-1951)

On this farm lived Mrs. Frank B. Black, a civic leader active in the county and State. Here on October 14, 1914, she organized the Society of Farm Women of Pennsylvania. In the ensuing years, groups in many Pennsylvania counties became Society affiliates, in furtherance of its aims to strengthen the role of farm women and promote better conditions in the State's farm homes.

US 219, 3 miles NW of Meyersdale. Dedicated Oct. 18, 1989.

71 NATIONAL ROAD

Out first national road; fathered by Albert Gallatin. Begun in 1811 at Cumberland, Md.; completed to Wheeling in 1818. Toll road under State control, 1835-1905. Rebuilt, it is present U. S. Route 40.

US 40 SE of Addison near State line. Erected Aug. 10, 1948.

71 TOLL HOUSE

One of the six original toll houses on the Cumberland or National Road is on the hill opposite. Built after the road was turned over to the State in 1835 by the U.S. Restored and preserved by the D. A. R.

Junction US 40 & SR 3002 (old US 40), Addison. Erected Oct. 24, 1947.

72 GREAT CROSSINGS

Since Indian days this was a major Youghiogheny River crossing place. In 1754 Washington's Virginians camped here. Braddock's army marched through here. The National Road bridged the river at this point in 1818.

US 40 at the Youghiogheny River. Erected Oct. 24, 1947.

73 FORT HILL

Archaeological study of the flat-top hill across the valley revealed two palisaded Indian villages with extensive house and burial remains, all dating from the Discovery Period.

PA 218, 2 miles NE of Ursina. Erected Oct. 24, 1947.

74 RURAL ELECTRIFICATION

In 1936 seventy-five percent of Pennsylvania farms had no electric service. During the next five years, with federal support, 14 consumer-owned cooperatives were formed in this State. Somerset Rural Electric Cooperative, serving four counties in Pennsylvania and one in Maryland, was incorporated on March 14, 1939.

SR 3015 (Water Level Rd.) between Somerset & Rockwood. Dedicated June 10, 1989.

75 ANKENY SQUARE

Set aside for burial ground and place of worship on the original plat of Milfordstown by Ulrich Bruner, 1787, and by Peter Ankeny in 1789 when he laid out the south side of the settlement renamed Somerset in 1795.

City type: Patriot St. at cemetery, Somerset. Erected June 28, 1954.

75 ADAM SCHNEIDER

Laid out the north half of the settlement renamed Somerset in 1795. Schneider and his brother Jacob conducted the first store in Somerset. It stood on this site.

City type: NW corner of Square, Somerset. Erected June 28, 1954.

75 HARMON HUSBAND

Leader of North Carolina revolt against the British, he fled under an assumed name in 1771. Somerset's first settler; lived at Coffee Springs farm some years. Became a pamphleteer and active in the Whiskey Rebellion. Died in 1795.

PA 31 W of junction with SR 3041 (old US 219), E of Somerset. Erected Oct. 24, 1947.

76 JEREMIAH S. BLACK

One of Pennsylvania's most noted jurists and lawyers, was born here Jan. 10, 1810. State Supreme Court Justice, 1851-57; U.S. Attorney-General, 1857-60. Later life spent at York as a famous lawyer. Died Aug. 19, 1883.

PA 31, 6.5 miles E of Somerset near Brotherton. Erected Oct. 24, 1947.

76 [JEREMIAH SULLIVAN BLACK]

Birthplace of Jeremiah Sullivan Black, 10 January, 1810. President Judge, Sixteenth Pennsylvania Judicial District, 1842-1851. Associate Justice and Chief Justice of Pennsylvania, 1851-1857. Attorney General of the United States, 1857-1860. Secretary of State of the United States, 1860-1861. Fearless and eloquent defender of Constitutional rights, of trial by jury, and of civil and religious liberty until his death, August 19, 1883. . . . Erected by the Pennsylvania Historical Commission and the Somerset County Bar Association, 1930.

Plaque: PA 31 (N side) E of Brotherton. Actually erected 1933.

77 FORBES ROAD (FORT DEWART)

"The fort on the top of Allegheny Hill" was erected in 1758 during the Gen. Forbes expedition against Fort Duquesne. The site is marked half a mile northeast of here, near the head of Breastwork Run.

US 30 near Bedford County line. Erected Jan. 30, 1952.

77 FORBES ROAD, 1758. FORT BEDFORD TO FORT DUQUESNE

Fort Dewart. Built by Colonel Henry Bouquet and garrisoned for several years, the Forbes Road leads westward to Edmond's Swamp. 17 miles from Fort Bedford. Erected by the Pennsylvania Historical Commission, 1930.

Plaque: private road .5 mile N of US 30 just W Bedford County line. Erected 1930.

78 FORBES ROAD, 1758. FORT BEDFORD TO FORT DUQUESNE

Edmond's Swamp. The fort stood a few rods west of this marker. The Forbes Road leads westward to Stony Creek Encampment. 18.5 miles from Fort Bedford. Erected by the Pennsylvania Historical Commission, 1930.

Plaque: old Central City-Buckstown Rd., 2 miles W of Central City. Erected 1930.

(79) FORBES ROAD (EDMUNDS SWAMP)

Named for Edmund Cartlidge, Indian trader. A camp located here, on the
Raystown Path, provided good grass for the horses of General Forbes' army in
1758. The site of the redoubt is marked two and a half miles north of here.

US 30 at Buckstown. Erected Jan. 30, 1952.

(80) FORBES ROAD, 1758. FORT BEDFORD TO FORT DUQUESNE

Stony Creek Encampment. "The Ovens" supply headquarters. Fortifications
were erected a few rods north of this site. The Forbes Road leads northward to
the encampment at the foot of Laurel Hill. 23.5 miles from Fort Bedford. Erected
by the Pennsylvania Historical Commission, 1930.

Plaque: grounds of Forbes High School, Kantner, just E of Stoystown (off US 30).
Erected 1930.

(81) LOG GRIST MILL

This reconstructed early log mill was built originally at Roxbury by a miller
named Cronin in 1805. It was in operation until 1918. It is now used as the
Mountain Playhouse. As restored, it is a fine example of an early mill.

PA 985 (old US 219) .5 mile N of Jennerstown. Erected Oct. 24, 1947.

(82) FORBES ROAD (THE CLEAR FIELDS)

Good forage found at open camps such as this on the Raystown Path, led
General Forbes to prefer this route to Braddock's Road. Site of Fort Dudgeon
(Tomahawk Camp) is a short distance to the north.

US 30 just W of Jennerstown. Erected Jan. 30, 1952.

(82) FORBES ROAD, 1758. FORT BEDFORD TO FORT DUQUESNE

Tomahawk Encampment. At foot of Laurel Hill. The Forbes Road leads
northwestward to Fort Ligonier. 35.5 miles from Fort Bedford. Erected by the
Pennsylvania Historical Commission, 1930.

Plaque: SR 4027 (former LR 55092) W of Jennerstown, N of US 30. Erected
1930.

REGION VI

The Southwest Borderland

Fayette, Green and *Washington* counties are in the southwest corner of Pennsylvania. In Washington County stood the most striking physical manifestation of ancient man in Pennsylvania, two large burial mounds of the Adena people, built two to three thousand years ago and excavated for their artifacts late in the nineteenth century. In the same way the written record, extending more than two hundred years, records the attempts of France to secure her territorial claims in the Ohio Basin by fortifying western Pennsylvania. The rebuff to her designs by her imperial arch-rival, Great Britain, was inevitable.

The first armed and deadly challenge to France's claim was made in 1754 by militia of the colony of Virginia under command of young Major George Washington. To throw up a defense against French retaliation, the Virginia militia hastily erected a palisaded enclosure, Fort Necessity, a replica of which stands at its site in Fayette County. Outnumbered, the Virginians were allowed to withdraw. Moreover, in the following year, General Edward Braddock's expedition to unseat the French at Fort Duquesne was turned to flight by a sudden and prolonged attack by French and Indians.

Ultimately, the British triumphed and the region was opened to settlement. Scotch-Irish families were the first settlers under a new nation to occupy this corner of the State; their lands, never highly productive, now support sheep, livestock and truck farming. Presbyterian churches and church-related colleges are their legacy. The most productive employment other than farming, until recently, was the mining of soft, bituminous coal. From this was made coke, which fired Pittsburgh-area steel manufacture and raised it to national leadership. The iron furnaces of Fayette County and the oil and gas wells of Washington County represent phases in the history of local industry.

General Braddock's ill-fated expedition traveled the first crude road into the region. Others followed, and in 1818 the National Road (now U.S. 40) was completed from Cumberland, Maryland, through Fayette and Washington counties to Wheeling, (now) West Virginia. Fathered by Albert Gallatin, Swiss-born Secretary of the Treasury whose home, Friendship Hill, still stands in Fayette County, the National Road was built by Congress in the interest of the frontier economy. Toll houses represent a later, pay-as-you-go phase of the highway's history.

The Whiskey Rebellion, which simmered in western Pennsylvania from 1791 to 1794 in opposition to the federal taxation of whiskey, allied Pennsylvania ever more closely with the Jeffersonian faction in the politics of the early republic. David Bradford, of Washington, Pennsylvania, was a leader in the agitation. Since these events, however, the representatives of the region have played a more temperate role in the affairs of state.

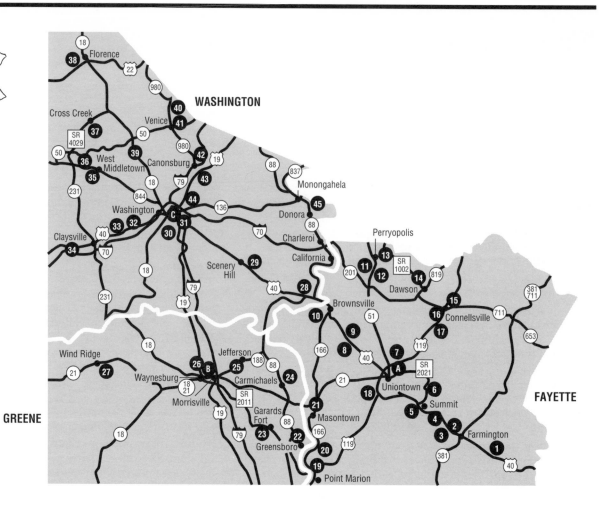

WASHINGTON

18
Florence
38
22
980
40
Cross Creek
Venice
41
50
37
SR
4029
39
Canonsburg
980
42
19
50
36
West
Middletown
43
35
231
18
79
844
44
136
Washington
C
33
32
31
Claysville
40
30
34
70
18
29
Scenery
Hill
231
79
40
28
19
GREENE
18
Wind Ridge
18
27
21
Waynesburg
18
21
26
B
25
188
88
24
Jefferson
Carmichaels
Morrisville
SR
2011
19
Garards
Fort
88
23
22
Greensboro
79
20
166
19
Point Marion

WASHINGTON
88
837
Monongahela
45
Donora
88
70
Charleroi
California
201
11
Perryopolis
13
SR
1002
12
14
Dawson
819
15
16
Connellsville
711
381
711
17
Brownsville
10
119
653
51
9
8
40
7
119
166
A
SR
2021
21
18
Uniontown
6
Masontown
166
5
Summit
119
4
2
Farmington
FAYETTE
3
381
1
40

Fayette County

A FAYETTE COUNTY
Formed September 26, 1783 from Westmoreland County. Named for the Marquis de Lafayette. Among the French and Indian War sites here is Fort Necessity. The county seat, Uniontown, was incorporated 1796. On the National Road, eventually U.S. Route 40.
City type: County Courthouse, Main St., Uniontown. Dedicated Oct. 21, 1982.

**Markers Located on or near US 40,
the National Road (or National Pike)**

1 BRADDOCK ROAD (TWELVE SPRINGS CAMP)
General Braddock's eighth camp, June 24, 1755, on the march to Fort Duquesne, was about half a mile SW. Chestnut Ridge, seen on the horizon to the west, was the last mountain range to be crossed. Axemen widened an Indian path for passage of supply wagons and artillery over it.
US 40, 3.5 miles SE of Farmington. Erected May 21, 1952.

2 FORT NECESSITY
Was located about 400 yards to the south in the Great Meadows. Built and commanded, 1754, by Lieutenant Colonel George Washington, aged 22. Here after 9 hours of engagement with M. Coulon de Villiers in command of 900 French regulars and their Indian allies, Washington and his 400 raw Virginia and South Carolina troops capitulated and early next morning, July 4, 1754, marched out with the honors of war. Marked by the Pennsylvania Historical Commission and Citizens of Fayette County, 1926.
Plaque: US 40, Mount Washington, 1 mile NW of Farmington. Dedicated July 4, 1926.

2 MOUNT WASHINGTON TAVERN
This building erected in 1816 was once a famous hostelry on the National Road. It is now used as a museum. Great Meadows nearby was once owned by George Washington.
US 40, 1.2 mile NW of Farmington. Erected Nov. 23, 1946.

3 NATIONAL ROAD
Our first national road; fathered by Albert Gallatin. Begun in 1811 at Cumberland, Md.; completed to Wheeling in 1818. Toll road under State control, 1835-1905. Rebuilt, it is present U.S. Route 40.
US 40, 1.7 mile NW of Farmington. Erected Oct. 12, 1948.

4 BRADDOCK PARK
Gen. Edward Braddock was buried here in 1755, after his disastrous defeat and death. The site of his original grave, the new grave to which his remains were moved in 1804, and a trace of the Braddock Road may be seen here.
US 40, 2.5 miles NW of Farmington. Erected Nov. 23, 1946.

5 BRADDOCK ROAD (ROCK FORT CAMP)
General Braddock's tenth camp, June 26, 1755, on the march to Fort Duquesne, was at the Half King's Rock, one mile NE of here. The Rock was named for Washington's friend, Tanacharisson, the Iroquois viceroy (half king) of the Ohio Indians. Washington met him here in 1754.
US 40 ca. 6 miles SE of Uniontown at Summit. Erected June 17, 1952.

6 BRADDOCK ROAD (DUNBAR'S CAMP)
General Braddock ascended the ridge east of this point and advanced toward Gist's Plantation. Col. Dunbar's detachment, following with the heavy baggage, made its last camp here. Later, as Braddock's defeated army streamed back, Dunbar destroyed his supples and withdrew.
SR 2021 (former LR 26115) ca. 3 miles N of US 40 at Jumonville. Erected June 17, 1952.

7 UNIONTOWN
Founded by Henry Beeson, who built a blockhouse on site of the county jail in 1774. Uniontown gained importance with the building of the National Road after 1811.
On main highways leading into city. Erected 1946 & 1947.

7 GEORGE C. MARSHALL
Soldier and statesman, born Dec. 31, 1880, on this site. Chief of Staff, U.S. Army, 1939-45. General of the Army from Dec. 1944. Secretary of State, 1947-49, and Defense, 1950-51. Author of Marshall Plan for European recovery. Awarded the Nobel Peace Prize. Died Oct. 16, 1959.
City type: 142 W. Main St. (US 40), Uniontown. Dedicated Jan. 17, 1981.

8 TOLL HOUSE
One of the six original toll houses on the Cumberland or National Road. It was built by the State after the road was turned over to it by the U.S. in 1835. The road was completed through this section in 1817-18.
US 40, 5 miles NW of Uniontown. Erected July 3, 1947.

8 SEARIGHT'S TOLLHOUSE
Erected by Pennsylvania, 1835, to collect tolls on the old national road. Administered by the Pennsylvania Historical and Museum Commission.
At site on US 40, 5 miles NW of Uniontown. Erected [1966].

9 NATIONAL ROAD
Same text as National Road above.
US 40 NW of Brier Hill. Erected Oct. 12, 1948.

10 BROWNSVILLE
Once called Redstone Old Fort, its history includes the Ohio Company's storehouse, 1754, and Fort Burd, 1759. It was on the route of Nemacolin's Trail, of Burd's Road, and of the National Road.
Off US 40 at Brownsville. Erected Nov. 22, 1946.

10 BRASHEAR HOUSE
John A. Brashear, astronomer, educator, was born here, 1840. His grandfather kept the Brashear House, a leading tavern. In 1825 Lafayette spoke from its doorway to the people of Brownsville.
Market, 6th & Union Sts., Brownsville. Erected Nov. 22, 1946.

10 PHILANDER KNOX
Born May 6, 1853, in a house still standing on Front Street. Attorney-General in 1901, leading the anti-trust fight. A U.S. Senator, 1904-09. Secretary of State under Taft. Re-elected Senator in 1917. Died in 1921.
Market, 6th & Union Sts., Brownsville. Erected Nov. 22, 1946.

Markers Located Elsewhere in Fayette County

11 COKE OVENS
The bee-hive ovens nearby are typical of the region. Coke was first made from coal near Connellsville in this type oven about 1840. Since 1870 use of coke has been vital to steel making.
PA 51 just W of Perryopolis. Erected Nov. 22, 1946.

12 WASHINGTON MILL
Opposite is the site of a grist mill built about 1774 by George Washington. It was sold by him in 1795 to Colonel Israel Shreve. The mill ruins still remain.
SR 4038 (former LR 26191), Perryopolis. Erected Nov. 22, 1946.

13 ALLIANCE FURNACE
First furnace west of the Alleghenies. Built 1789 on banks of nearby Jacob's Creek, its ruins are still observable. Supplied iron for Wayne's campaign in 1794 against the Indians.
SR 1002 (former LR 26015) ca. 6 miles NW of PA 819. Erected Nov. 22, 1946.

14 ALLIANCE FURNACE

Same text as above.

PA 819, 1 mile N of Dawson. Erected Nov. 22, 1946.

15 [COLONEL WILLIAM CRAWFORD]

In memory of Colonel William Crawford, born in Berkeley County, Virginia, in 1732. Friend of Washington — pioneer — patriot. The monument is situated 1260 yards S. 69 E. 16' of the spot where he built his log cabin in 1765 on the west bank of the Youghiogheny River, at the historic Stewart's Crossings. He first visited the region west of the mountains in 1758, as an officer in the expedition of General Forbes against Fort Duquesne. As Colonel of the Seventh Virginia Regiment, he crossed the Delaware with Washington in 1777, and shared in the victory at Trenton. Fighting in defense of the frontier, as commander of the Sandusky Expedition, he was captured by the Indians and burned at the stake near Crawfordsville, Ohio, June 11, 1782. Erected by the Pennsylvania Historical Commission, the City of Connellsville, and grateful citizens, 1917.

Plaque: S. Pittsburgh St. near Wills Rd., Connellsville. Dedicated Oct. 19, 1918.

16 COL. WILLIAM CRAWFORD

Hero of Indian wars, made his home about a half mile from Connellsville after 1766, and was Washington's land agent. During the Revolution, he led a campaign against Ohio Indians; he was captured and killed near Upper Sandusky in 1782.

US 119, .2 mile S of Connellsville. Erected 1966 (revised 1946 marker).

16 BRADDOCK ROAD (STEWART'S CROSSING)

General Braddock's twelfth camp, June 28, 1755, on the march to Fort Duquesne, was north of here, near the Youghiogheny River. On June 30, the army forded the River at Stewart's Crossing to a point about one-half mile northwest of present-day Connellsville.

US 119, .2 mile S of Connellsville. Erected Aug. 26, 1952.

17 MEASON HOUSE

The Georgian manor on the hill was built 1802 by Isaac Meason. Veteran of the Revolution, Meason was a pioneer ironmaster. In 1817 at Plumsock he built one of the first rolling mills.

US 119, 4.5 miles SW of Connellsville. Erected Nov. 22, 1946.

18 FORT GADDIS

Built on the Catawba Trail as a refuge from the Indians by Thomas Gaddis about 1764. Gaddis was later a colonel in the Pennsylvania Continental Line during the Revolution.

SR 3019 (old US 119) 2 miles S of Uniontown. Erected Nov. 23, 1946.

19 ALBERT GALLATIN

Friendship Hill, home of the Jeffersonian diplomat, financier, statesman, is a few miles from here. Built in 1789, it was his home for the greater part of his public life.

Junction US 119 & PA 166 N of Point Marion. Erected Nov. 23, 1946.

Friendship Hill National Historic Site

20 OLD GLASSWORKS

Half a mile east of here, 1794-1797, the first glass factory west of the Alleghenies was founded by Albert Gallatin, Secretary of the Treasury under Thomas Jefferson. He was aided by skillful glassworkers from the Amelung factory — Kramer, Gabler, Eberhart, Reppert, and Reitz. Factory closed in 1807.

PA 166 in New Geneva. Erected June 1955.

21 FORT MASON
Built as a blockhouse in 1774-78 by John Mason. It was a settler's refuge in Revolutionary days. The site of the fort was nearby. Later rebuilt on Main Street as a dwelling.
PA 166 at Masontown. Erected Nov. 23, 1946.

Greene County

B GREENE COUNTY
Formed February 9, 1796 from Washington County. Named for Gen. Nathanael Greene. Waynesburg, the county seat named for Gen. Anthony Wayne, was incorporated in 1816. Site of Waynesburg College, founded 1849. Near Ten Mile is birthplace of Gov. Edward Martin.
City type: County Courthouse, High St., Waynesburg. Dedicated May 3, 1982.

22 OLD GLASSWORKS
On this site, the first glass factory west of the Monongahela River was established in 1805 through the stimulating influence of Albert Gallatin, Secretary of the Treasury under Thomas Jefferson. Glass was made here until 1849.
SR 2014 (former LR 30068), Greensboro. Erected Mar. 28, 1955.

23 GARARD'S FORT
Site of frontier refuge in Revolutionary War; station in 1777 of small detachment of Virginia militia. Near here, on Sunday, May 12, 1782, Indians killed the wife and three children of Rev. John Corbly, a Baptist minister.
SR 2011 (former LR 616) .6 mile E of Garards Fort. Erected May 23, 1958.

24 GREENE ACADEMY
Established in 1810 by Act of Legislature. Was aided by State grant of $2000 and public subscriptions. Until 1860, a leading academy west of the mountains.Old building, no longer used for a school, is northeast of here, on Market St.
City type: PA 88, Carmichaels, near intersection Greene & Vine Sts. Erected May 22, 1953.

25 MONONGAHELA COLLEGE
This was first Baptist college in western Pennsylvania. It was begun by Ten Mile Baptist Assn. in 1867, opened in 1869, and in 1871 chartered by legislature. Operated 1869-1888; reopened 1890 and finally closed 1894. College building, erected 1871, lies 300 yards north of marker.
PA 188 in Jefferson at Green & Pine Sts. Dedicated May 8, 1960.

26 WAYNESBURG COLLEGE
Founded in 1849 by the Cumberland Presbyterian Church. Chartered by the State in 1850. One of the first two colleges in Pennsylvania to grant degrees to women, in 1857.
US 19 in Waynesburg. Erected Jan. 6, 1949.

27 RYERSON'S BLOCKHOUSE
Near here stood one of three blockhouses erected by Captain James Paul's company in 1792, durng the State's last troubles with the Indians. On April 17, 1792, soldiers carrying supplies from the Thomas Ryerson mill clashed with an Indian war party attacking the white settlements.
PA 21 at Wind Ridge. Erected Oct. 17, 1960.

Washington County

C WASHINGTON COUNTY
Formed March 28, 1781 out of Westmoreland County and named for Gen. George Washington. A scene of activity in the Whiskey Rebellion, 1791-94. The county seat, Washington, was made a borough in 1810; a city in 1924. On the National Road, eventually U.S. 40.
City type: County Courthouse, Main St. & Cherry Way, Washington. Dedicated Dec. 17, 1981.

Markers Located on or near US 40, the National Road (or National Pike)

28 JAMES G. BLAINE

Born, Jan. 31, 1830, on this site, of Pennsylvania pioneer ancestry. Washington College graduate. Moved to Maine in 1854. Served the nation as member of Congress, party leader and secretary of state.

238 Main St., West Brownsville. Erected May 28, 1947.

29 HILL'S TAVERN

This tavern, in continuous operation since 1794 when it was opened by Stephen Hill, is one of the oldest on the National Road. It was a popular stop for stage coaches and waggoners.

US 40 at Scenery Hill. Erected June 1952.

Entering Washington

30 LE MOYNE CREMATORY

This crematory, the first in the United States, was built in 1876 by Dr. Francis LeMoyne. From 1876 to 1900, there were 42 cremations. Dr. LeMoyne lies buried here.

City type: S. Main St. (SR 2001, former LR 62131), S end Washington. Erected Aug. 1953.

31 WASHINGTON

Laid out in 1781 by John and William Hoge. Site of Indian Catfish Camp. Boro charter, 1810; city, 1923. National Road center and rich in historic buildings and associations. Named for George Washington.

On main highways leading into city. Erected May 28, 1947.

31 WASHINGTON AND JEFFERSON COLLEGE

Chartered history starts with the founding of Washington Academy in 1787. A section of the Administration Building erected, 1793. Washington College (1806) and Jefferson College (1802) were united in 1865.

City type: campus (E of College Ave.), Washington. Erected Feb. 2, 1954.

31 LE MOYNE HOUSE

Built, 1812, by Dr. John LeMoyne. For many years, home of his son, Dr. Francis LeMoyne, noted abolitionist, and builder of first crematory in the U.S. Now the home of the Washington County Historical Society.

City type: 49 E. Maiden St., Washington. Erected Aug. 1953.

31 EDWARD ACHESON

The eminent American chemist was born in this house with the round corner, 1856. Was awarded many medals for his invention of carborundum, artificial graphite, and other valuable products of the electric furnace.

City type: SW corner Main & Maiden Sts., Washington. Erected Aug. 1953.

31 BRADFORD HOUSE

Built in 1788 by David Bradford, leader of the Whiskey Rebellion in 1794. Occupied by him until he fled to Spanish West Florida after the collapse of the Rebellion.

City type: 175 S. Main St., Washington. Erected Aug. 1953.

31 BRADFORD HOUSE

Home, built in 1788, of David Bradford, leader of the Whiskey Rebellion. Administered by the Pennsylvania Historical and Museum Commission.

At site, 175 S. Main St., Washington. Erected Apr. 7, 1966.

31 GLOBE INN

Stood on this site. It was opened in 1798 by David Morris. Among the noted guests during the National Road era were five presidents of the U.S. Lafayette was entertained here on May 25, 1825.

City type: 155 S. Main St., Washington. Erected Aug. 1953.

31 CAPT. PHILO McGIFFIN

Born Dec. 13, 1860, on this site. Graduate of U. S. Naval Academy. Went to China in 1885, built up and trained its Navy. Sept. 17, 1894, it fought the Japanese to a draw in a naval battle at Yalu River. McGiffin died in 1897 from his injuries.

Main & Beau Sts., Washington. Erected May 28, 1947.

31 GANTZ OIL WELL
Site of first oil well in Washington County. Oil was struck in Dec., 1884. First oil was shipped in 1885; last oil was pumped about 1916. This well led to the development of the Washington oil field.
City type: W. Chestnut St. at Brookside Ave., Washington. Erected Oct. 3, 1953.

Leaving Washington

32 AUGUSTA TOWN
Here met, in August, 1776, under Virginia's claim to western Pennsylvania, the first court west of the Monongahela River. The site is a mile south and marked by a monument.
US 40, 3 miles SW of Washington. Erected May 28, 1947.

32 WOLFF'S FORT
A stockaded house built here about 1780 by Jacob Wolff afforded a refuge for the settlers of this region. It was one of the most important forts in the area.
US 40, 3.3 miles SW of Washington. Erected May 28, 1947.

32 NATIONAL ROAD
Our first national road; fathered by Albert Gallatin. Begun in 1811 at Cumberland, Md.; completed to Wheeling in 1818. Toll road under State control, 1835-1905. Rebuilt, it is present U.S. Route 40.
US 40, 3.6 miles SW of Washington. Erected Apr. 1949.

33 ''S'' BRIDGE
This stone bridge was part of the National, or Cumberland Road. Originated in 1805, it was completed to Wheeling in 1818. Over it passed countless wagons and stages uniting the East and the growing West.
US 40, 5 miles SW of Washington. Erected May 28, 1947.

34 MILLER'S BLOCKHOUSE
Site 3 miles north. Built about 1780 by Jacob Miller, Sr. Rendezvous for settlers of the Dutch Fork area. Here, March 31, 1782, Ann Hupp led a heroic defense against attacking Indians.
US 40, 3.5 miles W of Claysville. Erected May 28, 1947.

34 RICE'S FORT
The site of this fortified blockhouse, built during the Revolution by Abraham Rice, was about six miles north of Buffalo Creek. It was attacked by a force of Indians in September, 1782, but withstood the siege.
US 40, 3.5 miles W of Claysville. Erected 1973 (revised 1947 marker).

Markers Located Elsewhere in Washington County

35 RALSTON THRESHER
Nearby was the site of the Robert McClure factory of pre-Civil War days. It pioneered in making Andrew Ralston's machine cleaning and threshing grain in a single operation, patented in 1842.
PA 844 at West Middletown. Erected May 28, 1947.

36 DODDRIDGE'S FORT
To the north were located the stockaded cabins of John Doddridge. Built about 1773, they served as a refuge for settlers of this region in Revolutionary days. Also boyhood home of Dr. Joseph Doddridge.
PA 844, 2.5 miles W of West Middletown. Erected May 28, 1947.

37 CROSS CREEK CHURCH
Founded by Scotch-Irish Presbyterians who began to hold services in 1775 at Vance's Fort, 1 mile north. Original church built here and first pastor called in 1779. The present church building was erected 1864.
SR 4029 (former LR 62185) at Cross Creek. Erected Oct. 16, 1950.

38 ELISHA McCURDY
The great Presbyterian revivalist is buried here where he served as pastor 46 years. At Cross Roads and Upper Buffalo he led, in Nov. 1802, the Great Revival meetings attended by many thousands from near and far.
SR 4004 (old US 22) at Florence. Erected May 28, 1947.

39 THE McGUGIN GAS WELL

Drilled in 1882, one mile west of here, with the then largest flow of gas in the world, and later piped to Pittsburgh for light and heat. This initiated the beginning and development of the great oil and gas fields in southwestern Pennsylvania.

PA 18 NW of Washington, S of PA 50. Erected Jan. 1967.

40 DAVID REED

Opposite was the log home of David Reed, leader of the Covenanter squatters on lands owned by George Washington. Here 13 of the Scotch-Irish pioneers met with him on Sept. 20, 1784, defying his effort to remove them.

PA 980 N of PA 50 at Venice. Erected May 9, 1950.

41 GEORGE WASHINGTON

Near here at the David Reed home, Washington met on Sept. 20, 1784, with 13 Covenanter squatters on his tract of 2813 acres. Failure to fix terms of purchase forced him to bring suit at Washington to eject the illegal tenants.

PA 50 at Venice. Erected May 9, 1950.

42 COL. GEORGE MORGAN

Here was the home, 1796-1810, of the noted Indian trader and agent. Site is marked by a monument. It was here that Morgan was visited by Aaron Burr. His conspiracy was first made known to Thomas Jefferson by Colonel Morgan.

Old PA 519 S of Morganza. Erected May 28, 1947.

43 THE REVEREND JOHN McMILLAN, D.D.

Born November 11, 1752. Died November 16, 1833. Pioneer preacher-educator-patriot lies buried in this churchyard. Served sixty years in the ministry. Leader in founding Western Theological Seminary — Jefferson College — Jefferson Medical College. His missionary labors resulted in the founding of Chartiers, Pigeon Creek, and many other Presbyterian churches in this region. With his faithful wife, he shared untold toil and privation in order that the Kingdom of God might be established on this rugged frontier. Marked by the Pennsylvania Historical Commission and the Board of Trustees of Chartiers Presbyterian Church, 1931.

Plaque: Junction US 19 & PA 519 NE of Washington. Erected 1931.

44 JOHN McMILLAN

First Presbyterian missioner in this area, 1775. Founder of Hill Church, 1776, and of Western Theological Seminary and Jefferson College. He died in 1833, after sixty years in the ministry, and is buried in the churchyard.

US 19, 5 miles NE of Washington. Erected Jan. 7, 1949.

44 HILL CHURCH

Founded 1776 by Rev. John McMillan, who served as its pastor until his death in 1833. The pioneer Presbyterian church in the region. Woodrow Wilson's father was once a pastor here.

US 19, 5 miles NE of Washington. Erected Jan. 7, 1949.

45 MONONGAHELA

Oldest settlement in the valley and transportation center since the days of Devore's Ferry, chartered 1775. Laid out in 1796 as Williamsport. A city since 1873. Here thousands of pioneers began the river journey to the West.

On main highways leading into city. Erected May 28, 1947.

45 THE MOUNDS

Site of two Indian Burial Mounds built between 2,000 and 3,000 years ago by the Adena people. Late 19th century excavations found skeletons, pottery, copper implements, and other antiquities.

City type: Memorial Park, Mound & Decker Sts., Monongahela. Erected July 15, 1954.

45 WHISKEY POINT

The bluff at Main St. and Park Ave. was the site on Aug. 14, 1794, of a meeting of 226 whiskey rebels. Albert Gallatin's eloquence turned the tide, resulting in peaceful ending of the Whiskey Rebellion and the possibility of civil strife.

PA 481 at Park Ave., Monongahela. Erected May 26, 1949.

REGION VII

Gateway to the Ohio Country

The eight-county region of westcentral Pennsylvania comprising *Allegheny, Armstrong, Beaver, Butler, Indiana, Jefferson, Lawrence,* and *Westmoreland* counties began its recorded history in the heat of conflict.

European settlement was still east of the Appalachians when displaced Indians, including refugee Delawares, seeking new hunting grounds, established Kittanning, the Kuskuskies and other towns in the west. Meanwhile, the British, with their Iroquois alliance and success in the Indian trade, threatened France's fragile link between Canada and Louisiana — the Ohio country.

To tighten this link, the Marquis Duquesne, Governor of Canada, began in 1753 to erect forts from Lake Erie to the Ohio Forks. The Ohio Company of Virginia and Governor Dinwiddie, whose colony claimed a portion of southwestern Pennsylvania, challenged the French "intrusion." Captain George Washington of Virginia militia, who carried to the French the command to withdraw, was rebuffed — diplomatically at Fort LeBoeuf and forcibly at Fort Necessity. General Braddock's ill-fated attempt in 1755 to seize Fort Duquesne at the Forks led the Forbes Expedition from Fort Ligonier to take Fort Duquesne in 1758, and to Colonel Bouquet's victory at Bushy Run, lifting the siege of Fort Pitt in the Pontiac Indian uprising of 1763.

With the frontier temporarily secured, the British were determined to ease the cost of defense by imposing new taxes in America and by halting the provocation caused by settlement west of the mountains. These enactments fomented the events that led to the American Revolution, a tax revolt that echoed in the tax resistance of the Whiskey Rebels to the federal government in 1794.

The building of Fort Pitt and Pittsburgh established the Ohio Forks as a military and commercial center and focus of migration. With the Native American claim north of the Allegheny River extinguished by treaty in 1784, affordable land was opened to veterans of the Revolution and to others. Pittsburgh became their supplier and manufacturer, and boatbuilding to reach these and other markets became Allegheny County's first industry. Moreover, the Pennsylvania Canal, in 1834, and the Pennsylvania Railroad, in 1852, linked the region competitively with industries and markets outside.

Using local iron at first, as well as coke produced from regional bituminous, the region became a leader in steel until the mid-twentieth century. Built on available resources — such as oil and natural gas — or on local genius and regional investment, the aluminum, glass, chemical, electrical and extraction industries have been among the mainstays of the regional economy.

Among those that prospered were the communal enterprises of the Harmony Society, a German religious body in exile, first in Butler County, later in Beaver. The peoples' migrations — Scotch-Irish; northern, southern and eastern European; southern African-American — are reflected in the institutions of the region and their vitality. Such vitality, in education, culture and industry and in securing the rights of citizens, prepared a foundation for civic renewal in the twentieth century.

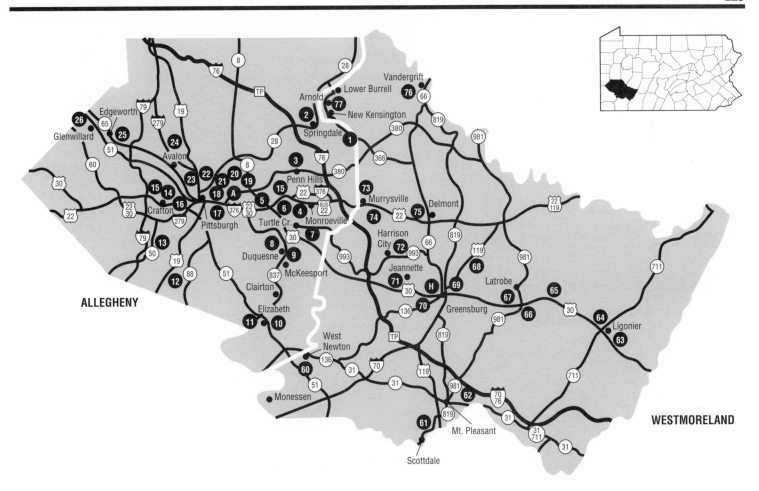

Glenwillard

26 Edgeworth
65 25

60

30

22
30

22

50

79

13

12

88

ALLEGHENY

11

24 Avalon

79

19

51

23 22 20 21 19
15 14 18 A 5
16
Crafton 376 22
17 279 30
Pittsburgh

8

Duquesne 9
837 McKeesport
Clairton

Elizabeth
10

8

76

TP

28

19

51

8

60

8

3

15

5
6 4
Turtle Cr.
30
7

Penn Hills
22 376
BUS
22
Monroeville

Arnold 2
77 New Kensington
Springdale 1

376

73

Murrysville

74 22

Harrison
City 72
993

Jeannette
71 993
30

70

136

West
Newton

60 136

31

70

51

Monessen

61

Scottdale

Mt. Pleasant

819 62

31

28

366

380

76

Vandergrift
76
66

819

981

380

Delmont
75

66 819

68

H 69 Latrobe
70 67 66
Greensburg
981

981

819

119

81

31

22
119

981

711

65 30 64
66 Ligonier
63

711

711

70
76

31
711
31

WESTMORELAND

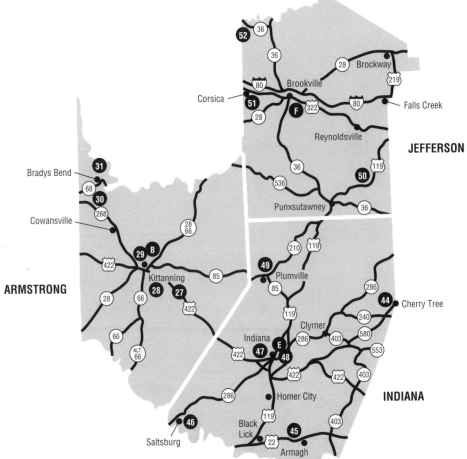

JEFFERSON

52

36

36

28 Brockway

80 Brookville

219

Corsica

51

F 322

80 Falls Creek

28

Reynoldsville

31 Bradys Bend

68

30

268 Cowansville

36

536

50 119

Punxsutawney 36

28
66

29 B

422 Kittanning

85

210 119

49 Plumville

85

286

44 Cherry Tree

ARMSTRONG

28

66

27

422

119

240

Clymer

580

66

Indiana

286

403

553

ALT.
66

47 E
48

422

422 403

286

422

INDIANA

Homer City

46

119

Black
Lick

45

Saltsburg

22

Armagh

403

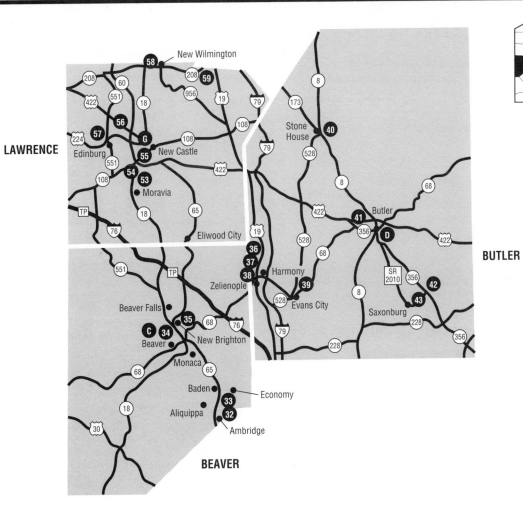

LAWRENCE

BUTLER

BEAVER

Allegheny County

A ALLEGHENY COUNTY

Formed September 24, 1788 out of Westmoreland and Washington counties. Named for the Allegheny River. County seat of Pittsburgh was laid out 1764; became a city in 1816. A center of the iron, steel and other industries and "Workshop of the World."

City type: County Courthouse, Grant St. between 5th & Forbes Aves., Pittsburgh. Dedicated Dec. 30, 1982.

1 WILLIAM D. BOYCE

Inspired by the good turn of an English Scout, he brought the Scouting movement to the United States. His efforts led to the incorporation of Boy Scouts in Washington, D.C., February 8, 1910, and to charter by Congress June 3, 1916. Born a mile south of this spot on June 16, 1858.

PA 366, Westmoreland County line, 2 miles SE of New Kensington. Dedicated June 11, 1960.

2 RACHEL CARSON

Scientist, naturalist and writer. Born 1907 at 613 Marion Avenue; died 1964. Her 1951 book "The Sea Around Us" was followed in 1962 by "Silent Spring." This book focused the nation's attention on the dangers of pesticides and helped launch the environmental movement.

City type: Pittsburgh St. (SR 1001, old PA 28) & Colfax St., in Springdale. Dedicated May 20, 1988.

3 BOUQUET CAMP

Bouquet Camp, supply base in Forbes' campaign against the French holding Fort Duquesne in 1758, was near here. Named in honor of Col. Bouquet, second-in-command and builder of Forbes Road.

PA 380 (Saltsburg & Frankstown Rds.), Petermans Corner, Penn Hills Twp. Erected Dec. 21, 1946.

3 FORBES ROAD, 1758. FORT BEDFORD TO FORT DUQUESNE

The Bouquet Encampment was located three miles east of this place which marks the farthest northern point of the Forbes Road, which leads westward to Fort Duquesne, 97 miles from Fort Bedford. Erected by the Pennsylvania Historical Commission, 1930.

Plaque: PA 380 (Saltsburg & Frankstown Rds.), Petermans Corner, Penn Hills Twp. Erected 1930.

4 FORBES ROAD (BOUQUET'S BREASTWORKS)

The last base of General Forbes' army. After crossing nearly "two hundred miles of wild and unknown country," the army entered Fort Duquesne on Nov. 25, 1758. Site is a mile north.

SR 2066 (Old Frankstown Rd.), Monroeville. Erected July 9, 1952.

5 JANE GREY SWISSHELM

Renowned editor, abolitionist, Civil War nurse, advocate of women's rights and temperance. Also author of "Half a Century, 1815-1865." Born Jane Grey Cannon at Pittsburgh December 6, 1815; died in old homestead on this site on July 22, 1884.

Braddock & Greendale Aves. in Edgewood, just N of I 376 exit 9. Erected Sept. 14, 1959.

5 FRANK CONRAD (1874-1941)

At his garage workshop here in 1919-1920, Conrad made broadcasts over his amateur station, 8XK, which introduced the concept of commercial radio and led to the start of KDKA. For 37 years a Westinghouse engineer, he held over 200 patents.

City type: PA 8 (Penn Ave.) & Peebles St., W end Wilkinsburg. Dedicated Dec. 1, 1990.

6 BRADDOCK'S DEFEAT

July 9, 1755, Gen. Braddock's British forces en route to capture Fort Duquesne were ambushed and routed by French and Indians within present limits of Braddock and North Braddock, forcing retreat and failure of the expedition.

US 30 at Forest Hills, S of I 376 exit 10. Erected Feb. 28, 1948.

7 GEORGE WESTINGHOUSE

Inventor of air brake and some 400 other devices. Developed AC transmission of electric current. Spent creative years in Pittsburgh and founded the industry which bears his name.

US 30 at George Westinghouse Bridge over Turtle Creek. Erected Dec. 23, 1946.

8 BRADDOCK'S CROSSING

Below this hill, about midday on July 9, 1755, a British army of 1300 made its second crossing of the river and advanced to drive the French from Fort Duquesne. A few hours later, with General Braddock mortally wounded and his army routed, survivors recrossed, pursued by the French and Indians.

PA 837 at Kennywood Park N of Duquesne. Erected Aug. 24, 1964.

9 NATIONAL TUBE WORKS

Incorporated 1869, the works began production here, 1872. By 1901, when it became a subsidiary of U.S. Steel, this was the world's largest pipe producer. Major advances in inspection techniques originated here. Plant operations ceased in 1987.

City type: PA 148 (Lysle Blvd.) subway entrance to plant, McKeesport. Dedicated Jan. 15, 1991.

10 ELIZABETH

Here were the boatyards of John and Samuel Walker, a major center for building boats for western waters. A ship launched in 1793 at these yards reached Philadelphia via New Orleans.

PA 51 just SE of Elizabeth. Erected Dec. 20, 1946.

11 YOHOGANIA COURTHOUSE

Governmental and judicial center for Yohogania, a county erected by Virginia in asserting its claim to western Pennsylvania from 1777 to 1780. The site is on the hilltop opposite.

PA 837 SW of West Elizabeth. Erected June 10, 1948.

12 BETHEL PRESBYTERIAN CHURCH

Founded, 1776, in the Old Stone Manse in South Park, by Rev. John McMillan, pioneer minister and educator. It is the mother of five nearby churches and has given its name to the community. In the cemetery, 14 Revolutionary War soldiers from this area are buried.

Bethel Church Rd. (county hwy.) between PA 88 & US 19. Erected Aug. 1, 1951.

13 NEVILLE HOUSE

Known as Woodville. Built 1785 by Gen. John Neville; later occupied by his son, Col. Presley Neville. Refuge of Gen. Neville's family when some Whiskey Rebels burned his home at Bower Hill, July 17, 1794.

PA 50 just S of Woodville. Erected Aug. 12, 1947.

13 [NEVILLE]

The residence of Gen. John Neville, soldier and U.S. revenue officer, one half mile southeast of this monument. On July 17, 1794, 500 men assembled at Mingo Church, marched to the Neville home, demanded the surrender of his commission. A skirmish took place, the insurgent leader was killed, and the mansion house burned. This was the first armed resistance to Federal authority in the United States; the culmination of widespread opposition to the enforcement of the excise tax imposed by Congress, known historically as the Whiskey Insurrection. . . . Erected by the Pennsylvania Historical Commission and Chartiers Historical Society, 1931.

Plaque: PA 50 at old entrance Woodville State Hospital, Woodville. Actually dedicated Oct. 27, 1935.

14 HAND'S HOSPITAL

On this site was located the isolation hospital erected 1777, by Gen. Edward Hand to care for troops at Fort Pitt. Blockhouses protected the original two-story log structure.

PA 60 (Steuben St.) at Linden St., Crafton. Erected Dec. 24, 1946.

Entering Pittsburgh

15 PITTSBURGH

Gateway to the West and steel center of the world. Named for William Pitt by Gen. Forbes after the fall of French Fort Duquesne in 1758. Laid out as a town by John Campbell in 1764. Incorporated as a city, 1816.

On main highways into city: PA 60 at Thornburg; PA 65, at N city line; US 19 N of city line; PA 28 at Millvale; US 30 westbound at Forest Hills. Erected Dec. 1946.

16 FIRST MINING OF PITTSBURGH COAL

This State's bituminous coal industry was born about 1760 on Coal Hill, now Mt. Washington. Here the Pittsburgh coal bed was mined to supply Fort Pitt. This was eventually to be judged the most valuable individual mineral deposit in the U.S.

City type: Grandview Ave. between Ulysses & Bertha Sts., Mount Washington. Dedicated Apr. 18, 1985.

17 POLISH ARMY

At hall on this site on April 3, 1917, a speech by I. J. Paderewski to delegates at convention of the Polish Falcons began the movement to recruit a Polish army in U.S. to fight in Europe with Allies for creating an independent Poland.

City type: 97 S. 18th St., South Side. Dedicated Apr. 3, 1960.

18 FORT PRINCE GEORGE

Named intended for fort begun here by Virginia force early in 1754 on site noted by Washington as "well situated for a Fort." Captured by the French, April 17, 1754, before its completion.

City type: Point State Park (main entrance Commonwealth Place). Erected May 8, 1959.

18 FORT DUQUESNE

Begun here April, 1754, by French after taking Virginia's fort. Key French position on the Ohio and base for raids on frontier after 1755. Burned by French before Forbes' army occupied it, November, 1758.

City type: Point State Park (adjacent to preceding marker). Erected May 8, 1959.

18 FORT PITT

Built by the English, 1759-61, to replace Mercer's Fort of 1758-59. Named for Prime Minister William Pitt of Great Britain. British stronghold in Ohio Valley and center for settlement.

City type: Point State Park (adjacent to preceding marker). Erected May 8, 1959.

18 FORT PITT BLOCKHOUSE

One of Fort Pitt's outworks, this blockhouse or redoubt stood near the western bastions and is the only surviving structure of that fort. Built in 1764 by Col. Henry Bouquet.

City type: Point State Park (adjacent to preceding marker). Erected May 8, 1959.

18 DAVID L. LAWRENCE

Pennsylvania's Governor, 1959-1963, was born in this area June 18, 1889. As a pioneer in urban renewal, he advocated the creation of Point Park as part of the redevelopment of the Golden Triangle.

City type: Point State Park. Erected Feb. 28, 1985.

18 FORBES ROAD, 1758. FORT BEDFORD TO FORT DUQUESNE

Fort Duquesne, end of Forbes Road. Occupied by General Forbes, November 25, 1758, and by him named Pittsburgh. His victory determined the destiny of the Great Northwest and established Anglo-Saxon supremacy in the United States. "His name for ages to come will be dear to Americans and appear with lustre among contemporary worthies in the British annals." — Col. Hugh Mercer to Colonel Bouquet, March 21, 1759. 104 miles from Fort Bedford. Erected by the Pennsylvania Historical Commission and the Daughters of the American Revolution of Allegheny County, 1930.

Plaque: Point State Park (between Fort Pitt Museum & Blockhouse). Erected 1930.

18 RADIO STATION KDKA

World's first commercial station began operating November 2, 1920, when KDKA reported Harding-Cox election returns from a makeshift studio at the East Pittsburgh Works of Westinghouse. Music, sports, talks, and special events were soon being regularly aired.

City type: plaza, KDKA hdqrs., 1 Gateway Center. Dedicated Nov. 30, 1990.

18 WESTINGHOUSE ELECTRIC CORPORATION

Pioneer in development of alternating current, permitting transmission of electricity over long distances. Founded 1886 by George Westinghouse, it first made AC motors, generators, transformers in a plant at Garrison Place and Penn Avenue.

City type: Westinghouse plaza, 6 Gateway Center. Erected Oct. 1986.

18 JOHN SCULL

His home and printing shop were in this block. The Pittsburgh Gazette was printed here in 1786, first newspaper west of the Alleghenies; also the first book in 1793. The first Post Office of Pittsburgh was here.

City type: Blvd. of the Allies just W of Market St. Erected Dec. 1958.

18 MARTIN R. DELANEY (1812-1885)

A promoter of African-American nationalism, Delany published a Black newspaper, The Mystery, at an office near here. He attended Harvard Medical School, practiced medicine in Pittsburgh, and was commissioned as a major in the Civil War.

City type: 5 PPG Place, 3rd Ave. & Market St. Dedicated May 11, 1991.

18 PITTSBURGH PLATE GLASS COMPANY

First commercially successful U.S. plate glass maker, founded 1883 by John Ford, John Pitcairn and others. First plant was at Creighton; office was half a block east of here on Fourth Avenue. The company became PPG Industries in 1968.

City type: plaza of PPG Place, between 4th Ave. & Market Sq. Dedicated Oct. 19, 1983.

18 UNITED STEELWORKERS OF AMERICA

In the Grant Building here on June 17, 1936, the Steel Workers Organizing Committee was founded. Renamed in 1942, the USWA became one of the world's largest unions, embracing over a million workers. Philip Murray was its first president.

City type: Grant St. between 3rd & 4th Aves. Dedicated June 17, 1986.

18 DUQUESNE UNIVERSITY

Founded by Holy Ghost Fathers from Germany in 1878. Incorporated 1882 as Pittsburgh Catholic College. Named Duquesne University in 1911, this Catholic institution has served students of many faiths in liberal arts and professional studies.

City type: Bluff St. at Administration Bldg. Dedicated Oct. 5, 1978.

19 STEPHEN C. FOSTER MEMORIAL

Tribute to Pittsburgh's beloved writer of songs and ballads, including "Oh Suzanna," "Old Folks at Home" and "My Old Kentucky Home." Born in 1826 and died in 1864.

City type: Forbes Ave. just E of Bigelow Blvd., Oakland. Erected Dec. 1958. (See also Stephen C. Foster below.)

19 V.F.W.

The Veterans of Foreign Wars organized September 14-17, 1914, at the former Schenley Hotel near here. Veterans who had served in Cuba, Puerto Rico, the Philippines and China were among its founders.

City type: 5th Ave. & Bigelow Blvd., Oakland. Dedicated Sept. 16, 1967.

19 UNIVERSITY OF PITTSBURGH

First institution of higher education west of the Alleghenies and north of the Ohio River. Founded in 1787 as the Pittsburgh Academy, it became the Western University of Pennsylvania in 1819. Present name was adopted in 1908.

City type: SE corner, 5th Ave. & Bigelow Blvd., Oakland. Dedicated Nov. 2, 1979.

19 STATION WQED

Television station, located here, opened April 1954, as first community-sponsored educational television station in America. In 1955 it was the first to telecast classes to elementary schools.

City type: 4802 5th Ave., Oakland. Dedicated Aug. 20, 1964.

19 SHADYSIDE IRON FURNACE

Built on lowlands here in 1792. Birth of the iron industry in the Pittsburgh region. It made stove and grate castings. Closed about a year later due to lack of ore and wood.

City type: SE corner, Bayard St. & Amberson Ave., Oakland. Erected Dec. 1958.

20 ALLEGHENY ARSENAL

Designed by Benjamin H. Latrobe and constructed in 1814. The Arsenal was used as a military garrison, in the manufacture and storing of supplies during the Civil War, Indian Wars, and Spanish-American War.

City type: opposite 257 40th St., Lawrenceville. Erected [1967].

20 SHANNOPIN TOWN

Name of a Delaware Indian village that covered this site from about 1731 to the French occupation, 1754. It was the Allegheny River terminus of the Raystown Indian and Traders Path from Carlisle to the west.

City type: 40th St. at bridge, Lawrenceville. Erected Dec. 1958.

20 STEPHEN C. FOSTER

America's beloved composer of folk songs and ballads was born nearby on July 4, 1826, and lived in the Pittsburgh area most of his life. After achieving fame in writing songs for Christy's Minstrels, he gradually declined in health and died in New York City on January 13, 1864.

3600 Penn Ave., Lawrenceville. Dedicated July 4, 1976. (See also Stephen C. Foster Memorial above.)

21 DAISY E. LAMPKIN

Outstanding as an NAACP organizer, Mrs. Lampkin was its National Field Secretary, 1935-47. President, Lucy Stone Civic League, 1915-65. A charter member, National Council of Negro Women, and Vice President, The Pittsburgh Courier. She lived here until her death in 1965.

City type: 2519 Webster Ave. Dedicated Aug. 9, 1983.

21 PENNSYLVANIA CANAL

The loading basin and western terminus of the State-built railroad, canal, and Portage over the Alleghenies uniting eastern and western Pennsylvania was here. Built in 1826-34. In 1857 sold to the Pennsylvania R. R.

City type: Liberty Ave. & Grant St. at railroad station. Erected Dec. 1958.

21 WESTINGHOUSE ELECTRIC CORPORATION

Pioneer in development of alternating current, permitting transmission of electricity over long distances. Founded 1886 by George Westinghouse, it first made AC motors, generators, transformers in a plant one block south, at Garrison Place.

City type: Fort Duquesne Blvd. near Garrison Pl. & Convention Center. Erection pending.

21 FORT LAFAYETTE

Stood on this site. It was completed in 1792. Built to protect Pittsburgh against Indian attacks and to serve as a chief supply base for Gen. Wayne's army, 1792-94. Reactivated during the War of 1812. Site sold in 1813.

City type: 9th St. just N of Penn Ave. Erected Dec. 1958.

22 AVERY COLLEGE

To the south, at Nash and Avery Streets, stood Avery College. Founded in 1849 by Charles Avery (1784-1858), Methodist lay preacher, philanthropist, abolitionist, to provide a classical education for Negroes.

City type: 619 E. Ohio St., North Side. Erected Jan. 1968.

22 JAMES HAY REED

Born Sept. 10, 1853, in a house standing in this square. Distinguished as a lawyer. Counselor to a majority of the leaders of business who built the corporations which made Pittsburgh leader in American industry.

City type: Buhl Planetarium (Federal St. between W. Ohio & N. Diamond Sts.), North Side. Erected Dec. 1958.

22 FERRIS WHEEL INVENTOR

Civil Engineer, George Washington Gale Ferris (1859-1896), lived at 204 Arch Street. He designed and constructed the world's first Ferris wheel for the Columbian Exposition in 1892.

City type: West Commons (Arch St. near S. Diamond St.), North Side. Erected [1967].

22 SITE OF THE WESTERN PENITENTIARY

Erected 1826 — Razed 1880. Where from August 5, 1863 to March 18, 1864 were incarcerated 118 officers of General John H. Morgan's Cavalry C.S.A. — the only Confederate prisoners of war held in Pittsburgh — who had surrendered near Lisbon, Ohio, July 26, 1863. Marked by the Pennsylvania Historical Commission and the Pittsburgh Chapter, United Daughters of the Confederacy, 1931.

Plaque: at West Commons (Courtyard of the Peacocks at the Conservatory Aviary), North Side. Actually dedicated June 2, 1934.

23 ALLEGHENY OBSERVATORY

Part of the University of Pittsburgh. Chartered 1860; located here since 1912. At the original site nearby, Professor Samuel P. Langley conducted experiments that would lead to the first sustained, mechanically powered flight in 1896.

City type: Riverview Ave. in Riverview Park (off US 19) near Observatory. Dedicated Nov. 2, 1979.

Leaving Pittsburgh

24 DAVIS ISLAND LOCK AND DAM

Below this bridge was the first lock and dam built (1878-1885) on the Ohio River. This was the world's largest movable dam yet constructed, and included the world's first rolling lock gate and widest lock chamber. Built and operated by the U.S. Army Corps of Engineers; replaced by the nearby Emsworth Locks and Dams in 1922.

PA 65 at E borough line, Avalon. Dedicated July 4, 1987.

25 ETHELBERT NEVIN

Composer of "Narcissus," "The Rosary," and other well-known musical works, was born Nov. 25, 1862, at Vineacre, a property adjoining the far end of this street. Died Feb. 17, 1901, at New Haven, Conn.

PA 65 northbound at Edgeworth. Erected May 7, 1948.

26 SHOUSETOWN BOATYARD

Founder, Peter Shouse, built "Kentuckian," its first steamboat, in 1829. Sold 1837 to E. & N. Porter. By 1866 over 80 steamboats had been launched. The last was the 1727-ton "Great Republic," famed on the Mississippi River for its size and elegance.

City type: PA 51, Honor Roll Park, Glenwillard. Dedicated June 14, 1987.

Armstrong County

B **ARMSTRONG COUNTY**
Formed March 12, 1800 out of Westmoreland, Allegheny and Lycoming counties. Named for Gen. John Armstrong, who had destroyed the Indian village at Kittanning, 1756. Here, county seat was laid out, 1803, and "Daugherty Visible" typewriter invented in 1881.
City type: Courthouse, N end Market St., Kittanning. Dedicated Oct. 15, 1982.

27 **BLANKET HILL**
So named from the blankets left by the Armstrong expedition after destroying Kittanning. Here also was a stopping point of the troops en route to attack the Indians, Sept. 7, 1756.
US 422, 6.5 miles SE of Kittanning. Erected Nov. 28, 1946.

28 **FORT ARMSTRONG**
Located on the nearby river bank. Erected in June 1779; abandoned in the fall of that year. An outpost of the Brodhead expedition against the Senecas. Named in honor of General John Armstrong.
PA 66, 1.8 miles S of Kittanning. Erected Nov. 28, 1946.

29 **KITTANNING**
The most notable Delaware Indian village west of the Alleghenies was situated here from about 1730 until destroyed by Armstrong's expedition in 1756. Its name means "great river," applying to the Ohio-Allegheny.
S. Water St. & W end Market St. Bridge, Kittanning. Erected Nov. 28, 1946.

29 **KITTANNING OR ATTIQUÉ INDIAN TOWN**
Was located on this river flat. The chief settlement as early as 1727 of the Lenni-Lenape or Delaware Indians in their early westward movement from the Susquehanna River. Became the most important Indian center west of the Allegheny Mountains. Destroyed September 8, 1756 by Colonel John Armstrong and his 300 frontier troops from the Cumberland Valley. Marked by the Pennsylvania Historical Commission and the Armstrong County Historical Society, 1926.
Plaque: at park on E bank Allegheny River, adjacent to bridge N. Water & Market Sts., Kittanning. Dedicated Sept. 8, 1926.

29 **[GENERAL JOHN ARMSTRONG]**
In memory of General John Armstrong, a Scottish Covenanter and a soldier of the American Revolution. Lieutenant Colonel, 2d Battalion Provincial troops 1756. Brigadier General Continental Army, 1776. Major General Pennsylvania Militia, 1778 to close of war. In command of Pennsylvania Militia at Brandywine and Germantown. Died 1795. Erected by the Pennsylvania Historical Commission and the Pennsylvania Daughters of the American Revolution to honor the memory of the hero of Kittanning for whom this county is named, 1917.
Plaque: entrance to Armstrong County Courthouse, N end Market St., Kittanning. Dedicated May 11, 1917.

30 **ST. PATRICK'S CHURCH**
A restored log church a few miles from here is a fine example of a pioneer place of worship. It memorializes the first Roman Catholic congregation in this region.
PA 268, 6 miles NW of Cowansville. Erected July 16, 1948.

31 **BRADY'S BEND WORKS**
Located near this point, 1839-73. Organized as the Great Western and later known as the Brady's Bend Iron Company. One of that era's largest iron works, and first to make iron rails west of the Alleghenies.
PA 68 Bradys Bend, at Allegheny River bridge. Erected Nov. 28, 1946.

Beaver County

C **BEAVER COUNTY**
Formed March 12, 1800 from Washington and Allegheny counties. The county seat, Beaver, was laid out 1792-93. County's waterways have spurred its industrial growth. At Shippingport was the world's first full-scale atomic power station devoted to civilian needs.
City type: County Courthouse, at park on 3rd St., Beaver. Dedicated July 5, 1982.

32 **OLD ECONOMY**
Third and last home, 1825-1905, of the Harmony Society, religious community founded by George Rapp in 1805. Administered by the Pennsylvania Historical and Museum Commission.
PA 65 in Ambridge, across from site. Erected [1948].

32 **OLD ECONOMY MEMORIAL**
Maintained by the Pennsylvania Historical and Museum Commission as a State memorial to the HARMONY SOCIETY, Organized February 15, 1805, Dissolved December 15, 1905. These buildings, erected 1824-1831, comprise a portion of the third settlement by the society. 1st Settlement — Harmony, Butler Co., Pa., 1804-15; 2nd Settlement — New Harmony, Posey Co., Ind., 1814-25; 3rd Settlement — Economy, Beaver Co., Pa., 1824-1905.
Old Economy, 13th & Church Sts., Ambridge. Erected 1947.

32 **HARMONY SOCIETY CEMETERY 1823-1951**
On this site are buried 594 members and workers of the Harmony Society, the people of Old Economy.
City type: Church St., center of cemetery, Ambridge. Erected Dec. 2, 1963.

32 **HARMONY SOCIETY CHURCH**
Constructed, 1828-1831, with bricks made by the Society members, this is the second building erected for worship. It is believed designed by Frederick Rapp. The spiritual life of the Society centered here.
City type: Church St. near Creese St., Ambridge. Erected Sept. 11, 1967.

33 **LOGSTOWN**
One of the large Indian towns on the upper Ohio was located nearby in 1727-58. Important conferences were held here between the British, French, and Indians in the struggle for the Ohio country.
Duss Ave. (old PA 65) at Anthony Wayne Dr. N of Ambridge. Erected Oct. 31, 1946.

33 **[LOGSTOWN]**
A short distance southeast of this spot, along the banks of the river, was situated the village of Logstown, one of the largest Indian settlements on the upper Ohio. It was the scene of many important conferences between the French, the British and the Indians during the period from 1748 to 1758. The first official council between the British and the Indians west of the mountains was held at this place by Conrad Weiser, on behalf of the Province of Pennsylvania, in 1748. George Washington met the Indian chiefs at this place in 1753, when on his mission to the French forts. After the capture of Fort Duquesne by the British in 1758, the site was deserted by the Indians, who had moved westward to the Beaver and Muskingum Rivers. Erected by the Pennsylvania Historical Commission and the Historical Society of Western Pennsylvania, 1918.
Plaque: Duss Ave. at Anthony Wayne Dr. N of Ambridge. Unveiled June 22, 1918.

33 **LEGIONVILLE**
Gen. Anthony Wayne's army camped here Nov. 1792 to April 1793, preparing for the campaign which led to the Battle of Fallen Timbers with the Northwest Indians.
Duss Ave. at Anthony Wayne Dr. N of Ambridge. Erected Sept. 25, 1946.

33 **[GENERAL WAYNE'S CAMP]**
On the plateau, southwest of this spot, was situated the camp of the army of General Anthony Wayne. This army, known as the Legion of the United States, encamped at this place when on the expedition against the Indians west of the Ohio from November 1792 until April 1793. The expedition resulted in the Treaty of Greenville, which was signed in the summer of 1795. Erected by the Pennsylvania Historical Commission and the Historical Society of Western Pennsylvania, 1918.
Plaque: Duss Ave. at Anthony Wayne Dr. N of Ambridge. Unveiled June 22, 1918.

(34) KING BEAVER'S TOWN

Present Beaver perpetuates the name of a Delaware chief and of his village near here. Its location along the Ohio-Beaver River trails gave it importance in the fur trade.

PA 68 (3rd St.) at Wilson Ave., Beaver. Erected Sept. 25, 1946.

(34) FORT McINTOSH

The first U.S. military post north of the Ohio. Located on River Road in the area between Bank, Insurance, and Market Streets. Built in 1778 and scene of Treaty of Fort McIntosh in 1785; also a survey base. Abandoned 1791.

PA 68 (3rd St.) at Insurance St., Beaver. Erected Oct. 31, 1946.

(34) MATTHEW S. QUAY

Home of the noted state and national political leader is near here. He rose between 1856-87 from local and state offices to U.S. Senator. A Republican Party leader from 1887 until his death in 1904.

PA 68 (3rd St.) at Insurance St., Beaver. Erected July 22, 1947.

(35) "WHITE COTTAGE"

Home of Grace Greenwood (Sara J. Clarke Lippincott, 1823-1904), pioneer woman correspondent, poetess and authoress. While living here during the mid-19th Century, she wrote many of her popular juvenile stories.

City type: 1221 3rd Ave., New Brighton. Dedicated May 27, 1969.

Butler County

(D) BUTLER COUNTY

Formed March 12, 1800 from Allegheny County. Named for Gen. Richard Butler, Revolutionary officer. A young George Washington had crossed this area, 1753. County seat was established at Butler in 1803, and the county was home of the Harmony Society, 1804-15.

City type: County Courthouse, Main St. (PA 8), Butler. Dedicated June 11, 1982.

(36) HARMONY

First home of Harmony Society, founded 1804, by George Rapp and German followers. In 1814 moved to New Harmony, Indiana, and settled at Economy in present Ambridge, Beaver County, in 1825.

PA 68 in Harmony. Erected Oct. 3, 1947.

(36) HARMONIST CEMETERY

Burial place of Harmonist Society, 1805-1815. Graves were not marked. The stone wall was built in 1869, after the Harmonists had returned from Indiana and settled at "Old Economy," in Beaver County.

PA 68 in Harmony. Erected Oct. 3, 1947.

(37) HARMONY MENNONITES

Church organized 1816 by Abraham Ziegler, purchaser of the Harmonist property. The Rev. John Boyer was the first pastor. Present stone church built 1825.

US 19 N of Zelienople. Erected Oct. 3, 1947.

(38) ZELIENOPLE

Founded by Baron Dettmar Basse in 1802. Named for his daughter Zelie. On the hill overlooking the town, he built Bassenheim, a palatial wooden "castle," which burned in 1842.

US 19 in Zelienople. Erected Oct. 3, 1947.

39 GEORGE WASHINGTON

Returning to Virginia from his historic visit at Fort Le Boeuf, Washington used the adjacent Venango Indian Trail. In this locality, on Dec. 27, 1753, he narrowly escaped death, being shot at by an Indian less than fifteen paces from him.

PA 68, 1.8 miles NE of Evans City. Erected Dec. 15, 1970.

40 OLD STONE HOUSE

A haven for lumbermen, drovers and travelers, this important landmark and once famous hostelry was built in 1822 at the crossroads of the old Venango Trail and Butler to Mercer Pike by John K. Brown of Oliver. The Marquis de Lafayette may have stopped here on June 1, 1825.

PA 8 at junction PA 173, Stone House. Erected [1968].

Harmonist Cemetery, with turnstile entrance, Harmony

40 OLD STONE HOUSE

Pioneer wayside inn, built in 1822 and reconstructed in 1963. Administered by the Pennsylvania Historical and Museum Commission.

At site, PA 8 at junction PA 173, Stone House. Erected [1968].

41 [GENERAL RICHARD BUTLER]

In memory of General Richard Butler, born in Ireland, one of five brothers soldiers distinguished for bravery and devoted service, Captain 2d Pennsylvania Battalion, 1776, Colonel 9th Pennsylvania Regiment, 1777, Major General United States Levies, 1791, killed in action against the Indians on the Miami, 1791, and in whose honor Butler County was named. Placed by the Pennsylvania Historical Commission and the Pennsylvania Daughters of the American Revolution, 1917. ''When I want a thing well done I order a Butler to do it.'' Lafayette.

Plaque: wall County Courthouse, Main St. (PA 8), Butler. Dedicated May 30, 1917.

42 WILLIAM A. SMITH

Known as ''Uncle Billy'' Smith. In 1859, he drilled the world's first successful oil well with tools that he made in his blacksmith shop near Tarentum. The well, $69^{1}/_{2}$ ft. deep, was drilled near Titusville for Col. Edwin Drake. ''Uncle Billy'' died in 1890. He lies buried about 120 ft. southeast of here.

PA 356, 9 miles SE of Butler. Erected Jan. 1, 1955.

43 THE ROEBLINGS

John A. Roebling, inventor of steel wire rope and designer of the Brooklyn Bridge, began business at Saxonburg, founded by him in 1832. His son, Washington A. Roebling, who built the Brooklyn Bridge, was born here in 1837.

SR 2010 (former LR 387), Saxonburg. Erected Oct. 6, 1947.

Indiana County

E ## INDIANA COUNTY
Formed March 30, 1803 from Westmoreland and Lycoming counties, and once densely forested. Its name memorializes the first inhabitants. County seat, Indiana, was laid out 1805 on land given by George Clymer, signer of the Declaration of Independence.
City type: New Courthouse Sq., 8th & Philadelphia Sts., Indiana. Dedicated Sept. 10, 1982.

44 ## PURCHASE OF 1768
The northern corner of the Indian land purchase based on the Fort Stanwix Treaty was a huge cherry tree at Canoe Place, now Cherry Tree village. This point is now the junction of the Counties of Cambria, Clearfield, and Indiana.
US 219 at Cherry Tree. Erected July 2, 1948.

45 ## JOHN B. McCORMICK
Designed the first of the modern mixed-flow type of water turbine, thus making an important contribution to American industry. Began his experiments in 1868 on the water wheel of a sawmill at nearby Armagh. He died near Smicksburg in 1924.
US 22 W of Armagh. Erected Sept. 15, 1951.

46 ## SALTSBURG
First salt well in the vicinity was drilled, 1813-14. By the 1830's this area had become a leading U.S. salt producer. Important to its shipment was the Pennsylvania Canal's Western Division. The canal crossed here, 1829-1864, and was the lifeline of this small town.
City type: PA 286 (Washington St.), Saltsburg. Dedicated Feb. 4, 1984.

47 ## MOORHEAD'S FORT
About 1781, Fergus Moorhead, pioneer settler, built a fort near the buildings about 200 yards south, to protect his family and neighbors from hostile Indians. It was the first permanent settlement in this vicinity.
SR 4032 (Philadelphia St., old US 422) .6 mile W of Indiana. Erected July 9, 1951.

48 ## WILLIAM H. SYLVIS
American labor pioneer. Born in Indiana County, 1828. Founder, National Union of Iron Molders, 1859. President, National Labor Union, 1868-1869. Sylvis strove for unity among working men and women regardless of race or nationality. He died, ''labor's champion,'' 1869.
City type: at Keith Hall, Indiana University, Indiana. Dedicated Sept. 1, 1990.

48 ## RURAL ELECTRIFICATION
In 1936 seventy-five percent of Pennsylvania farms had no electric service. During the next five years, with Federal support, 14 consumer-owned cooperatives were formed in this State. Southwest Central Rural Electric Cooperative Corporation, serving users in seven counties, was incorporated on March 4, 1937.
Airport Rd. just off PA 286 at E end Indiana. Erected 1988.

49 ## JOHN S. FISHER
Governor of Pennsylvania, 1927-1931, was born on a farm, 1 mile NE of here, in 1867. He supported an extensive State building program, revised the State fiscal system, and promoted the conservation of natural resources. Died in 1940.
Junction PA 85 & 210 E of Plumville. Erected Sept. 14, 1950.

Jefferson County

F JEFFERSON COUNTY
Formed March 26, 1804 out of Lycoming County and named for President Thomas Jefferson. Until 1806 attached to Westmoreland County, then to Indiana County until 1830. Noted for its coal and lumber industries. Brookville, county seat, was incorporated 1834.
City type: County Courthouse, Main St., Brookville. Dedicated May 25, 1982.

50 GREAT SHAMOKIN PATH
An Indian trail followed the ridge of hills north of the present highway. It was used by Delaware and Shawnee war parties striking east against distant settlements. Marie le Roy and other captives were taken this way to Kittanning.
US 119, 4 miles NE of Punxsutawney. Erected Oct. 16, 1950.

51 OLEAN ROAD
This early road from Olean to Kittanning followed the Catawba Path, formerly used by Five Nations war parties attacking the Catawbas of South Carolina. Near here it crossed the Indian path from Venango (Franklin) to Chinklacamoose (Clearfield).
US 322 in Corsica. Erected Oct. 16, 1950.

52 COOKSBURG
Named for John Cook who came to this section in 1826 and started lumber industry along Tom's Run. Here is Cook Forest State Park. In this park, there is one of the finest stands of large white pine-hemlock in the State.
PA 36 near Clarion River bridge. Erected Sept. 17, 1954.

Lawrence County

G LAWRENCE COUNTY
Formed March 20, 1849 from Beaver and Mercer counties. Its name honors naval hero Capt. James Lawrence. County seat, New Castle, was laid out in 1802. Between 1890 and 1920 it was one of America's fastest growing cities and center of the tin-plate industry.
City type: Clavelli History Center (Lawrence County Historical Society), 408 N. Jefferson St., New Castle. Dedicated Oct. 2, 1982.

53 FRIEDENSSTADT
Founded 1770 by Christian Delaware Indians brought from upper Allegheny by the Rev. David Zeisberger. Settling on the eastern river-bank on May 3, they moved to the west side about three months later.
PA 18 (near junction PA 168) N of Moravia. Erected Mar. 12, 1948.

53 FRIEDENSSTADT
Abandoned April 13, 1773, when its inhabitants, with the Rev. John Heckewelder, moved to new towns on the Muskingum in present Ohio. There some of them were massacred, March 8, 1782, by Pennsylvania militia.
PA 18 N of Moravia. Erected Mar. 12, 1948.

53 [FRIEDENSSTADT]
This stone marks the site of the former Moravian Indian village of Languntoutenunk or Friedensstadt, or City of Peace, settled by the Moravian Indians in the spring of 1770. The majority of the members of this mission had formerly belonged to the mission at Wyalusing, before removing to Lawunakhannek on the Allegheny River, from which place they removed to this site. In the spring of 1773 the inhabitants of this village moved to Gnadenhuetten and Schoenbrunn in the Tuscarawas Valley, where other Moravian missions were organized. Erected by the Pennsylvania Historical Commission, the Moravian Historical Society, and the Lawrence Chapter, Daughters of the American Revolution, 1921.
Plaque: PA 18 (W side) N of Moravia. Dedicated June 14, 1922.

54 KUSKUSKIES TOWNS

Important group of Indian towns on and near site of present New Castle. First inhabited by Senecas; but after 1756 settled chiefly by Delawares from eastern Pennsylvania. Abandoned during Revolutionary War.

Junction PA 18 & 108 S of New Castle. Erected Mar. 19, 1948.

54 C. FREDERICK POST

Sent by Provincial officials to draw Indian friendship away from the French, the Moravian missionary held councils at Kuskuskies Towns, August to November, 1758. His work, and the threat of Gen. Forbes' army, forced the French to leave present-day Pittsburgh on November 24, 1758.

PA 18 & 108 S of New Castle. Erected Aug. 1, 1968 (revised 1948 marker).

55 "SQUAW CAMPAIGN"

500 unruly militia, under command of Gen. Edward Hand, left Pittsburgh to attack British at present Cleveland, February 1778. At an Indian town in the river-fork below here, they killed a man and an old woman; then returned home.

SR 3007 (Elmwood St., former LR 37091) just S of New Castle. Erected Mar. 19, 1948.

56 HARBOR CREEK

Northern terminus, Beaver Division of Pennsylvania Canal system, completed to this point, 1834. Important shipping point before completing "Cross-Cut Canal" to Ohio, 1838, and Erie Extension to Greenville, 1840.

US 422 just NW of New Castle. Erected Mar. 19, 1948.

57 KUSKUSKIES TOWNS

Of this group of towns, the last one occupied by the Indians stood near here in 1785, when Gen. Wm. Irvine toured the Donation Lands just before their division into tracts given to Revolutionary soldiers.

Junction US 224 & PA 551 at Edinburg. Erected Mar. 19, 1948.

57 IRA D. SANKEY

Famous singing evangelist, fellow-worker with Dwight L. Moody in Europe and America, was born Aug. 26, 1840, at Edinburg, in a house since removed. He died in Brooklyn, New York, on Aug. 13, 1908.

Junction US 224 & PA 551 at Edinburg. Erected Mar. 19, 1948.

57 "CROSS-CUT CANAL"

The Pennsylvania and Ohio Canal, in use 1838-1872. Chartered by both states, 1827. Joined Beaver Canal just below New Castle, linking Pittsburgh with Youngstown and Cleveland. Followed Mahoning River on line of present railroad.

US 224 just N of Edinburg at bridge. Erected Mar. 19, 1948.

58 WESTMINSTER COLLEGE

Founded by the Associate, now United Presbyterian Church. Chartered 1852. One of the first two colleges in Pennsylvania to grant degrees to women, and the first to grant them the A.B. degree, in 1857. Its home is New Wilmington.

Junction PA 18 & 208 W of New Wilmington. Erected Jan. 25, 1949. (Now Presbyterian Church USA.)

59 NESHANNOCK POTATO

The once widely-known and choice variety originated just west of here, on a farm occupied by John Gilkey, 1798-1826. A brother, James, was fellow-worker. Their potato was also called Mercer or Gilkey.

US 19 at SR 1004 (Shaw Rd.) just S of Mercer County line. Erected Mar. 19, 1948.

Westmoreland County

H WESTMORELAND COUNTY

Formed on Feb. 26, 1773 out of Bedford County, it once embraced southwestern Pennsylvania. First seat of English justice west of Alleghenies. Site of 1775 "Hanna's Town Resolves." Greensburg, county seat, was incorporated 1799.

City type: NE corner, Courthouse Sq., Main & Otterman Sts., Greensburg. Dedicated Nov. 25, 1981.

60 WEST NEWTON

Led by Gen. Rufus Putnam, the first settlers to establish American government in the Northwest Territory, built boats here to continue their journey from New England and to found Marietta, Ohio. They embarked on their river trip Apr. 2, 1788.

PA 136 at Youghiogheny River bridge, West Newton. Erected Dec. 10, 1946.

61 HENRY CLAY FRICK

The steel and coke magnate was born about one mile from here on Dec. 19, 1849. Birthplace and Historical House, the Overholt home, are now preserved as a historical museum.

PA 819 at SR 3089 (old US 119), N end Scottdale. Erected Dec. 10, 1946.

Henry Clay Frick birthplace, Scottdale

Westmoreland-Fayette Historical Society

62 JOHN W. GEARY

Governor of Pennsylvania, 1867-73; born, 1819, in Mt. Pleasant. His active career included other important offices: First Mayor of San Francisco, 1850; Governor of Kansas Territory, 1856; Major General, Civil War. Died, 1873.

PA 31 near SR 2003 (former LR 64131) E of Mount Pleasant. Erected Aug. 23, 1951.

63 LOYALHANNING

Indian village settled by the Delawares soon after their departure from the Susquehanna area in 1727, was located here. The name refers to "middle stream."

US 30 just SE of Ligonier. Erected Dec. 10, 1946.

64 FORT LIGONIER

Built here 1758 as a base of Forbes expedition. Under Col. James Burd withstood a French and Indian attack, Oct. 12, 1758. Only small fort in West not taken in Pontiac's War, 1763, it made possible Bouquet's rescue of Fort Pitt.

Main & Market Sts., Ligonier. Erected Dec. 10, 1946.

64 FORBES ROAD, 1758. FORT BEDFORD TO FORT DUQUESNE

Fort Ligonier, built by order of General Forbes, was located 200 yards west of this marker. The road leads southwestward to 12-mile encampment. Eminent service was rendered here by Colonel Henry Bouquet and Colonel John Armstrong, and in engagements with the French and Indians near this place Colonel George Washington, Colonel James Burd and Lieutenant Colonel Hugh Mercer distinguished themselves. 50 miles from Fort Bedford. Erected by the Pennsylvania Historical Commission, 1930.

Plaque: 301 E. Main St. (SE corner, Main & Market Sts.), Ligonier. Erected 1930.

65 ARTHUR ST. CLAIR

At the head of the hollow to the south was the last home of Gen. St. Clair. He served in the Revolutionary army, in the Continental Congress, and was first Governor of the Northwest Territory. His grave is at Greensburg.

US 30, 6.5 miles NW of Ligonier. Erected Dec. 10, 1946.

65 # JOHNSTON HOUSE
Wm. F. Johnston, Governor of Pennsylvania, 1848-52, was born near here, 1808. This house, built by his father, 1815, was his boyhood home. Known as Kingston House, it has been cited as a fine example of colonial style.
US 30, 7 miles NW of Ligonier. Erected Dec. 10, 1946.

66 # TWELVE MILE CAMP
George Washington in 1758 set up a camp a mile north of this point while building Forbes Road. In 1774 Fort Shippen was built at the same site.
Junction US 30 & PA 981, 7.1 miles E of Greensburg. Erected Dec. 10, 1946.

67 # ST. VINCENT
St. Vincent Archabbey was the first of Benedictine Institutions in the U.S. Founded 1846, its College was incorporated in 1870. From here ten abbeys and colleges in eight states were founded.
US 30, 6.6 miles E of Greensburg at College. Erected Dec. 10, 1946.

67 # ST. XAVIER'S
This Convent and Academy is the oldest institution of the Sisters of Mercy who came from Ireland in 1843. From here many Sisters have gone to various parts of the United States as nurses and teachers.
US 30, 6 miles E of Greensburg at Academy. Erected Dec. 10, 1946.

68 # HANNASTOWN
Site of former county seat of Westmoreland County is just west of here. First county seat west of mountains, 1773. Citizens adopted a Declaration in support of the Revolution, 1775. Burned by the Indians in 1782.
US 119 at SR 1032 (Forbes Rd.) N of Greensburg. Erected Dec. 6, 1946 on PA 819; relocated 1980 with "east" changed to "west" in first sentence.

69 # TOLL HOUSE
Site of toll house of the Stoyestown-Greensburg Turnpike Road Co. The turnpike, a section of the Philadelphia-Pittsburgh road, was completed in 1819 at a cost of about $6,000 a mile. State took over the turnpike in 1911.
City type: E. Pittsburgh St. E of Stark St., Greensburg. Erected May 28, 1955.

69 # TOLL HOUSE
Just northeast of here stood 1 of 5 gates of Greensburg-Pittsburgh Turnpike Road Co. The turnpike, a section of the Pittsburgh-Philadelphia road, was completed in 1817. Over it, passed goods in trade between east and west.
City type: Mount Odin Park, Greensburg. Erected May 28, 1955.

70 # FORT ALLEN
A little south, site of post built 1774 by Pennsylvania German pioneers of Brush Creek and Harrold's settlements. A refuge from the Indians in Dunmore's War and American Revolution.
PA 136 at SR 3097 (former LR 64113) SW of Greensburg. Erected Dec. 10, 1946.

70 # FORT ALLEN
Built and commanded by Colonel Christopher Truby, officer of the War of the Revolution, was located 150 yards to the south of this marker. A frontier fort of the Dunmore War of 1774, the Indian War and the War of the Revolution. It was also known as Truby's Block-house. From here a petition to Gov. John Penn sent by eighty inhabitants of Westmoreland County headed by Wendel Oury asked for aid in the threatened Indian uprising of 1774. Marked by the Pennsylvania Historical Commission and Citizens of Westmoreland County, 1929.
Plaque: at church, SR 3097 (former 64113) & St. Johns Rd., .5 mile S of PA 136 SW of Greensburg. Dedicated May 30, 1929.

71 # BUSHY RUN
Four miles to the north, at Bushy Run, an army under Col. Henry Bouquet defeated the Indians Aug. 5-6, 1763. This raised the siege of Fort Pitt and opened the gateway for settlement of the West. It is now a State Park.
US 30 at Lowry Ave., S end Jeannette. Erected Dec. 10, 1946.

72 # BUSHY RUN BATTLEFIELD
British and Americans under Col. Henry Bouquet defeated the Indians here, Aug. 5-6, 1763, during the Pontiac War, and lifted the siege of Ft. Pitt. Administered by the Pennsylvania Historical and Museum Commission.
At site, PA 993, 1 mile E of Harrison City. Erected Sept. 14, 1964.

73 MURRYSVILLE GAS WELL
First gas well in county, and one of the world's most productive. Drilled, 1878. Caught fire in 1881, burning for years with tremendous roar and brilliance. Later was controlled and piped to Pittsburgh. Site lies 500 yards S. E. near railroad.

US 22 at SR 4033 (Mill St.), Murrysville. Erected July 13, 1960 (revised 1946 marker).

73 FORBES ROAD, 1758. FORT BEDFORD TO FORT DUQUESNE
Turtle Creek Defile. Two and one-half miles to the eastward was located the Washington camp. The Forbes Road leads northwestward to the Bouquet encampment. 89 miles from Fort Bedford. Erected by the Pennsylvania Historical Commission, 1930.

Plaque: post office, Murrysville. Erected 1930 on old US 22, Murrysville; relocated & rededicated Nov. 11, 1967.

74 FORBES ROAD
On the hill one mile south was located the Washington Camp. This base for Forbes Road was built Nov. 1758 by Col. George Washington, ''Commanding the Troops to ye Westward,'' on the order of Colonel Henry Bouquet.

US 22, 1.2 miles E of Murrysville. 2 markers, erected July 13, 1960 (revision of 1946 & 1949 markers).

75 BUSHY RUN
Three miles to the south, at Bushy Run, an army under Col. Henry Bouquet defeated the Indians Aug. 5-6, 1763. This raised the siege of Fort Pitt and opened the gateway for settlement of the West. It is now a State Park.

PA 66 at Pittsburgh St. (old US 22), Delmont. Erected Dec. 10, 1946.

76 VANDERGRIFT
Hailed by historian Ida Tarbell as America's ''most important industrial town,'' with homes owned by the workers. Founded 1895 by Geo. G. McMurtry, president, Apollo Iron & Steel Co. Named for Capt. Jacob J. Vandergrift and designed by the firm of Frederick Law Olmstead.

City type: E lawn, Municipal Bldg., Washington Ave., Vandergrift. Dedicated May 17, 1990.

77 FANNIE SELLINS (1872-1919)
An organizer for the United Mine Workers, Fannie Sellins was brutally gunned down in Brackenridge on the eve of a nationwide steel strike, on August 26, 1919. Her devotion to the workers' cause made her an important symbolic figure. Both she and Joseph Starzelski, a miner who also was killed that same day, lie buried here in Union Cemetery where a monument to the pair was erected.

Front of Union Cemetery, PA 366, Arnold. Dedicated Sept. 3, 1989.

REGION VIII

Earth's Ample Storehouse

The history of the European occupation of the northwesternmost counties — *Clarion, Crawford, Erie, Mercer,* and *Venango* — begins with France's seizure of western Pennsylvania in 1753 and the erection there of Forts Presque Isle, LeBoeuf and Machault. George Washington, a major of the Virginia militia, was sent to demand France's withdrawal. After refusing his demand, the French departed only when forced to do so in 1758. The British then replaced France's little wooden strongholds with forts of their own.

The purchase by Pennsylvania in 1768 and 1785 of two huge tracts of Native American lands, and more to the point, the withdrawal of the British and the end of the War of Revolution called upon the ingenuity and resourcefulness of the Commonwealth to distribute the millions of acres now available for settlement through public and private sales.

Added to this expanse was a large tract called the Erie Triangle, facing Lake Erie and purchased from the United States government in 1792. For Pennsylvania to gain access to this, however, required military action in 1794 by General Anthony Wayne to extinguish Indian resistance. Many of the land-hungry who seized this opportunity to begin a more productive life were rooted directly or indirectly in New England, and its stamp remains in the region.

Lake Erie was also an international frontier, as the customhouse at Erie attests, and it was not until the triumph of U.S. warships — partly Erie built — over a British naval flotilla on the lake in 1813 that the fear of British designs on the frontier was removed. For many years afterward the U.S.S. *Wolverine* was the only warship assigned to the Great Lakes.

Meanwhile, transportation took several forms, including that of the "Underground Railroad," whereby slaves from the southern states were assisted in escaping to freedom, often to Canada, a country beyond the reach of slave-hunters. The most efficient transportation before the railroad, however, was the Erie Extension Canal, which penetrated the region and connected the city of Erie with New Castle.

The major early nineteenth-century economic endeavor of the five-county district, other than iron, coal and timber, was farming, particularly in Clarion County. However, in 1859 near Titusville, Edwin L. Drake, borrowing the techniques of well-drilling, found a way to extract petroleum from abundant reservoirs. A revolution in industry (and ultimately in transportation) was begun, founded on local petroleum. (Although it is no longer a major producer, the region is still a small but significant source of oil.) Meanwhile, the port city of Erie became the region's largest urban center, attracting people to its industry and commerce from rural America and from Europe.

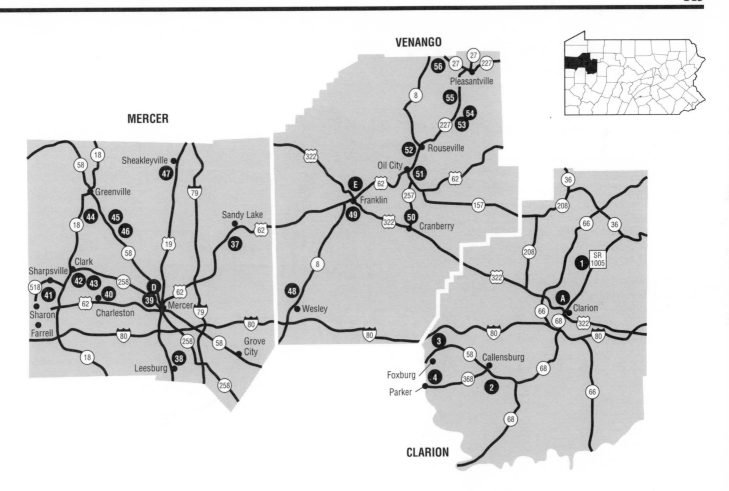

MERCER

VENANGO

CLARION

Sheakleyville
Greenville
Sandy Lake
Clark
Sharpsville
Charleston
Mercer
Sharon
Farrell
Grove City
Leesburg

Pleasantville
Rouseville
Oil City
Franklin
Cranberry
Wesley

Clarion
Callensburg
Foxburg
Parker

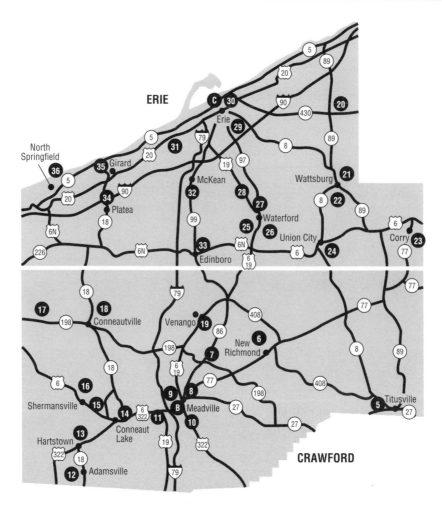

ERIE

North
Springfield

Girard

McKean

Wattsburg

Erie

Platea

Waterford

Union City

Corry

Edinboro

Conneautville

Venango

New
Richmond

Shermansville

Meadville

Titusville

Hartstown

Conneaut
Lake

Adamsville

CRAWFORD

Clarion County

Ⓐ CLARION COUNTY
Formed March 11, 1839 out of Armstrong and Venango counties. Named for the Clarion River. Early center of iron industry. Noted also for its coal resources and lumbering. The county seat, Clarion, was incorporated as a borough on April 6, 1841.
City type: Courthouse, Main St. at 5th Ave., Clarion. Dedicated Apr. 26, 1982.

① HELEN FURNACE
Just west of this point can be seen the well-preserved interior of cold blast furnace built in 1845. It was one of numerous iron furnaces operated in Clarion County from about 1829-1867. The County, then, was often referred to as "The Iron County."
SR 1005 (old PA 966) 7 miles NE of Clarion. Erected Mar. 31, 1950.

② BUCHANAN FURNACE
A short distance NW of here is the well-preserved cold blast furnace, named for James Buchanan. It was built in 1844; abandoned, 1858, due to lack of timber. At the time of its operation, the iron industry was very prosperous in Clarion County.
PA 58 E of Callensburg. Erected Apr. 3, 1950.

③ FOXBURG GOLF COURSE
Oldest golf course in continuous use in the U.S. In 1867, land was made available to the newly formed Foxburg Golf Club by Joseph M. Fox, its first president. Course was enlarged from five to nine holes in 1888. The Foxburg Country Club purchased, in 1924, the original land which it had been leasing.
PA 58 NE of Foxburg. Erected June 1955.

④ RURAL ELECTRIFICATION
In 1936 seventy-five percent of Pennsylvania farms had no electric service. During the next five years, with Federal support, 14 consumer-owned cooperatives were formed in this State. Serving users in seven counties of western Pennsylvania, Central Electric Cooperative at Parker was incorporated July 12, 1937.
PA 368, 1 mile E of Parker. Dedicated July 11, 1987.

Crawford County

Ⓑ CRAWFORD COUNTY
Formed March 12, 1800 from Allegheny County. Meadville, in 1788, was the first permanent settlement in northwest Pennsylvania. In 1842 the nation's first direct primary was held here. Cradle of the oil and zipper industries. Named for Col. William Crawford.
City type: County Courthouse, 903 Diamond Park, Meadville. Dedicated May 12, 1982.

Entering Titusville

⑤ EARLY REFINERY
The first refinery in the Oil Creek Region for crude petroleum was built nearby in 1860. The first run of oil was made in 1861. Oil was first refined at Pittsburgh, about 1854, by Samuel Kier.
City type: E. Main St. (PA 27), Titusville. Erected Sept. 29, 1954.

⑤ JOHN A. MATHER
Photographer of oil industry from 1860, lived in this house. His thousands of views form an extraordinary record of an industry that began here. Born, Bury, England, in 1829; died Titusville, 1915.
City type: 407 E. Main St. (PA 27), Titusville. Dedicated Sept. 14, 1964.

⑤ IDA M. TARBELL

Noted oil historian, biographer of Lincoln, journalist, lived in this house about six years. She was graduated from the Titusville High School in 1875.

City type: 324 E. Main St. (PA 27), Titusville. Erected Sept. 30, 1954.

⑤ OIL CREEK

Along this stream the first white explorers found Indians skimming surface oil. From 1859 to 1865, the center of oil production and its refining was along the banks of Oil Creek.

City type: Smock Blvd. (PA 8), Titusville. Erected Sept. 30, 1954.

⑤ ROBERTS TORPEDO

First successful device for increasing the flow of oil by setting off an explosion deep in a well. It was publicly demonstrated in 1865. The nitroglycerin was made .4 mile south of here, along Hammond Run.

City type: Smock Blvd. (PA 8), Titusville. Erected Sept. 29, 1954.

⑤ FIRST OIL EXCHANGE

Organized, 1871, in the American Hotel which stood on this site. After occupying other buildings, oil men returned to this site and in 1881 dedicated an Oil Exchange building.

City type: W. Spring St. (PA 8 eastbound), Titusville. Erected Sept. 29, 1954.

⑤ EDWIN L. DRAKE

The man who first sank an oil well is buried in Woodlawn Cemetery and is commemorated by Niehaus's bronze figure, "The Driller." Drake Well is now a State park, a mile and a half south of Titusville.

PA 8 near Woodlawn Cemetery, Titusville. Erected Nov. 18, 1946.

Leaving Titusville

⑥ JOHN BROWN'S TANNERY

On the side road, a short distance south, are the remains of the tannery and home built by the noted abolitionist of Harper's Ferry fame. Here, he lived and worked from 1825 to 1835, employing as many as 15 men in producing leather.

PA 77 at New Richmond. Erected 1969.

⑦ JOHN BROWN TANNERY

John Brown of Ossawatomie and Harper's Ferry worked here as a tanner, 1825-35. The nearby house was then his home. His first wife and a son are buried near.

Twp. road (former LR 20118) S of PA 77, New Richmond. Erected Nov. 18, 1946.

Edwin L. Drake tomb and memorial, Titusville

Drake Well Museum

8 RURAL ELECTRIFICATION
Here on August 5, 1936, the State's first rural electric pole was placed by the Northwestern Rural Electric Cooperative Association. Incorporated on April 30, 1936, this was Pennsylvania's first such cooperative. By 1941, thirteen more had been formed in this State.
PA 198, Woodcock Creek Lake, E of PA 86. Dedicated Aug. 2, 1986.

Entering Meadville

9 BISHOP JAMES M. THOBURN
Methodist missionary to India, south Asia, and the Philippines, 1859 to 1908. Upon retirement he lived in Meadville until his death in 1922. He is buried in Greendale Cemetery.
PA 77 at E end of Meadville. Erected Nov. 18, 1946.

9 MEADVILLE
Founded in 1788 by David Mead and other settlers from the Wyoming region. In 1800 made county seat. First direct primary in U.S. held here in 1842. Making of hookless fasteners was pioneered here.
On main highways leading into city. Erected Nov. 1946.

9 BALDWIN-REYNOLDS HOUSE
Two blocks west is the home built in 1843 by Justice Henry Baldwin, who was appointed to the U.S. Supreme Court in 1830. As a member of Congress from 1816 to 1822, he was an early advocate of protective tariff. The house is now maintained as a museum by the Crawford County Historical Society.
Baldwin St. & Reynolds Ave., Meadville. Erected 1975 (revised 1947 marker).

9 UNITARIAN CHURCH
A fine example of Greek Revival architecture. It was erected in 1835-36 at a cost of $3500, mostly given by Shippen and Huidekoper families. Planned by the builder of Fort Sumter, General George W. Cullum.
City type: Main & Chestnut Sts., Meadville. Erected June 29, 1967.

9 RICHARD HENDERSON
Born a slave in Maryland in 1801, he escaped as a boy and about 1824 came to Meadville. A barber, he was long active in the Underground Railroad. His Arch Street house, since torn down, is estimated to have harbored some 500 runaway slaves prior to the Civil War.
City type: Liberty & Arch Sts., Meadville. Dedicated June 1, 1980.

Leaving Meadville

10 FRENCH CREEK FEEDER
The canal bed beside the road is part of a channel constructed 1827-1834 to take water from Meadville to Conneaut Lake for the Erie Extension Canal. Two miles below here the Feeder crossed the creek by aqueduct.
US 322 S of Meadville. Erected July 13, 1948.

11 FRENCH CREEK FEEDER
The canal visible beyond the field was built 1827-1834. Repaired in 1841, it carried water from French Creek to Conneaut Lake, reservoir for the Erie Extension Canal, which operated between Erie and New Castle, 1844-71.
US 19 SW of Meadville. Erected July 12, 1948.

12 ERIE EXTENSION CANAL
Canal bed visible at foot of the slope, toward the railroad. Extended from Beaver Division Canal, at New Castle, to Erie; this part of the Shenango Line, north to Conneaut Lake, was completed in 1842, and in use until 1871.
PA 18 S of Adamsville. Erected July 13, 1948.

13 ERIE EXTENSION CANAL
Cut off from the rest of Pymatuning Swamp by a 3-mile bank, this became the 600-acre "Pymatuning Reservoir" of the canal, which lay at its western edge. Begun by the State, 1838; finished by the Erie Canal Co., 1843-44.
US 322 E of Hartstown. Erected Sept. 20, 1948.

14 ERIE EXTENSION CANAL
Begun by the State, 1836, as part of a system of internal improvements. Completed 1843-44 by a private company. In use until 1871. Extended 105 miles from New Castle to Erie; French Creek Feeder joined it with Meadville.
US 6 & 322 E of Conneaut Lake. Erected July 12, 1948.

14 CONNEAUT RESERVOIR
Raised some 10 feet by a 23-mile "feeder" from Meadville, this lake was the vital source of water for the highest part of the canal, 4 miles west. Lake water and traffic flowed north to Erie, and south to the Ohio River.
US 6 & 322 E of Conneaut Lake. Erected Sept. 20, 1948.

15 ERIE EXTENSION CANAL
By this channel Conneaut Lake, raised 9 feet above normal level, fed water to the canal at its highest point, the junction of the Shenango and Conneaut Lines, about 2 miles west from here. The canal was in use 1844-1871.
PA 618 S of Conneaut Lake Park. Erected July 12, 1948.

16 ERIE EXTENSION CANAL
Remains of the canal bed may be seen beside the railroad, below the bridge. Less than 2 miles away this Shenango Line, from New Castle, united with the Conneaut Line, from Erie. The entire canal was in use 1844-1871.
US 6 W of Shermansville. Erected July 13, 1948.

17 OIL-PRODUCING SALT WELL
Drilled here in 1815 by Samuel Magaw and William Clark to reach brine, a frontier source of salt. When it was deepened by Daniel Shryock to 300 feet in 1819, oil was struck. Because of this unwanted byproduct, the well and salt works here were closed, 1821. This early yield of oil from a drilled well occurred 40 years before Edwin L. Drake's 1859 discovery near Titusville.
PA 198, Lawrence Corners, 1 mile E of Ohio line. Dedicated May 17, 1985.

18 ERIE EXTENSION CANAL
Part of the old channel lies near the highway. The Conneaut Line, from Erie to near Conneaut Lake, was begun by the State, 1838, and completed by the Erie Canal Company, 1843-44. Canal in use until 1871.
PA 18 N of Conneautville. Erected July 14, 1948.

19 FRENCH CREEK
The Riviere aux Boeufs of the French, renamed by George Washington in 1753. It had an important part in the French and Indian War and the settlement of northwestern Pennsylvania.
US 6 & 19 S of Venango. Erected Nov. 19, 1946.

Erie County

C ERIE COUNTY
Formed March 12, 1800 from Allegheny County. Named for Lake Erie, which took its own name from the Erie Indians. Erie, the county seat, was laid out 1795; made a city in 1851. Ships of Perry's fleet which won the 1813 Battle of Lake Erie were built here.
City type: County Courthouse, W. 6th St. between Peach & Sassafras, Erie. Dedicated Aug. 28, 1981.

20 COLT'S STATION
Judah Colt, Agent, began the first Pennsylvania Population Co. development here in 1797. He set up the first organized settlement in Erie County, at the head of flatboat navigation on French Creek.
PA 89 at PA 430, Colt Station. Erected Oct. 29, 1951.

21 OLD STATE LINE
The northern boundary of Pennsylvania, before the purchase of the Erie Triangle in 1792, crossed the highway at this point. The State paid $151,640.25 for the Erie tract and its port on the Lakes.
PA 8 at Wattsburg. Erected Nov. 1946.

22 IDA M. TARBELL
Noted writer; biographer of Lincoln, historian of Standard Oil; born Nov. 5, 1857, in her grandfather's log home at Hatch Hollow, about two miles to east. She died Jan. 6, 1944, at Bridgeport, Connecticut.
PA 8 SW of Wattsburg. Erected Sept. 26, 1950.

23 CLIMAX LOCOMOTIVE

Over 1000 geared steam locomotives were built at the Climax plant here from 1888 to 1928. These were widely used on logging railroads in the United States and other countries. By making new areas accessible to large-scale lumbering, geared locomotives were a key to the industry's growth.

PA 77 at S end of Corry. Dedicated May 17, 1987.

24 DRAKE WELL PARK

Near Titusville. The Park and Museum are owned by the State. On the site Col. Edwin Drake struck oil Aug. 27, 1859, marking the birth of the petroleum industry. Historical and museum material center.

PA 8 just S of Union City. Erected Nov. 20, 1946.

25 FRENCH CREEK

The Riviere aux Boeufs of the French, renamed by George Washington in 1753. It had an important part in the French and Indian War and the settlement of northwestern Pennsylvania.

US 19 S of Waterford. Erected Nov. 1946.

Entering Waterford

26 FORT LE BOEUF

Three forts have stood on this site. French fort, built 1753, to guard road into Ohio Valley, abandoned 1759. British fort built in 1760, burned by Indians in 1763. American fort to protect settlers, built in 1794.

US 19 in Waterford. Erected Nov. 1946.

26 FORT LE BOEUF MEMORIAL

The Judson House, built in 1820, stands on the site of the old French fort. This was the scene of Washington's first public mission. Administered by the Pennsylvania Historical and Museum Commission.

Property on US 19, Waterford. Erected Sept. 19, 1951.

26 [FORT LE BOEUF]

This monument marks the site of Fort Le Boeuf. Erected by the French in 1752 [actually 1753]. George Washington, as a Major representing the Governor of Virginia, came here in 1753, bearing a letter to the commander of the fort, warning the French to withdraw their forces from this region claimed by Great Britain. This mission was one of the first links in the chain of events that settled forever the dominance of our land by the Anglo-Saxon. Erected by the Pennsylvania Historical Commission and the People of Waterford and Friends, 1921.

Plaque: US 19 opposite Fort Le Boeuf Museum, Waterford. Dedicated Aug. 30, 1922. (Atop the pedestal of this monument is a large statue of the young Washington, referred to on the next marker.)

26 GEORGE WASHINGTON

In December, 1753, George Washington came here with notice from the Governor of Virginia to the French that they were trespassing on British soil. The statue shows Washington carrying out his first public mission.

US 19 in Waterford. Erected Nov. 1946.

26 LP-GAS INDUSTRY

The liquefied petroleum gas industry originated in this vicinity. The first domestic customer, John W. Garhing, had "bottled gas" for lighting and cooking installed May 17, 1912, at his farm home about five miles southeast of Waterford at Le Boeuf Station.

US 19 at square in Waterford. Dedicated May 17, 1962.

Leaving Waterford

27 PRESQUE ISLE PORTAGE

The old portage, part of the historic Venango Trail from Lake Erie to the Ohio River, crossed today's road here. The Indian trail became a French military road in 1753.

US 19 N of Waterford. Erected Nov. 1946.

28 OLD STATE LINE

Same text as Old State Line above.

US 19 at Strongs Corners. Erected Nov. 1946.

29 OLD FRENCH ROAD
Here today's highway leaves the course of the Presque Isle Portage, part of the historic Venango Trail. The French Road, built in 1753, following an Indian path, turned down into the valley.

PA 97 S of Erie. Erected Nov. 1946.

Entering Erie

30 ERIE
The State's only lake port, bought with Erie Triangle, 1797. Laid out in 1795 by Ellicott and Irvine. Site of French, British and U.S. forts. Perry built his fleet here in 1813.

On main highways leading into city. Erected Nov. 1946.

30 CAPTAIN C. V. GRIDLEY
Grave of Capt. Gridley, commander of Dewey's flagship Olympia in the Battle of Manila Bay, 1898, is in this cemetery. Dewey's order, ''You may fire when you are ready, Gridley,'' opened the battle.

E. Lake Rd. (Alternate PA 5), Erie. Erected Nov. 1946.

30 ANTHONY WAYNE
On the Soldiers and Sailors Home grounds near the foot of this street is a restored blockhouse on the site of American Fort Presque Isle. It is the original burial place of General Wayne, who died there on December 15, 1796.

E. 6th St. (Alternate PA 5) at Ash St., Erie. Erected Nov. 1946.

30 FORT PRESQUE ISLE
Two forts stood four blocks north. French fort, built by Marin, 1753, abandoned, 1759. British fort, built by Col. Bouquet, 1760, and captured 1763 by Pontiac's Indians. The French Road to Fort Le Boeuf began there.

6th & Parade Sts., Erie. Erected Oct. 1946.

30 HARRY T. BURLEIGH
Eminent American baritone, composer, and arranger, was born 3 blocks north in 1866. He arranged ''Deep River'' and other spirituals, and set to music poems by Walt Whitman. Was a student and associate of Dvorak. He died in 1949.

E. 6th St. (Alternate PA 5), Erie. Erected Feb. 21, 1952.

30 OLD CUSTOM HOUSE
Built in 1839 to house a branch of the U.S. Bank of Pennsylvania. Later used as custom house, post office, and G. A. R. hall. A famed example of Greek Revival architecture.

State St., Erie. Erected Nov. 1946. Now home of Erie Art Museum.

The Old Custom House, Erie

30 CASHIER'S HOUSE
Erected as a residence for the cashier of a branch of the U.S. Bank of Pennsylvania, which occupied the adjacent building. Completed 1839. Under a series of owners after 1849. Administered by the Pennsylvania Historical and Museum Commission.

417 State St. in Erie. Erected 1980.

30 CANAL BASIN
End of Erie Extension of the Pennsylvania Canal system. Work begun here July 4, 1838. Canal formally opened December 5, 1844, by arrival of ''R. S. Reed'' with Mercer County coal, and ''Queen of the West'' with passengers.
N end of State St., Erie. Erected Apr. 5, 1948.

30 USS WOLVERINE
This is the bowsprit of the Wolverine, originally named the Michigan. Launched in 1843, it was the U.S. Navy's first iron ship. In use until 1923. Only warship on the Lakes for many years.
City type: N end State St., Erie. Erected Sept. 3, 1953.

30 FLAGSHIP NIAGARA
Restored flagship of Capt. Oliver Hazard Perry in the Battle of Lake Erie, Sept. 10, 1813. Administered by the Pennsylvania Historical and Museum Commission.
At property on State St., Erie. Erected 1948.

30 PERRY'S SHIPYARDS
Perry's ships, the Lawrence, the Niagara, and the Ariel, were built in spring, 1813, at the foot of this street. His warehouses, blockhouse, and lookout station were also located there.
6th & Cascade Sts., Erie. Erected Nov. 1946.

Leaving Erie

31 ERIE EXTENSION CANAL
A section of this canal, linking New Castle and Erie, lies at foot of the slope, to left of side road. Conneaut Line, Erie to Conneaut Lake, begun by State, 1838; finished by company headed by R. S. Reed, of Erie, 1843-44.
US 20 at Asbury Chapel, W of Erie. Erected Apr. 30, 1948.

32 OLD STATE LINE
Same text as Old State Line above.
PA 99 at McKean. Erected Nov. 1946.

33 EDINBORO STATE COLLEGE
Founded in 1857, it was established in 1861 as a State Normal School, second oldest in the Commonwealth and first west of the mountains. It became a Teachers College in 1926, and a State College in 1960.
City type: US 6N at campus in Edinboro. Erected May 31, 1968. Became Edinboro University in 1983.

34 ERIE EXTENSION CANAL
Part of the old channel is visible by the present railroad, which replaced the canal. Lockport, now Platea, was founded 1839 at a point where a series of locks, 28 in two miles, lowered boats bound for Erie. Canal open 1844-71.
PA 18 at Platea. Erected Apr. 30, 1948.

35 CIRCUS HISTORY
America's most famous clown of the Nineteenth Century. Dan Rice (1823-1900), had the winter quarters of his circus in Girard from 1852 to 1875. The nearby Soldiers' Monument was donated by the versatile clown and showman, whose home stood opposite.
US 20 at the Diamond in Girard. Dedicated Aug. 21, 1974.

36 OLD STATE LINE
Same text as Old State Line above.
PA 5 E of North Springfield. Erected Nov. 1946.

Mercer County

D MERCER COUNTY
Formed March 12, 1800 from Allegheny County. The U.S. census reported 3228 residents in 1800. Named for General Hugh Mercer, Revolutionary hero killed at Battle of Princeton, 1777. Early iron and coal center. Mercer, the county seat, was incorporated 1814.
City type: County Courthouse, at Courthouse Sq., Mercer. Dedicated May 12, 1983.

37 "FREEDOM ROAD"

In search of freedom, men and women brought from the South by the "Underground Railroad" settled near here about 1825 and later. After 1850, most of them went on to Canada. Their cemetery, still in use, lies a short distance above the road.

US 62 SW of Sandy Lake. Erected Aug. 23, 1948.

38 JOHNSTON TAVERN

Kept by Arthur Johnston; licensed in 1827. Present building erected in 1831. Served travelers on the Pittsburgh-Mercer road, and stood conveniently near Springfield Furnace, in operation after 1837.

US 19 N of Leesburg. Erected Aug. 24, 1948.

39 [GENERAL HUGH MERCER]

In memory of General Hugh Mercer. Born in Scotland. Colonel in General Forbes Expedition against Fort Duquesne, 1758. Commandant at Fort Pitt, 1759. Colonel 3d Virginia Regiment, 1776. Brigadier General Continental Army, 1776. Killed in the Battle of Princeton, 1777. This tablet placed by the Pennsylvania Historical Commission and the Pennsylvania Daughters of the American Revolution to honor the soldier for whom Mercer County is named, 1917. "I am willing to serve my adopted country in any capacity she may need me."

Plaque: N entrance, County Courthouse, Mercer. Dedicated May 19, 1917.

40 CLAY FURNACE

First successful use of raw bituminous coal in place of charcoal, 1846; and of unmixed Lake Superior iron ore in 1856. Built 1845 by Vincent & Himrod; named for Henry Clay. Abandoned in 1861. The site is 2 miles away.

US 62 W of Charleston. Erected Jan. 20, 1949.

41 ERIE EXTENSION CANAL

Route of travel and trade, Pittsburgh to Great Lakes 1840-1871. Important to the western Pennsylvania iron industry before the rise of the railroads. The only remaining canal lock still stands in Sharpsville.

Junction PA 18 & 518 E of Sharpsville. Erected Nov. 12, 1946.

42 ALBERT BUSHNELL HART

Distinguished scholar and historian, Harvard graduate and member of its faculty for sixty years, was born nearby, July 1, 1854, and lived here six years. He died July 16, 1943, at Cambridge, Massachusetts.

PA 258 at Clark. Erected Apr. 30, 1948.

43 PYMATUNING

Delaware Indian village on opposite river bank about 1764-1785. Name was once used for upper Shenango River, which flowed from Pymatuning Swamp, now Pymatuning Reservoir.

PA 258 E of Clark. Erected Nov. 12, 1946.

44 ERIE EXTENSION CANAL

The channel is clearly visible from here. Part of the Shenango Line, from New Castle to near Conneaut Lake. Built by the State; formally opened to Greenville, Aug. 23, 1840. Run by the Erie Canal Co., 1844-70. Closed 1871.

Wasser Bridge Rd. (SR 4003) just E of PA 18, S of Greenville. Erected Apr. 30, 1948.

45 BIGLER GRAVES

Jacob and Susan Bigler, parents of two governors, are buried here. Their son William was Governor of Pennsylvania, 1852-55; and their son John, Governor of California, 1852-56.

PA 58 SE of Greenville, junction SR 4003. Erected Nov. 12, 1946.

46 BIGLER HOME

Jacob and Susan Bigler, parents of two governors, resided nearby after 1822. In January 1852 their son John became Governor of California, and their son William became Governor of Pennsylvania.

PA 58 SE of Greenville & W of Kremis. Erected Nov. 12, 1946.

47 JAMES SHEAKLEY

Fourth Territorial Governor of Alaska, 1893-1897, James Sheakley (1829-1917), was born in Sheakleyville, which was named for his uncle George. Appointed by President Cleveland, he also served as United States Commissioner of Schools for Alaska, 1887-1892.

US 19 at Sheakleyville. Erected Mar. 6, 1967.

Venango County

(E) VENANGO COUNTY

Formed March 12, 1800 out of Allegheny and Lycoming counties. The name (an Indian term) refers to French Creek. Franklin, county seat, was laid out in 1795. It became a city in 1868, as did Oil City in 1871. At Drake Well the oil industry was born, 1859.

City type: County Courthouse, 12th & Liberty Sts., Franklin. Dedicated Oct. 18, 1981.

(48) VENANGO PATH

A major Indian path from the Forks of the Ohio (Pittsburgh) to Venango (Franklin) was located just west of here. George Washington used it in traveling north to Fort Le Boeuf in 1753. Capt. Jonathan Hart widened the path in 1787 on his way to build Fort Franklin. Here at Mayes Forks, the house on the NW corner was a major hotel — and a mail and stagecoach stop — during the early nineteenth century.

Intersection SR 3013 (old PA 8) & SR 3003 just N of Wesley. Dedicated Aug. 23, 1987.

Entering Franklin

(49) JOHNNY APPLESEED

John Chapman, an actual person as well as a folk hero, lived nearby along French Creek between 1797 and 1804. Records indicate he had a nursery there and one near Warren, Pa., before moving on to Ohio. Born 1774 in Massachusetts, he died in Indiana, 1845.

City type: 13th St. (US 322) & Franklin Ave., Franklin. Dedicated Sept. 26, 1982.

(49) FORT FRANKLIN

Site just west of here. Built in 1787 by U. S. troops under Captain Heart [Hart]. First American fort in the region and base for protecting northwestern Pennsylvania's early settlements.

13th St. (US 322) & Franklin Ave., Franklin. Erected Mar. 20, 1947.

(49) OLD GARRISON

Built in 1796 to replace Fort Franklin. Commanded both French Creek and the Allegheny River. Occupied until 1799 by U.S. troops. Was later the first jail of Venango County. The site at the foot of Tenth Street is now under water.

10th & Liberty Sts. (on U.S. 322), Franklin. Erected Mar. 20, 1947.

(49) FORT MACHAULT

Built by the French in 1756 to guard the route to the Ohio, it was evacuated and burned by them after the siege and fall of Fort Niagara in 1759. Site of fort is one block south.

City type: 8th & Elk Sts. (on US 322), Franklin. Erected Apr. 7, 1969 (revised 1947 marker).

(49) FORT VENANGO

To assert control over the area, Fort Venango was built near this point by the British in 1760. The fort was attacked and destroyed by Indians in 1763 during Pontiac's uprising.

City type: 8th & Elk Sts. (on US 322), Franklin. Erected Oct. 10, 1972 (revised 1947 marker).

Leaving Franklin

(50) DRAKE WELL PARK

Near Titusville. The Park and Museum are owned by the State. On the site Col. Edwin Drake struck oil Aug. 27, 1859, marking the birth of the petroleum industry. Historical and museum material center.

US 322 at Cranberry. Erected Mar. 20, 1947.

(51) JOHN DEWEY

After graduation from the University of Vermont in 1879, the noted philosopher, liberal, and advocate of progressive education (1859-1952) taught for the first two years of his distinguished career at Oil City's first high school, located on this site.

City type: Central Ave. & W. 4th St., Oil City. Dedicated July 20, 1980.

52 OLDEST PRODUCING OIL WELL
McClintock No. 1 Oil Well has produced continuously since August, 1861.
Drilled only two years after the famous Drake Well, it is located 240 yards away,
across the railroad.
PA 8 just S of Rouseville. Erected Aug 5, 1958.

53 PITHOLE
Created in 1865 by the discovery of oil. Within a few months it was a boom town
of 15,000 with banks, churches, hotels, newspaper, post office, water system,
and railroad. Oil wells began to go dry in less than a year, and in time only
excavations and street lines remained. Site is about two miles northeast.
Intersection PA 227 & SR 1006 (former LR 60049) 5.6 miles SW of Pleasantville.
Erected July 1986 (revised 1954 marker).

54 PITHOLE
Created in 1865 by the discovery of oil; became a city of 15,000 within a few
months. Center of the city was at the foot of this hill. Reservoir stands just NW
of here. The Methodist Church, last building to be torn down, was about 150 feet
to the east.
SR 1006 (former LR 60049) on the hill. Erected Dec. 1973 (revised 1954 marker).

54 PITHOLE CITY
Site of oil-boom town of 15,000. Established in 1865, a ghost town by 1868.
Administered by the Pennsylvania Historical and Museum Commission.
At property on SR 1006. Erected July 26, 1966.

55 FIRST OIL PIPELINE
Constructed in the fall of 1865. Following a straight course about 5 miles in
length, it transported oil by pumps from Pithole to a railhead at Miller Farm,
thus revolutionizing the transportation of petroleum. Dug up when Pithole
wells were pumped dry. Trench is visible here and at points along the course of
the old pipeline.
PA 227, 4 miles SW of Pleasantville. Erected Nov. 15, 1954.

56 DRAKE WELL PARK
On this site "Col." Edwin Drake struck oil Aug. 27, 1859; the birth of the
petroleum industry. Administered by the Pennsylvania Historical and Museum
Commission.
At Drake Well Museum SE of Titusville. Erected 1948.

REGION IX

Trails Through the Forest

The five counties of *Cameron, Elk, Forest, McKean, Potter* and *Warren* in northeast and northcentral Pennsylvania, clustered on the boundary of New York, are covered mainly by miles of forest, interrupted for the most part by an occasional small town.

Part of this was hunting ground for the Seneca Indians, and it was crossed by several important Indian paths. French traders visited here each year. In 1749 a French military detachment under Celoron de Blainville, on orders of the Governor of New France (Canada), entered the Allegheny River at Conewango Indian town, at the later borough of Warren, and planted the first of the inscribed lead plates that promulgated France's claim to jurisdiction throughout the Ohio basin. This claim challenged that of her imperial rival, Great Britain.

In 1767 the missionary David Zeisberger came from the Moravian town of Bethlehem to minister to displaced Delaware Indians who had established three towns under Seneca patronage in Forest County. The Senecas were the tribe of the Iroquois confederation — known as the Six Nations — that was situated farthest to its west. After the American Revolution, in which the Iroquois had remained constant in their alliance with the British, a Seneca leader, Cornplanter, decided that it was in the interest of his people to cast their lot with the fledgling government of the United States. In gratitude the State of Pennsylvania in 1791 granted a tract of land in Warren County to him and his heirs.

However, other than a portion of Potter County, there was little in the region to attract the farmer, and so the early immigrant came primarily to engage in lumbering or the tanning of leather. Another wave of population was attracted in the 1860's and 1870's by the drilling of oil, primarily in Warren and McKean counties. Because of the New England origin of the settlers, it was inevitable that its influence would be implanted here, as it was in much of northern Pennsylvania.

Foreign influence on the other hand was small but real. In 1852 Ole Bull, a world-renowned Norwegian violinist, established a colony for poor fellow countrymen in Potter County. Serious miscalculations, however, brought the venture to ruin. Other communities were established in the region by German brotherhoods and cooperative groups. Such was the origin under Roman Catholic auspices in 1842 of the Elk County borough of St. Marys.

Lumbering was a major industry until 1900. Reforestation, however, has again made the region productive of lumber products. Recreation is also a major enterprise, with the establishment of State and national forests and State-owned game lands. Other industries, such as electronics manufacture, have been introduced, but mountainous terrain and forest have limited the growth of the area's population.

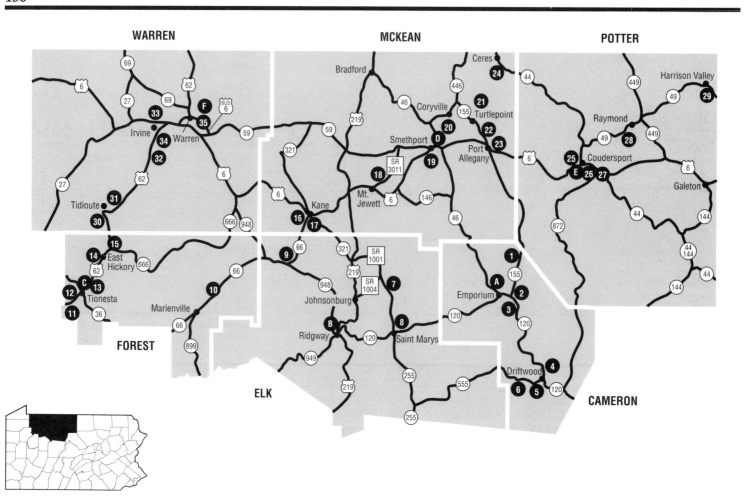

WARREN

MCKEAN

POTTER

FOREST

ELK

CAMERON

Cameron County

A CAMERON COUNTY

Formed March 29, 1860 from Clinton, McKean, Potter and Elk counties. Named for Sen. Simon Cameron. County seat, Emporium, was incorporated 1864. Lumbering was of early importance, and flagstone at Tomb of the Unknown Soldier was later quarried here.

City type: County Courthouse, PA 120, Emporium. Dedicated Sept. 14, 1982.

1 PORTAGE PATH

The railroad along Portage Creek follows the course of an Indian path connecting heads of navigation, known as "Canoe Places," on the Sinnemahoning and the Allegheny at present Emporium Junction and Port Allegany.

PA 155, 5.5 miles N of Emporium Junction. Erected Oct. 10, 1950.

2 ALLEGHENY PORTAGE

The 23-mile crossing from Susquehanna West Branch to the Allegheny River began at a "canoe place" near this point. Indians and pioneers went north to Portage Creek, and at present Port Allegany resumed travel by canoe.

Junction PA 120 & 155 E of Emporium. Erected Aug. 25, 1949.

3 SINNEMAHONING PATH

An Indian path ran up the valley of the Sinnemahoning Creek to Canoe Place, now Emporium Junction, and on to the Seneca villages at the Big Bend of the Allegheny. Early settlers in Clinton, McKean, Cameron, and Potter Counties used this path.

PA 120, 3.8 miles S of Emporium. Erected Feb. 9, 1950.

4 SINNEMAHONING PATH

One of the earliest paths through the Allegheny Mts. followed this valley. It connected the Upper Allegheny River with the Susquehanna. In 17th century the Senecas used it in war against the Susquehannocks.

PA 120, 1.5 miles N of Driftwood. Erected Feb. 9, 1950.

5 "THE BUCKTAILS"

Famed Civil War volunteers, departed from this point for Harrisburg, April 1861, where they were mustered into State service. A monument, erected in their honor, is just south of here. The highway and a State park are named for the Bucktails.

Junction PA 120 & 555, Driftwood. Erected Feb. 8, 1950.

6 TOM MIX

The famous cowboy star of cinema and circus was born here, January 6, 1880. A soldier during the Spanish-American War, he won renown for his "wild west" roles in hundreds of motion pictures — both silent and sound — between 1910 and 1935. Tom Mix died in an auto accident in Arizona on October 12, 1940.

At birthplace, Mix Run Rd. off PA 555 W of Driftwood. Dedicated May 28, 1988 (revised 1968 marker).

Elk County

B ELK COUNTY

Formed April 18, 1843 from parts of McKean, Clearfield and Jefferson counties. Named for the large elk herd that roamed the area. First State Game Lands established in Pennsylvania, in 1920, are here. The county seat, Ridgway, was settled in 1824.

City type: County Courthouse, Main St., Ridgway. Dedicated July 24, 1982.

7 FIRST STATE GAME LANDS

A tract of 6288 acres lying north and east of here was the first purchase of State Game Lands by the Pennsylvania Game Commission. The purchase was made in 1920 with funds obtained from hunting license fees.

SR 1001 (former LR 24013) SE of Glen Hazel. Erected Oct. 20, 1950.

8 ST. MARYS

Founded, 1842, as Marienstadt, by the German-American Catholic Brotherhood, St. Marys was a haven from persecution. It was aided by the Roman Catholic Church, Baltimore merchants, and Ludwig I, King of Bavaria.

St. Marys near the Diamond. Erected 1967.

9 IROQUOIS "MAIN ROAD"

An ancient Indian trail from Ichsua (Olean) and all parts of the Iroquois country, passed this way for the south. At Kittanning the path forked, one branch going to the Mississippi and the other to the Carolinas.

PA 66 & 948, Highland Twp. Erected Oct. 7, 1950.

Forest County

C FOREST COUNTY

Formed April 11, 1848 from Jefferson County. Named for its extensive forests. Part of Venango County was added, 1866, and county seat moved from Marienville to Tionesta. Area notable for its Indian paths, and Zeisberger's mission to the Munsees, 1767-1770.

City type: County Courthouse, Elm St. (US 62), Tionesta. Dedicated Aug. 21, 1982.

10 PIGEON

The name of this town recalls the now-extinct passenger pigeon, which in vast flights nested in the beech groves of this area. The nestlings were taken as food each spring by the Seneca Indians.

PA 66, 5 miles NE of Marienville. Erected June 3, 1948.

11 HOLEMAN FERRY

Established by Eli Holeman about 1804. Crossing the Allegheny River here, it was an important link on the old State Road, or "Bald Eagle Road," leading from Milesburg (Centre County) to Waterford (Erie County). Most of the early settlers crossed at this point. In the War of 1812, troops and supplies were transported on the Ferry.

US 62, 3 miles SW of Tionesta. Erected Aug. 5, 1954.

12 REFUGEE TOWNS

This part of the Allegheny was allotted to Munsee and other displaced Indians by the Seneca before 1750. In 1767-70 Zeisberger worked among these refugee groups, then occupying three towns along the river here.

US 62, 1.5 miles S of Tionesta Station. Erected July 29, 1947.

13 DAMASCUS

Later name of Zeisberger's "Lower Town," located on opposite side of the river here. Residence of a Seneca sentinel chief at the time. Town name was taken from the Munsee word, "muskrat."

US 62 at Tionesta. Erected July 29, 1947.

14 INDIAN PATHS

Across the river here paths led over the hills to Oil Creek. Each year, in spring, the Indians used to travel westward to gather petroleum from the oil pits, boil maple sugar and make bark canoes.

US 62, 2.3 miles S of East Hickory. Erected July 29, 1947.

14 HICKORY TOWN

Site across the river of Zeisberger's "Middle Town," later called Hickory Town. Here his noted dispute with Wangomen took place in 1767. Here too ended Indian paths from the south, by which trade goods were obtained.

US 62, 2 miles S of East Hickory. Erected July 29, 1947.

15 GOSCHGOSCHINK

Name applied at the time of Zeisberger's arrival in 1767 to all three of the refugee Indian towns. Later the name was given to "Upper Town," located across the river at this point.

US 62, .9 mile S of East Hickory. Erected July 29, 1947.

15 REFUGEE TOWNS

Same text as Refugee Towns above.

US 52, .5 mile S of East Hickory. Erected July 29, 1947.

15 LAWUNAKHANNEK

Name of Indian mission near here, at which the first Protestant church building west of the Allegheny Mountains was built by Zeisberger in 1769. Term is Delaware word meaning "northerly stream place."

US 62, .2 mile N of East Hickory. Erected July 29, 1947.

18 KINZUA VIADUCT

Originally built 1882 for a branch of the Erie Railroad to ship coal northward. It was the world's highest and longest rail viaduct. Rebuilt 1900 to carry heavier loads, it was in service until 1959. Kinzua Bridge State Park was created here, 1963.

City type: Kinzua Bridge State Park, off SR 3011 (former LR 42044) 3.5 miles NE of Mount Jewett. Dedicated Aug. 15, 1982.

The Kinzua Bridge State Park

Department of Environmental Resources

McKean County

D McKEAN COUNTY

Formed March 26, 1804 out of Lycoming County. Named for Gov. Thomas McKean. Smethport, the county seat, was incorporated 1853; here the "Bucktails," famed Civil War regiment, assembled in 1861. Oil, gas and lumber spurred the county's early economic growth.

City type: County Courthouse, US 6 in Smethport. Dedicated Oct. 14, 1981.

16 THOMAS L. KANE

Commander of the Civil War "Bucktail Regiment" and founder of the borough of Kane. Breveted Major General in 1863. A friend of Brigham Young and stanch supporter of the Mormon pioneers. He died, 1883, and was buried at this chapel, built at his direction in 1876-78.

City type: 30 Chestnut St. (Kane Memorial Chapel), Kane. Dedicated June 29, 1980.

17 SENECA SPRING

The spring, 200 yards SW of here, was a stopping place on an ancient Indian trail which crossed the Big Level on the way south. The trail was once the main route from Onondaga, the Iroquois capital, to the Ohio and the Carolinas.

PA 321 S of Kane. Erected Sept. 28, 1951.

19 SMETHPORT

County seat for McKean County since 1807, when land agent Francis King surveyed town lots. The first cabin was built in 1811 by Arnold Hunter; but permanent settlement was delayed until 1822. First courthouse built in 1827.

US 6 at Courthouse, Smethport. Erected Aug. 8, 1949.

19 "THE BUCKTAILS"
At the call of Col. Thos. L. Kane, 100 Civil War volunteers assembled here on Apr. 24, 1861, to go to Harrisburg. Tails of buck deer, worn as distinctive insignia, provided the name of the famed 42d Regiment, of which they were the core.
US 6 at Courthouse, Smethport. Erected Aug. 8, 1949.

20 TIDEWATER PIPE CO.
Opposite here was station No. 1 of the first pipe line to carry oil across the Alleghenies. Built by an early competitor of Standard Oil, it began May 28, 1879, to pump oil 109 miles to Williamsport, Pa.
PA 445, .3 mile SW of Coryville. Erected Aug. 9, 1949.

21 ST. MARY'S CHURCH
Parish organized 1847 at Sartwell in the "Irish Settlement," originally formed 1842-60. Log church built 1848; present one completed 1871. Resident pastor long served Roman Catholics throughout McKean and Potter counties, and this was the "mother church" of those at Port Allegany, Bradford, Smethport, Eldred, Duke Center, and Costello. It later became a mission of St. Raphael's at Eldred.
Newell Creek Rd. at church, off PA 155 NE of Turtlepoint. Dedicated July 7, 1985.

22 MT. EQUITY PLANTATION
Gov. McKean, for whom the county was named, purchased here, in 1805, a 299-acre tract. Its name derived from the fact that the purchase was made in part to give Pennsylvania equity of power in lands settled by Connecticut.
PA 155, 3 miles NW of Port Allegany. Erected Aug. 11, 1949.

23 PORT ALLEGANY
Travel point since pioneer days, when travelers coming overland from the Susquehanna continued by water from "Canoe Place." The town grew as a center of lumber and tanning industry. Its descriptive present name came into use about 1840.
US 6, .2 mile W of & at square, Port Allegany. Erected Oct. 12, 1948.

23 ALLEGHENY PORTAGE
The 23-mile crossing from Susquehanna West Branch to the Allegheny River followed Portage Creek to a "canoe place" near this point. From here Indians and pioneers continued on their way by boat down the Allegheny River.
Junction US 6 & PA 155, Port Allegany. Erected Aug. 10, 1949.

24 CERES
One mile south of here the first permanent white settlement in present McKean County was made in 1798 by Francis King, agent and surveyor for the John Keating land company of Philadelphia.
PA 44 near Ceres at bridge. Erected Aug. 8, 1949.

Potter County

E POTTER COUNTY
Formed March 26, 1804 out of Lycoming County, and fully organized in 1835. Named for Revolutionary hero, General James Potter. An early center of the lumbering and tanning industries. Coudersport, the county seat, was laid out in 1807; incorporated 1848.
City type: County Courthouse, 2nd & East Sts., Coudersport. Dedicated July 31, 1982.

25 [DAVID ZEISBERGER]
Erected as a memorial to David Zeisberger, who encamped near this place on the night of October 8, 1767, when on his way from Bethlehem to the mouth of Tionesta Creek to visit the Indians on the Allegheny River. He was accompanied by two Delaware Indians, Anthony and Papunhank. This visit led to the establishment of the various Moravian missions among the Delaware in western Pennsylvania and eastern Ohio. David Zeisberger was, so far as all records show, the first white man to pass through the primeval forests of the upper Allegheny River. Erected by the Pennsylvania Historical Commission in co-operation with the Allegewe Chapter, Daughters of the American Revolution, 1916.
Plaque: 2nd (US 6) & Main Sts., at County Courthouse, Coudersport. Dedicated October 13, 1916.

25 DAVID ZEISBERGER

Noted Moravian missionary, camped near here Oct. 8, 1767, en route from Bethlehem to found missions among the Delaware Indians to the West. He was the first white man to pass through the primeval forests of this region.

2nd St. (US 6), Coudersport. Erected Aug. 22, 1947.

26 LYMANSVILLE

The pioneer settlement in this region was made here in 1808 by Major Isaac Lyman, land agent and a Revolutionary officer. The first saw and grist mill, post office, and court were also located here.

Junction US 6 & PA 872, 2 miles E of Coudersport. Erected Aug. 19, 1947.

27 OLE BULL'S COLONY

The 11,144 acres of land within the tract acquired by the noted Norwegian violinist in 1852 were SE of here. Here were village sites, New Norway, Oleona, New Bergen, Walhalla, and Ole Bull's Castle.

US 6, 3.5 miles E of Coudersport. Erected Aug. 19, 1947.

27 JERSEY SHORE PIKE

Lymansville was the north terminus for the early pack trail and wagon road south to Jersey Shore. In 1834 a Turnpike toll road was completed between the two points. For many years it was a major trade route.

US 6, 3.5 miles E of Coudersport. Erected Aug. 19, 1947.

28 ALLEGHENY RIVER

Here is the head stream of this historic river, pathway of Indians, and white traders and settlers for over 200 years. It unites with the Monongahela, 352 miles away at Pittsburgh, forming the Ohio.

PA 49, 11 miles NE of Coudersport near Raymond. Erected Aug. 22, 1947.

28 DAVID ZEISBERGER

Noted Moravian missionary, passed through here in Oct. 1767, en route from Bethlehem to found missions among the Delaware Indians to the West. He was the first white man to travel through the primeval forests of this region.

PA 49, 11 miles NE of Coudersport near Raymond. Erected Aug. 22, 1947.

29 DAVID ZEISBERGER

Same text as above.

PA 49, 1 mile E of Harrison Valley. Erected Aug 22, 1947.

Warren County

F WARREN COUNTY

Formed March 12, 1800 from Allegheny and Lycoming counties. Named for Gen. Joseph Warren, killed at Bunker Hill. Warren, the county seat, was laid out in 1795. Long known for its oil and timber operations, and site of the Cornplanter Indian Grant.

City type: County Courthouse, 4th Ave. at Market St., Warren. Dedicated March 12, 1981.

30 THE GRANDIN WELL

At oil spring across river at this point J. L. Grandin began second well drilled specifically for oil, Aug., 1859, after Drake's success. It was dry, showing risks involved in oil drilling.

US 62, .4 mile S of Allegheny River bridge near Tidioute. Erected July 15, 1959.

31 INDIAN PAINT HILL

Across the river from here deposits of red ochre and adjacent petroleum springs provided the Indians with raw materials for face and body paint.

US 62, 3 miles NE of Tidioute. Erected Oct. 23, 1947.

32 THOMPSON'S ISLAND

An advance party of Brodhead's expedition of 1779 into the Seneca Country had a skirmish here with 30 or 40 Indians, the only fighting which took place in that campaign and the only Revolutionary battle in northwestern Pennsylvania.

US 62, 9 miles SW of Warren. Erected Oct. 23, 1947.

33 GEN. WILLIAM IRVINE
Surveyed Donation Lands in this area in 1785. Later bought a large tract of land
developed by his son Callender and grandson, Dr. William Irvine. One of the
tenant houses of the estate stands opposite.
Old US 6 (SR 3022) W of US 62, Irvine. Erected Oct. 23, 1947.

34 BUCKALOONS
A famous Indian village at the junction of Brokenstraw Creek and the Allegheny,
visited by Celoron in 1749, and destroyed by Brodhead in 1779. Burial mounds
excavated here show the antiquity of this site.
In Buckaloons Park near US 62 E of Irvine. Erected Oct. 23, 1947.

35 CELORON'S EXPEDITION
In 1749 a French force under Celoron de Blainville entered the Ohio valley by
way of Chautauqua Lake and Conewango Creek. A lead plate was buried at the
mouth of the Conewango claiming the area for France.
Pennsylvania Ave. (Business US 6) at Hickory St., Warren. Erected Oct. 23, 1947.

35 CONEWANGO
Mid-18th century Seneca village located on site of present Warren. First
mentioned by Bonnecamps in 1749, as composed of 12 or 13 cabins. Name in
Iroquois means ''below the rifles.''
Pennsylvania Ave. (Business US 6), Conewango Creek bridge, Warren. Erected
Oct. 23, 1947.

REGION X

The Pennsylvania Heartland

Located at the center of the State, the five counties of *Clearfield, Clinton, Centre, Juniata* and *Mifflin* sit astride the Allegheny Front. The front ascends from valleys and ridges to the Allegheny Plateau, setting the wooded plateau to the northwest apart, with its deep and narrow valleys, from the high ridges and wider valleys characteristic of the Appalachian Mountains on the southeast.

With fear of the Native American relieved, with the question of "title" to Pennsylvania's western lands resolved in 1768 by the Treaty of Fort Stanwix, and with the completion of the Revolutionary War, the pace of settlement in this region quickened. Settlers began, in increasing numbers, to cultivate their farms and grow their livestock, lay out building lots and towns, erect iron furnaces, and harvest the abundant forests.

If oral tradition is to be credited, one of the earliest and most notable events among the first settlers, who were beyond the reach of local government, was a resolution of independence from Great Britain on July 4, 1776, passed under the famous Tiadaghton Elm, which stood until recent years several miles from Lock Haven.

Several important paths upon which the Indians journeyed through the region were later adapted to vehicular travel, including in 1804 the first road to the northwest frontier and the Allegheny River. Economic life and, particularly, the industries of the larger towns received a major boost from the opening in 1834 of the Pennsylvania Canal to Lock Haven and a branch to Bellefonte, and from erection in 1829 of the Juniata Division of the canal to Lewistown. Railroad construction began soon after and added to the accessibility of industry to markets. In the 1920's Bellefonte airfield provided an essential link in the U.S. airmail service.

Ruins of ironworks, which flourished particularly in Centre County, are numerous. The economic strength of Clearfield County, on the other hand, was in its coal mining and lumbering, and that of Clinton County and the borough of Renovo in the railroad. Livestock have been the principal product of farming.

The fact that several governors, including Civil War executive Andrew G. Curtin, who began a nearly century-long dominance of Pennsylvania politics by the Republican party, and other notables lived and prospered in this rural and productive area should surprise no one. Moreover, the opening in 1859, in the geographical center of the Commonwealth, of what was to become the Pennsylvania State University, though at that time a great distance from most of its potential students, should need no justification today in light of both the demography and the athletic enthusiasms of the late twentieth century. Just as have the high technology and service industries that are gaining importance in the State's economy, the university has helped to stimulate the economies of many of its neighbors.

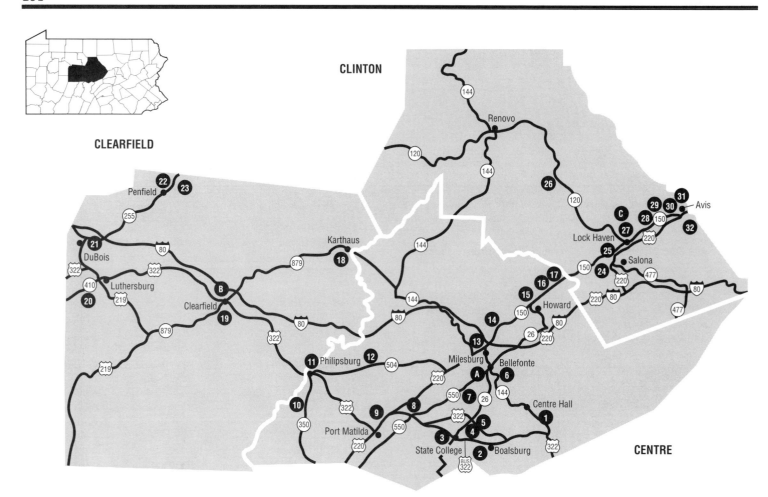

CLINTON

CLEARFIELD

CENTRE

Renovo

Penfield

DuBois

Lutersburg

Clearfield

Karthaus

Lock Haven

Avis

Salona

Howard

Philipsburg

Milesburg

Bellefonte

Centre Hall

Port Matilda

State College

Boalsburg

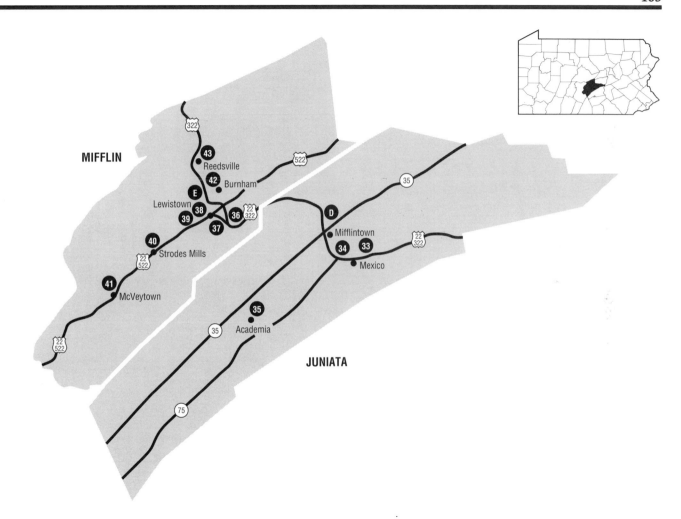

MIFFLIN

322

43
Reedsville

42
Burnham

522

E
Lewistown
38
39
36
22
322
37

40
Strodes Mills
22
522

41
McVeytown

22
522

D
Mifflintown
34
33
Mexico

35
Academia

35

22
322

35

75

JUNIATA

Centre County

Ⓐ CENTRE COUNTY
Formed on Feb. 13, 1800 from Huntingdon, Mifflin, Lycoming and Northumberland counties. Named for its location in the State, and home of The Pennsylvania State University. Five governors of Pennsylvania lived in Bellefonte, county seat laid out in 1795.
City type: County Courthouse, Allegheny St., Bellefonte. Dedicated May 10, 1982.

❶ POTTER'S FORT
Built 1777 by Gen. James Potter. A stockaded fort refuge for the settlers of the valley region. The site is on the nearby rise.
PA 144 SE of Centre Hall. Erected May 5, 1947.

❷ 28TH DIVISION SHRINE
Dedicated to heroic dead of Pennsylvania's famed 28th in two world wars. The Division was created Sept., 1917. The shrine was founded by Col. Theodore Boal and made a State memorial in 1932.
Business US 322 at Pennsylvania Military Museum, Boalsburg. Erected May 6, 1947.

❸ THE PENNSYLVANIA STATE UNIVERSITY
Chartered 1855. Opened Feb. 16, 1859. Gen. James Irvin gave the original land. April 1, 1863, by Act of Assembly made the land grant College of the State for "liberal and practical education."
Business US 322, State College. Erected Apr. 30, 1947.

❹ CENTRE FURNACE
Here Cols. John Patton and Samuel Miles operated the first charcoal iron furnace in the region, 1792-1809. Present stack used 1825-1858. In this era Centre County led in the making of Juniata iron.
PA 26 just NE of State College, adjacent to Centre Furnace Mansion. Erected Apr. 29, 1947.

❹ CENTRE FURNACE
This stack is part of the plant of the Centre Iron Company which was erected in 1792 by Col. John Patton and Colonel Samuel Miles, officers in the war of the American Revolution. The product of this furnace was the first iron melted in Centre County and was carried on mule-back to Pittsburgh. The furnace was operated from 1792 to 1809 and from 1825 to 1858. Tablet placed on the 130th anniversary by the Pennsylvania Historical Commission and the Department of History of the Pennsylvania State College, 1922.
Plaque: Centre Furnace Mansion, 1001 E. College Ave. (PA 26), State College. Dedicated Oct. 30, 1922 at adjacent furnace; relocated about 1980.

❺ PHILIP BENNER
The ironmaster's home was at Rock. Here also were the first forge, 1794, and a nail and slitting mill. A founder of Bellefonte; leader in Centre County affairs until his death in 1832.
PA 26 NE of State College. Erected May 2, 1947.

❻ BELLEFONTE
Laid out by James Dunlop and James Harris, 1795. Named by Talleyrand for "beautiful fountain." Early center of the iron industry. One-time home of five of Pennsylvania's governors.
PA 150 at Bellefonte. Erected May 8, 1947.

❻ ANDREW G. CURTIN
Governor of Pennsylvania, 1861-67, was born on this site. He brought about the establishment of State Normal Schools; organized the famed Pennsylvania Reserve Corps; obtained funds for the erection of State Orphan Schools.
City type: Allegheny St. at Cherry Ln., Bellefonte. Erected Oct. 9, 1950.

❻ BELLEFONTE AIR MAIL FIELD
The initial stop on the first scheduled west-bound air mail flight was made here by Pilot Leon D. Smith on December 18, 1918. The site for the field was chosen by pioneer aviator Max Miller and was in regular use for air mail until 1925.
PA 550 (E. Bishop St.) at high school, Bellefonte. Erected June 1969.

7 PHILIP BENNER
Same text as Philip Benner above.
PA 550 SW of Bellefonte. Erected May 2, 1947.

8 SCOTIA
Two miles southwest of here, an iron center called Scotia was established by Andrew Carnegie in 1881. Here houses were erected, a railroad built, and machinery set up. Some physical traces of the center have remained.
US 322 NW of State College. Erected Aug. 1954.

9 JUNIATA IRON
Along the streams of this region are ruins of many charcoal iron furnaces and forges built between 1790-1850. Juniata iron was the best in America. Its reign ended with the rise of coal and coke iron making.
US 220 & 322, 1.8 miles NE of Port Matilda. Erected May 6, 1947.

10 INDIAN PATHS
The Warriors Mark Path intersected the Bald Eagle Path at about this point, then proceeded north to join the Great Shamokin Path, east of Chinklacamoose (Clearfield). The Warriors (Mark) Path came north from Cumberland, Maryland, and the Bald Eagle Path came west from Milesburg.
PA 350 S of Philipsburg. Dedicated Oct. 25, 1972.

11 UNION CHURCH
Built of logs in 1820 by Philipsburg pioneers to serve as school and place of worship for all faiths. Remodeled in 1842, church is outstanding example of simplified American gothic architecture.
City type: Presqueisle St. (US 322), Philipsburg. Erected Nov. 2, 1967.

12 PLUMBE FORGE
About six-tenths mile north are the remains of the forge built by Dr. John Plumbe in 1828. Here, "blooms" were made from pig iron carried from the Bald Eagle Valley by mule. Costs of hauling products to the Pennsylvania Canal caused the forge to close in 1842.
PA 504, 6 miles E of Philipsburg. Erected May 1969.

13 BALD EAGLE'S NEST
A Delaware Indian village name for a noted Munsee chief Woapalanne or "Bald Eagle." Located at union of Spring and Bald Eagle Creeks. From here raids on the frontier were made in Revolutionary days.
US 220 & PA 144 at Milesburg. Erected Aug. 26, 1947.

14 EAGLE IRONWORKS
At nearby Curtin, making iron was begun about 1810 by Roland Curtin. The last old-style furnace in the U.S. was in blast here and ceased operation in 1922.
PA 150 (former US 220) 2.8 miles NE of Milesburg. Erected Apr. 29, 1947.

Eagle Ironworks, Curtin Village restoration

15 WILLIAM F. PACKER
The newspaper editor and publisher, and Governor of the Commonwealth, 1858-61, was born April 2, 1807, in a house which stood nearby. He died, 1870, in Williamsport and is chiefly remembered for his interest in improved transportation facilities.
PA 150 at PA 26, Howard. Erected May 19, 1971.

16 WARRIORS PATH
Paths from all parts of the Six Nations country converged at Great Island. Thence the Warriors Path ran up his valley to Bald Eagle's Nest, now Milesburg; then on south toward the Carolinas.
PA 150, 2.2 miles NE of Howard. Erected Mar. 23, 1949.

17 GREAT SHAMOKIN PATH
The Indian highway from Shamokin, now Sunbury, to Kittanning, left the Bald Eagle Valley to follow Marsh Creek and Little Marsh Creek. It crossed the Allegheny Mt. by way of Snow Show and Moshannon.
PA 150, 4 miles NE of Howard. Erected Aug. 23, 1950.

Clearfield County

B CLEARFIELD COUNTY
Formed March 26, 1804 out of Huntingdon and Lycoming counties. Clear fields, found by early travelers, gave rise to the name. County was important for logging and rafting on the West Branch, 1850-1901. The county seat, Clearfield, was incorporated 1840.
City type: County Historical Museum, E. Pine & Front Sts., Clearfield. Dedicated Sept. 17, 1982.

18 KARTHAUS FURNACE
Near here stood the iron furnace erected 1817 by Peter Karthaus. Rebuilt 1836 by Peter Ritner and John Say, it became in 1839 one of the earliest to use coke in place of charcoal. Abandoned at the end of the same year.
PA 879 in Karthaus. Erected Mar. 2, 1948.

19 CHINKLACAMOOSE
Name of the Indian village located here, and visited by C. F. Post while traveling to an Indian council at Kuskuski in 1758. The later Clearfield is said to get its name from clearings made by grazing bison along nearby creeks.
US 322 E end & PA 879 W end, Clearfield. Erected May 28, 1947.

20 THE BIG SPRING
Former camping place at the junction of two Indian paths: the Great Shamokin, running from Sunbury to Kittanning; and the path to Venango, now Franklin. During War of 1812, Maj. McClelland's force camped here. Spring is 60 yards SW.
PA 410, .5 mile SW of Luthersburg. Erected Dec. 29, 1950.

21 OLD STATE ROAD (MILESBURG TO WATERFORD)
The first road to the northwest frontier of Pennsylvania. Opened to the Allegheny River in 1804. In this section, it followed, generally, the course of the Chinklacamoose Path. During the War of 1812, troops under Major McClellan were transported over it to Erie. Highway crosses the route of old Road at this point.
US 322, 6 miles NW of Luthersburg. Erected Feb. 8, 1955.

22 GEORGE ROSENKRANS
Noted band composer (1881-1955) lived most of his life in Penfield and was church organist here. Rosenkrans wrote piano and organ music and hymns, as well as over 200 band numbers. Among his marches are ''Triumphant Battalions'' and ''Our Glorious Flag.''
City type: PA 255 at Methodist Church, Penfield. Dedicated Sept. 15, 1984.

23 PHILIP P. BLISS
The great singing evangelist and gospel song writer was born July 9, 1838, in a log house which stood a little distance from here. He lived and worked on the farm and in nearby lumber camps until the age of 16.
PA 255, 2.2 miles NE of Penfield. Erected May 27, 1947.

Clinton County

C CLINTON COUNTY

Formed on June 21, 1839 out of Lycoming and Centre counties. Named probably for New York's Gov. DeWitt Clinton. Site of "Tiadaghton Declaration of Independence," 1776. In 19th century a lumbering center. Lock Haven, the county seat, became a city in 1870.

City type: Heisey Museum, 362 E. Water St., Lock Haven. Dedicated June 12, 1982.

24 DANIEL H. HASTINGS

Governor of Pennsylvania, 1895-1899; born, 1849, on a farm 4.5 miles SE of here. During his term, the State Department of Agriculture was created and the present State Capitol planned. Lived most of his life in Bellefonte. Died there in 1903.

PA 64 at PA 477 NW of Salona. Erected Oct. 9, 1950.

25 GREAT SHAMOKIN PATH

By the Indian path along Bald Eagle Creek, in 1772, Bishop Ettwein, Moravian, brought some 200 Christian Mohicans and Delawares from Friedenshuetten, near Wyalusing, to Friedensstadt on the Beaver.

PA 150 (old US 220) 2.3 miles SW of Lock Haven. Erected Jan. 24, 1950.

26 SINNEMAHONING PATH

An ancient Indian trail connected the West Branch of the Susquehanna with the Upper Allegheny. From the Great Island at Lock Haven it followed the West Branch, the Sinnemahoning, and Portage Creek, to the Seneca country.

PA 120, 14 miles NW of Lock Haven. Erected Feb. 2, 1950.

27 FORT REED

William Reed's stockaded house was the westernmost defense for Susquehanna Valley settlers. The site of the pioneer outpost is a few blocks ahead at the monument near the bridge.

PA 120 (W. Main & W. Water Sts.), Lock Haven. Erected Apr. 29, 1947.

27 PENNSYLVANIA CANAL (WEST BRANCH DIVISION)

Division was built from Northumberland to Lock Haven in 1828-34. Until 1889, boats carried iron, lumber, and manufactures from this area to eastern markets. Here, Bald Eagle Cross-Cut Canal joined the Division, connecting with it by two locks, a dam, and a towpath bridge.

PA 120 (E. Water St. near Jay St.), Lock Haven. Erected June 16, 1952.

28 THE GREAT ISLAND

Many Indian nations have occupied the Great Island in the river just south of here. Trails led from the Genesee, Ohio, Potomac, and Susquehanna North Branch. Delawares and Shawnees stopped here for a time on their migration west.

PA 150 (old US 220) 1.3 miles NE of Lock Haven. Erected May 3, 1949.

29 FORT HORN

A stockaded log house used as a frontier refuge in 1777-78. It was on the Susquehanna's south bank opposite here. In 1778 it was abandoned.

PA 150, 4 miles NE of Lock Haven. Erected July 14, 1949.

30 SHAMOKIN PATH

Much-traveled Indian path; followed north shore of Susquehanna from present Sunbury to Great Island near Lock Haven. It was used by Delawares and Shawnees on migration to the Ohio country before French and Indian War.

PA 150, 6 miles NE of Lock Haven. Erected May 3, 1949.

31 TIADAGHTON ELM

Here July 4, 1776, pioneer settlers of the West Branch resolved independence from Britain. This historic tree still stands about two miles from here at the junction of the Susquehanna and Pine Creek.

SR 1016 (old US 220) 8.5 miles NE of Lock Haven near Avis. Erected Apr. 30, 1947. The tree no longer stands.

32 TIADAGHTON ELM

Under this elm, on July 4, 1776, resolves declaring independence were drawn prior to news of action by Congress at Philadelphia. This was an expression of the spirit common to the frontier and led by the famous Fair Play men.

2 miles S of SR 1016, just off twp. road E of Avis. Erected May 6, 1947.

Juniata County

D JUNIATA COUNTY
Formed on March 2, 1831 from Mifflin County. Named for the Juniata River, and noted for its scenery and wildlife. Indian trails, turnpike, canal and railroad made the area a major route for trade and travel. Mifflintown, county seat, was incorporated 1833.
City type: County Courthouse, Mifflintown. Dedicated June 27, 1982.

33 PATTERSON'S FORT
A stockade built about 1755 to protect settlers from Indian marauders. Capt. James Patterson was builder and commandant. It was located nearby to overlook the Juniata.
SR 3001 (old US 22 & 322), .1 mile E of Mexico. Erected Apr. 1947.

34 FORT BIGHAM
The site of this stockaded blockhouse is a few miles west in Tuscarora Valley. Built about 1754 to protect traders and settlers in this region. In 1756 it was destroyed by Indians.
SR 3001 (old US 22 & 322), .8 mile NW of Mexico. Erected. Apr. 1947.

34 TUSCARORA PATH
Used by the Five Nations Iroquois in raiding tribes to the south, and later by early traders and settlers. It began one mile west of here and terminated in the Tuscarora region of North Carolina.
SR 3001 (old US 22 & 322), .9 mile NW of Mexico. Erected Apr. 1947.

35 TUSCARORA ACADEMY
Founded in 1836, it operated as an academy until 1912. Building, erected 1816, was used as a church until 1849. Administered by the Pennsylvania Historical and Museum Commission.
At site, SR 3017 (former LR 34005), Academia. Erected Mar. 20, 1968.

Mifflin County

E MIFFLIN COUNTY
Formed September 19, 1789 from Cumberland and Northumberland counties, and named for Thomas Mifflin, Governor, 1790-99. County seat, Lewistown, was laid out 1790; incorporated 1795. Important in Pennsylvania's canal development and early iron industry.
City type: Old Courthouse, Monument Sq., Lewistown. Dedicated Sept. 19, 1981.

36 TRAVEL HISTORY
Five stages of travel can be recalled here. Concrete covers the old turnpike. Opposite are the ruins of the old canal. The Juniata was once filled with river craft. Across the river is the Pennsylvania Railroad.
US 22 & 322, 1.7 mile E of Lewistown. Erected Mar. 28, 1947.

37 OLD ARCH BRIDGE
The restored stone bridge opposite was built 1813. It was a part of the turnpike from Harrisburg to Pittsburgh. The arch is without a keystone.
US 22 just E of Lewistown. Erected Mar. 28, 1947.

1813 stone-arch bridge, near Lewistown

D. Turnitsa

38 McCOY HOME

The birthplace of Major General Frank R. McCoy, 1874-1954, graduate of West Point, who took part in Spanish-American War, World Wars I & II. He was also President of the Foreign Policy Association.

City type: 17 N. Main St., Lewistown. Erected Mar. 27, 1967.

39 FORT GRANVILLE

Erected in 1755-56 along the river just south. An important link in the chain of early frontier defenses. Destroyed July 30, 1756 by French and Indians under Capt. Coulon de Villiers.

1200 W. 4th St. (US 22 & 522), Lewistown. Erected Mar. 24, 1947.

39 [FORT GRANVILLE]

About 650 yards south of this spot, on the high bank of the Juniata River, was the site of Fort Granville, which was erected in 1755-56. This fort was twice attacked by the Indians. It was destroyed on July 30, 1756, when in command of Lieut. Edward Armstrong, who was killed in the battle with a large body of French and Indians. The entire garrison was either killed or carried into captivity. Erected by the Pennsylvania Historical Commission in co-operation with the Committee of Historical Research of Mifflin County, 1916.

Plaque: 1200 W. 4th St. (US 22 & 522), Lewistown. Dedicated May 16, 1916.

40 THREE LOCKS

Preserved here are three locks of the Pennsylvania Canal, Juniata Division. Unique in that three locks and levels were adjacent. Stonework and the old bed of the canal can be seen.

US 22 & 522 at Strodes Mills, 4.6 miles SW of Lewistown. Erected Apr. 1, 1947.

40 JUNIATA IRON

Along the streams of this region are ruins of many charcoal iron furnaces and forges built between 1790-1850. Juniata iron was the best in America. Its reign ended with the rise of coal and coke iron making.

US 22 & 522 at Strodes Mills, 4.9 miles SW of Lewistown. Erected Aug. 21, 1947.

41 JOSEPH T. ROTHROCK

Born here April 9, 1839. Conservationist and father of the State Forest idea in Pennsylvania. Pioneer in development of forest fire control, reforestation, and scientific forestry.

US 22 & 522 at McVeytown. Erected Apr. 1, 1947.

42 FREEDOM FORGE

Iron and steel have been made here for over 150 years. Freedom Forge, 1795, became Freedom Iron and Steel Co., 1867. The third Bessemer plant in nation. Open hearth steel first made here in 1895.

SR 1005 (old US 322) at Burnham. Erected Mar. 31, 1947.

43 CHIEF LOGAN

Logan, son of Shikellamy, and famous Mingo chief, lived in a cabin near the spring opposite. It was his home from about 1766 to 1771, when he moved to the Ohio country.

SR 1005 (old US 322) .5 mile N of Reedsville. Erected Mar. 31, 1947.

REGION XI

Pathways to the Iroquois

In the north-central counties of *Bradford, Columbia, Lycoming, Montour, Northumberland, Snyder, Sullivan, Tioga* and *Union* the historical record begins with a challenge to William Penn's Indian policy of just and peaceful relations. Threatening this peaceful strategy was the migration of displaced Native Americans into the Susquehanna Valley.

To maintain the peace, James Logan, Penn's Provincial Secretary, devised a policy in 1732 to strengthen New York's six Iroquois nations' influence over the smaller refugee groups of Indians in Pennsylvania. Thus, the Iroquois would keep the peace by restraining at the same time the discontent of dependent tribes and the encroachment of white settlers upon the Native Americans.

The Iroquois overseer was the Oneida diplomat, Schickellamy. Representing Pennsylvania was the wilderness envoy, Conrad Weiser. Together they trod the Sheshequin Path from the Indian town of Shamokin (now Sunbury) to meet the Iroquois Council at Onondaga, New York.

Pennsylvania's Indian relations became embroiled, inevitably, in the rivalry of Britain and France. With the 1754 purchase of Indian territory west of the Susquehanna River arousing indignation among the native inhabitants, and with the conflict in the west triggering the French and Indian War, Native Americans who had been attracted to the side of the French made a devastating assault on the frontier. Killings in Snyder and Union counties in 1755 prompted the erection of a chain of forts, of which the major stronghold, Fort Augusta, was built at Sunbury in 1756-57. The final opening to white settlement in the region was effected in the Treaty of Fort Stanwix in 1768.

In the Revolution, however, the alliance of Britain with the Iroquois held. Fortifications against them were erected and settlers took refuge when they could. In 1799 Major General John Sullivan, with four thousand men assembled at Tioga Point, marched into New York to destroy their villages and crops.

Beginning in 1795, in the wake of the French Revolution, upheavals in France and Haiti deposited refugees who formed the Bradford County settlement of Azilum, which endured for a time. In much of the region, however, lumbering and, later, small industries were the chief attraction. Williamsport, site of the great log boom of the Susquehanna, thrived on lumber, while Montour and Columbia counties produced iron and Tioga and Northumberland counties coal, both of which were shipped on the canal networks of the region.

Meanwhile, in 1794 the Englishman Joseph Priestley, political exile and discoverer of oxygen, settled his family in Northumberland; in 1868 Christopher Sholes, born in Danville, invented the typewriter; in 1883 Thomas A. Edison installed the world's first three-wire electric-lighting system in Sunbury; and in 1846 David Wilmot of Towanda began the national struggle over slavery extension as author in the U.S. Congress of the Wilmot Proviso, a struggle that reached its climax in the Civil War of 1861-65.

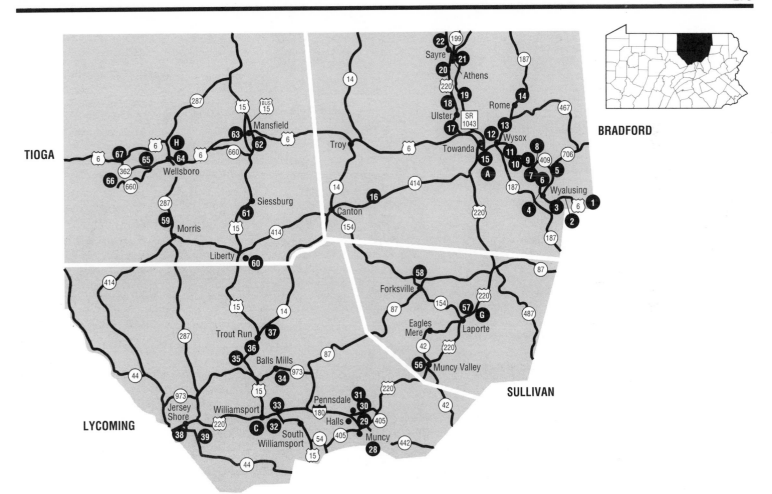

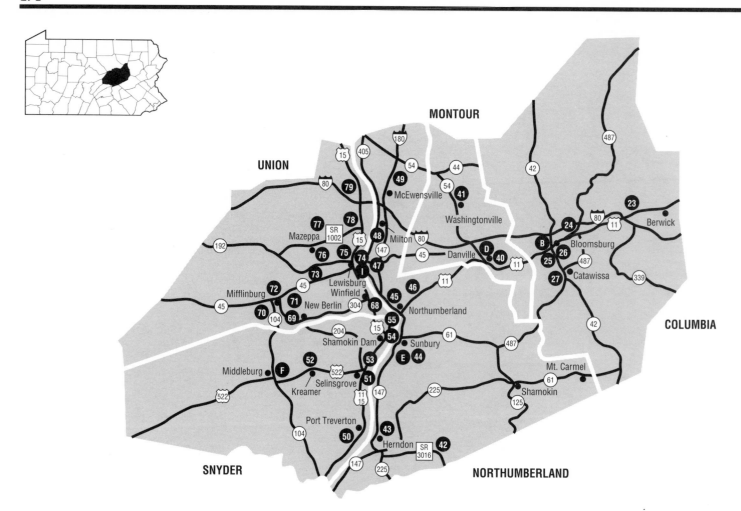

MONTOUR

UNION

COLUMBIA

SNYDER

NORTHUMBERLAND

McEwensville
Washingtonville
Berwick
Bloomsburg
Catawissa
Danville
Milton
Mazeppa
Lewisburg
Winfield
Mifflinburg
New Berlin
Northumberland
Shamokin Dam
Sunbury
Middleburg
Selinsgrove
Kreamer
Mt. Carmel
Shamokin
Port Treverton
Herndon

Bradford County

A BRADFORD COUNTY

Formed on February 21, 1810 from Lycoming and Luzerne counties. Named Ontario County until 1812; renamed for the second U.S. Attorney General, William Bradford. County seat of Towanda was incorporated 1828. Famous for Sullivan's March and David Wilmot.

City type: County Courthouse, Main St., Towanda. Dedicated July 10, 1982.

1 INDIAN HILL

The hill just southeast was the scene, Sept. 29, 1778, of a battle between Col. Thos. Hartley's men from Fort Muncy, and the Indians. Two days before, Hartley had burned Queen Esther's town near present Athens.

US 6, 4.6 miles E of Wyalusing. Erected May 12, 1947.

2 INDIAN HILL BATTLEFIELD

On September 29th, 1778 on the hill one mile southeast of this marker in the most desperate engagement between Indians and white men in Bradford County, Colonel Thomas Hartley defeated the Indians. He left Fort Muncy September 21st, on the 27th burned Tioga, Queen Esther's Town, and reached Wyalusing at eleven o'clock on the night of September 28th. Hardby on the east of this marker led the Old Warrior Path and the Sullivan Trail. This campaign ended Indian incursions in Bradford County and prepared the way for the Sullivan Expedition. Marked by the Pennsylvania Historical Commission and the Bradford County Historical Society, 1928.

Plaque: old US 6, 4 miles E of Wyalusing. Dedicated Oct. 13, 1928.

3 SULLIVAN'S MARCH

Gen. John Sullivan's army camped just west, Aug. 5-7, 1779, en route to attack the New York Iroquois. A major campaign, destroying 40 villages and ending the Indian-Tory frontier menace.

US 6, 1.4 miles SE of Wyalusing. Erected May 12, 1947.

3 THE SULLIVAN EXPEDITION AGAINST THE IROQUOIS INDIANS, 1779

Wyalusing, 10½ miles from Vanderlip's farm. Fifth encampment of Sullivan's army on the march from Wyoming to Teaoga, Aug. 6-7, 1779, was on site just west of this road marked by the Moravian Indian Town Monument. Marked by the Pennsylvania Historical Commission and Mach-Wi-Hi-Lusing Chapter, D.A.R., 1929.

Plaque: US 6, 1.4 miles SE of Wyalusing. Erected 1929.

4 WYALUSING

Named for an early town of the Munsee Delawares, which occupied the flats south of the present town. In 1760 Munsees under Papoonhank welcomed Post here, on his way toward a great Indian council beyond Allegheny River.

US 6 at Wyalusing. Erected Mar. 15, 1949.

4 WARRIORS PATH

A great Indian highway from Six Nations country, New York, to the Catawba country in the Carolinas. It made its way through the Allegheny Mountains by following the Susquehanna and Juniata valleys.

US 6, 1.3 miles N of Wyalusing. Erected Mar. 15, 1949.

5 CAMPTOWN

Stephen Foster's well-known song, "Camptown Races," was probably inspired by the horse races run from this village to Wyalusing. "The Tioga Waltz," Foster's first music, was completed during his residence in nearby Towanda and Athens in 1840-41.

Junction PA 706 & 409 at Camptown. Erected May 15, 1969.

6 LIME HILL

Here Apr. 14, 1782, a party held by Sgt. Thos. Baldwin tried to rescue a woman and her children held as Indian captives. In a four-hour battle, three children were saved but the mother was killed.

US 6 at Limehill, 3.7 miles N of Wyalusing. Erected May 12, 1947.

6 LIME HILL BATTLEFIELD

April 14, 1782, Sergeant Thomas Baldwin's party in attempting to rescue Mrs. Roswell Franklin and her four children, who had been captured by Indians, met the enemy near this spot. After four hours of fighting, three of the children were rescued but Mrs. Franklin was killed. Sergeant Baldwin's breastworks were located seventy rods northwest of this marker. Marked by the Pennsylvania Historical Commission and the Bradford County Historical Society, 1928.

Plaque: US 6, 3.7 miles N of Wyalusing. Dedicated Nov. 9, 1928.

(In August 1988, while the manuscript for this *Guide* was in preparation, the above plaque — and a companion plaque which had been privately erected — were found to have been stolen. Still in place is the large stone to which both had been attached, and efforts are under way for their recovery or replacement.)

7 CAMPTOWN RACES

Stephen Foster's title for the well-known song is said to have been taken from nearby Camptown. Foster's residence at Towanda and Athens may have created the association.

Junction US 6 & PA 409, 4.2 miles N of Wyalusing. Erected May 12, 1949.

7 AZILUM

The broad plain which can be seen from this point was the site, 1793-1803, of the French refugee colony. The Great House, built for Marie Antoinette and her son, was there and an entire village founded.

US 6, 4.5 miles N of Wyalusing at lookout. Erected May 12, 1947.

8 ASYLUM

A settlement of French royalists, who fled the French Revolution in 1793, was established in the valley directly opposite this marker. It was laid out and settled under the direction of Viscount de Noailles and Marquis Antoine Omer Talon. It was hoped that Queen Marie Antoinette might here find safety. Among many distinguished visitors to this place were Louis Philippe, Duke of Orleans, later King of France, Prince de Talleyrand, Duke de Montpensier and the Duke de la Rochefoucauld-Liancourt. Marked by the Pennsylvania Historical Commission and the Bradford County Historical Society, 1930.

Plaque: Mount Rock lookout off US 6, 5 miles N of Wyalusing. Dedicated June 24, 1930.

9 SULLIVAN'S MARCH

Gen. John Sullivan's army camped on the nearby river lowlands August 8-9, 1779, en route to attack the Six Nations Iroquois. Sixth camp between Wyoming and Fort Sullivan.

US 6, 7.2 miles NW of Wyalusing. Erected May 12, 1947.

10 THE SULLIVAN EXPEDITION AGAINST THE IROQUOIS INDIANS, 1779

Standing Stone, 9½ miles from Wyalusing. Sixth encampment of Sullivan's army on the march from Wyoming to Teaoga, August 8-9, 1779, was on river lowlands opposite the Standing Stone. Marked by the Pennsylvania Historical Commission and Lt. Asa Stephens Chapter, D.A.R., 1929.

Plaque: old US 6 (SR 2016, former LR 08023), Standing Stone. Erected 1929.

11 RURAL ELECTRIFICATION

In 1936 seventy-five percent of Pennsylvania farms had no electric service. During the next five years, with Federal support, 14 consumer-owned cooperatives were formed in the State. Claverack Rural Electric Cooperative, serving parts of eight northeastern Pennsylvania counties, was incorporated October 24, 1936.

US 6, 3.2 miles E of Wysox. Dedicated Oct. 24, 1986.

12 AZILUM

Site of the famed French refugee colony is a few miles south. Here exiles laid out a town and built La Grande Maison for the Queen and her son, the heir to the throne of France.

Junction US 6 & PA 187 at Wysox. Erected May 12, 1947.

13 LESTER FRANK WARD

"Father of American Sociology," geologist, and Civil War veteran L. F. Ward (1841-1923), spent his youth in Myersburg working with his brother, Cyrenus Osborne Ward, labor historian, in their hub factory. He has been called "the American Aristotle."

PA 187 at Myersburg. Erected Jan. 30, 1967.

14 PHILIP P. BLISS

The great singing evangelist and gospel song writer lived and taught school at one time in Bradford County. The cemetery monument was built by Sunday School gifts from England and U.S. after his death in 1876.

PA 187 in Rome at cemetery. Erected May 12, 1947.

15 DAVID WILMOT

The great Free-Soiler, who began the fight on slavery extension with the Wilmot Proviso in 1846, lived in this house. Republican Party founder; its first candidate for Governor. He died here in 1868.

US 6 (York Ave.) above Barstow Ave., Towanda. Erected May 12, 1947.

15 DAVID WILMOT

The great Free-Soiler is buried here. Born at Bethany, 1814. Studied law at Wilkes-Barre, 1834. Began practice in Towanda, his home until his death, 1868. His famed Wilmot Proviso introduced August 8, 1846.

William St. at Riverside Cemetery, Towanda. Erected May 12, 1947.

15 STEPHEN FOSTER

The great writer of folk songs and ballads lived in Towanda in 1840-41. He attended Towanda Academy on the hill a short time and stayed with his brother William, a canal official.

US 6 (Main St.) near State St., Towanda. Erected May 12, 1947.

16 SHESHEQUIN PATH

A branch of the Warriors Path. Left the Susquehanna at Sheshequin, now Ulster; crossed Sugar Creek; and by valleys of Towanda and Lycoming Creeks reached West Branch, near present Montoursville, where it joined the Shamokin Path.

PA 414 near Le Roy, 5.6 miles SW of West Franklin. Erected Mar. 16, 1949.

17 SHESHEQUIN PATH

Indian trail joining the Iroquois country and the Shamokin area, passed near here. Conrad Weiser took this route to Onondaga, capital of the League, to represent the Province in council with the Iroquois.

US 220, 3.1 miles NW of Towanda. Erected Sept. 6, 1948.

18 SULLIVAN'S MARCH

Gen. John Sullivan's army camped on the Sheshequin Flats opposite, Aug. 9-10, 1779. The seventh and last overnight stop on the way to Tioga Point.

US 220, 1.3 miles N of Ulster. Erected Mar. 15, 1949.

19 THE SULLIVAN EXPEDITION AGAINST THE IROQUOIS INDIANS, 1779

Sheshecunnunck, 15 miles from Standing Stone. Seventh and last encampment of Sullivan's army on march from Wyoming to Teaoga, August 10, 1779, lay on these lowlands by the river. Marked by the Pennsylvania Historical Commission and the Tioga Point Chapter, D.A.R., 1929.

Plaque: E side of SR 1043 (former LR 08077) in Sheshequin Twp., 1.2 miles N of the bridge into Ulster. Erected 1929.

19 SULLIVAN'S MARCH

Same text as Sullivan's March just above.

SR 1043 near plaque immediately above. Erected May 12, 1947.

20 [TEAOGA AND QUEEN ESTHER'S TOWN]

Teaoga, a watch town: The south door of Iroquois Long House was situated on the point at the meeting of the rivers 200 rods to the northeast. Queen Esther's Town of the Delaware Indians was 100 rods to the east along the Chemung River bank. Both towns were destroyed by Colonel Thomas Hartley and his troops, September 27, 1778. These flats for five miles known as Queen Esther's Flats were grazing grounds for their herds. Marked by the Pennsylvania Historical Commission and Tioga Point Chapter, Daughters of the American Revolution, Athens, Pa., 1928.

Plaque: US 220 (E side) .3 mile N of Milan. Erected 1928.

21 COLONEL JOHN FRANKLIN

Leader of Connecticut land claimants. Served in Sullivan Campaign, 1779. Imprisoned in 1787-89 for leading new state movement. Later served in Pa. legislature. Moved here in 1789; died in 1831. Homesite and grave are east of road.

SR 1043 (former LR 08077) 1.2 miles SE of Athens at cemetery. Dedicated Sept. 23, 1959.

Entering Athens

21 ATHENS

Known also as Tioga Point. Connecticut settlers laid out the village in 1786. Site of ancient Indian village of Teaoga. Base for the Sullivan campaign into central N.Y. Gateway from southern N.Y. into Pennsylvania for centuries.

PA 199 (old US 220) at Athens. Erected May 12, 1947.

21 TEAOGA

This strategic locality between the Chemung and the Susquehanna shows signs of age-old residence by various Indian groups. Graves of an Andaste chief and his followers were unearthed here in 1883-95.

PA 199, S end Chemung River bridge into Athens. Erected Sept. 6, 1948.

21 CARRYING PATH

Here the Indian voyager down the Chemung lifted his canoe and carried it a hundred and ninety yards across the neck to ascend the Susquehanna.

PA 199 at Chemung River bridge into Athens. Erected Sept. 6, 1948.

21 THE CARRYING PATH

Here was the western end of the Indian carrying path from the Chemung to the Susquehanna River. The eastern end was 190 rods southeast. Fort Sullivan was built across this path. Marked by the Pennsylvania Historical Commission and the Tioga Point Chapter, D.A.R., 1929.

Plaque: PA 199 at N end of bridge into Athens. Erected 1929.

21 FORT SULLIVAN

Here, between the Chemung and Susquehanna commanding both rivers, Gen. John Sullivan built a fort Aug. 18, 1779. With a camp on the flats, it was base for the central N.Y. campaign and defeat of the Tory-Indian alliance.

PA 199 in southern Athens. Erected May 12, 1947.

21 [FORT SULLIVAN ''SOLDIERS' BURIAL'']

Here within the confines of Fort Sullivan were buried, August 14, 1779, several soldiers killed the previous day in a skirmish at Chemung as attested by Solomon Talada, soldier in the ranks, who returned to live in Athens the rest of his life. This statement was corroborated by finding skeletons previous to 1839. Marked by the Pennsylvania Historical Commission and the Tioga Point Chapter, D.A.R., 1929.

Plaque: 731 S. Main St., Athens. Erected 1929.

21 THE SULLIVAN EXPEDITION AGAINST THE IROQUOIS INDIANS, 1779

Teaoga, Indian village, 3 miles distant from Sheshecunnunck. Site of Sullivan's army encampment, August 11-26, 1779, lay one and one-fourth miles south of this point. Marked by the Pennsylvania Historical Commission and the Tioga Point Chapter, D.A.R., 1929.

Plaque: corner Tioga (PA 199) & Main Sts., Athens. Erected 1929.

21 STEPHEN FOSTER

America's beloved writer of folk tunes and ballads attended, 1840-41, Athens Academy which stood here. The Tioga Waltz, Foster's first music, was composed at that time.

PA 199 (old US 220) in Athens. Erected May 12, 1947.

Leaving Athens

22 PINE PLAINS

This area was known by pioneers as the ''Pine Plains.'' In 1790 near this spot Timothy Pickering met Red Jacket and his Senecas. They were on the way to the peace council at Tioga Point.

PA 199 (Keystone Ave.), Sayre-South Waverly borough line. Erected May 12, 1947.

Columbia County

B COLUMBIA COUNTY
Formed March 22, 1813 out of Northumberland County. Named in honor of America. County seat, Bloomsburg, became this State's only incorporated town in 1870. A Friends meetinghouse was built at Catawissa about 1789. "Twin covered bridges" at Forks are a unique site.
City type: County Courthouse, Main St., Bloomsburg. Dedicated July 11, 1983.

23 FORT JENKINS
A stockaded house used as a settler's refuge was situated here on the bank overlooking the river, 1778-80, when it was destroyed by the Indians. The land was later owned by James Wilson, an author of the Constitution.
Old US 11 (SR 1004, former LR 19117) 6.5 miles NE of Bloomsburg. Erected May 8, 1948.

24 FORT WHEELER
A stockade-type fort was built here in 1778 along Fishing Creek by Moses Van Campen. It served during the Revolution as a refuge against the Indians, by whom it was once attacked. Van Campen was the noted Indian scout of this region.
PA 487, 1.2 miles NE of Bloomsburg. Erected May 10, 1948.

25 WYOMING PATH
Important path linking the many Indian settlements in the Wyoming Valley with Shamokin, now Sunbury. In 1742 Count Zinzendorf, organizer of Moravian missions, came this way after visiting the Shawnees at Wyoming.
US 11 at Fairgrounds, Bloomsburg. Erected May 3, 1949.

25 FORT McCLURE
Early in 1781 the McClure house was stockaded by the noted Indian fighter, Moses Van Campen, to protect settlers in this region after destruction of Fort Jenkins in 1780. Site on the north bank of the Susquehanna in present Bloomsburg.
US 11 at Fairgrounds, Bloomsburg. Erected May 8, 1948.

26 CATAWISSA FRIENDS MEETING
At Catawissa, three miles distant, is the Friends meetinghouse built about 1790. The log structure is still standing and is a fine example of a pioneer place of worship.
Junction US 11 & PA 42, .7 mile SW of Bloomsburg. Erected May 8, 1948.

27 CATAWISSA FRIENDS MEETING
The nearby Friends meetinghouse, built about 1790, was the place of worship for early Quaker settlers among the pioneers of this region. Catawissa itself was laid out by William Hughes, a Berks County Quaker.
South St. between 3rd & 4th Sts., Catawissa. Erected May 10, 1948.

Lycoming County

C LYCOMING COUNTY
Formed April 13, 1795 out of Northumberland County. The name (from a Delaware Indian word) honors Lycoming Creek. Williamsport, the county seat, became a borough, 1806, and a city, 1866. Once a great lumbering center. Birthplace of Little League Baseball.
City type: County Courthouse, W. 3rd St., Williamsport. Dedicated Apr. 13, 1981.

28 MUNCY MILLS
The nearby memorial is at the site of this valley's first grist mill. It was built by John Alward about 1772 and burned by Indians 1779. Other mills built on the site in 1783 and 1800. Last mill was used until 1872.
Junction PA 405 & 442 E of Muncy. Erected May 28, 1947.

29 MUNCY
Laid out, 1799, by Benjamin McCarty. Named for the Monsey Indians, tribe of Delawares, who inhabited this area before arrival of the whites. Four Indian paths — Shamokin, Wyalusing, Wyoming, Towanda — formed a junction here.
PA 405 E & SR 2014 (old PA 147) N of Muncy. Erected Jan. 21, 1952.

29 CAPT. JOHN BRADY

The famed Indian fighter and hero of the colonial wars and the Revolution was killed in ambush by Indians near here April 11, 1779. He commanded Fort Brady at present Muncy at the time.

SR 2014 (old PA 147) .8 mile N of Muncy. Erected May 28, 1947.

30 PENNSYLVANIA CANAL (WEST BRANCH DIVISION)

This Division, built 1828-1834, extended from Northumberland to Farrandsville. Used to Lock Haven until 1889, to Muncy Dam until 1901. Beyond the woods to the south, 1400 feet of vertical wall, 22 feet high, built along the river, support the old towpath.

Near junction SR 2014 (old PA 147) & SR 2036 (old US 220), Halls. Erected July 9, 1952.

31 PENNSDALE MEETING

The Friends Meeting House opposite was built in 1799. It was erected to provide a place of worship for the numerous Quaker settlers of this region.

Junction SR 2051 (former LR 41054) & township road (former LR 41154) near Pennsdale. Erected May 1947.

32 SUSQUEHANNA LOG BOOM

Six-mile series of piers, built by a company incorporated in 1846; used to collect and store logs during spring log drives down the West Branch. Helped make Williamsport the world's lumber capital prior to 1900. Badly damaged in 1889 flood, the boom declined thereafter.

US 15 just S of Williamsport. Erected Dec. 19, 1962.

33 WILLIAMSPORT

Laid out 1795 by Michael Ross. Incorporated as a borough 1806; as a city 1866. At one time a leading lumber center of the nation. Trade and travel center for over a century.

On main highways leading into city. Erected May 1947.

34 BLOOMING GROVE DUNKARD MEETING HOUSE

Built 1828 by German colonists who came to this valley beginning 1805 seeking religious freedom, led by Dr. Frederick Haller and including the following families: Heim-Ulmer-Staiger-Waltz-Kiess-Young-Harmon-Gross-Biehl-Scheel-Burghardt. Marked by the Pennsylvania Historical Commission and the Lycoming Historical Society, 1930.

Plaque: meetinghouse 2 miles E of Balls Mills, .7 mile S of PA 973. Dedicated Aug. 8, 1931.

35 SHESHEQUIN PATH

Branch of Warriors Path; provided a short cut from Tioga to the Great Island, traversing "the dismal wilderness" of Lycoming Creek. Dense forest, swamp, windfall, and storm made Indians believe a demon had power in this valley.

US 15, 2.2 miles S of Trout Run. Erected Mar. 1949.

36 WILLIAMSON ROAD

Built in 1792-96 by land agent Charles Williamson to open the Genesee lands in N.Y. From Trout Run, it cut through the wilderness to Lawrenceville by the same general route as the present highway.

US 15 at Trout Run. Erected May 1947.

37 SHESHEQUIN PATH

By this path up Lycoming Creek, Conrad Weiser, with Lewis Evans, map-maker, and John Bartram, botanist, traveled to Onondaga in 1743 on a peace mission for Virginia: "To take the hatchet out of the head of the Six Nations."

PA 14, 1.4 miles NE of Trout Run. Erected Mar. 1949.

38 FORT ANTES

Built 1776 by Col. Henry Antes. Site on opposite side of the river at the mouth of Antes Creek. Nearby was Antes Mill, first in the region. The stockade was abandoned during the Great Runaway; burned by Indians.

Main & Seminary Sts. (on old US 220). Erected May 1947.

38 PINE CREEK PRESBYTERIAN CHURCH

Just south along Pine Creek was the site of the first Presbyterian Church in this area, organized in 1792. It was the ancestor of the Jersey Shore Presbyterian Church, organized in 1851.

SR 3028 (old US 220) .5 mile SW of Jersey Shore. Erected Feb. 25, 1949.

39 [ANTES FORT]

About one half of a mile southwest of this spot, on the high bluff above the river, stood the stockade known as Antes Fort. Erected by Lieut. Col. John Henry Antes in the summer of 1777. This fort was an important rallying point for the settlers in this region. It was destroyed by the Indians and Tories in July, 1778, at the time of the big runaway, when the entire valley was abandoned by the white settlers. In memory of the following who lost their lives during the Indian raids in this region. At Fort Antes, July 1777: Zephaniah Miller, Abel Cady, James Armstrong, Isaac Bouser. At Fort Horn, July 1778: Robert Fleming, Robin Donaldson, James McMichael. Erected by the Pennsylvania Historical Commission and the Fort Antes Chapter, Daughters of the American Revolution, 1917.

Plaque: PA 44, 1 mile E of Jersey Shore. Dedicated June 8, 1917.

40 CHRISTOPHER SHOLES

Typewriter inventor, born at Mooresburg, Feb. 14, 1819. Went to school and worked as a printer at Danville. Migrated to Wisconsin at the age of 20. His first writing machine patent was issued June 23, 1868.

US 11 in Danville at Mahoning Creek. Erected Mar. 23, 1948.

40 FIRST IRON RAILS

The first rolling mill built to make the iron T railroad rails was nearby. T rails were first rolled Oct. 8, 1845. The first 30 foot rails made on order in the U.S. were rolled here in 1859 for the Sunbury and Erie Railroad.

US 11 in Danville at Mahoning Creek. Erected May 12, 1947.

41 FORT BOSLEY

Located in the forks of the Chillisquaque on east bank of the north branch. Here in 1777 a small force stockaded and garrisoned Bosley's mill for protection against Indian marauders.

PA 54 at Washingtonville. Erected May 12, 1947.

Montour County

D MONTOUR COUNTY

Formed May 3, 1850 from Columbia County. Named for the Indian woman leader, Madame Montour. Site of the first manufacture of iron T rails for railroads. Inventor of typewriter, Christopher Sholes, born here. County seat, Danville, was incorporated 1849.

City type: County Courthouse, Mill St., Danville. Dedicated Nov. 10, 1982.

40 MONTGOMERY HOUSE

Built in 1792 as the residence of General William Montgomery, pioneer settler and father of the founder of Danville. The house is now occupied by the Montour County Historical Society.

City type: 1 Bloom St., Danville. Erected May 6, 1952.

Northumberland County

E NORTHUMBERLAND COUNTY

Formed March 21, 1772 from Lancaster, Cumberland, Berks, Bedford and Northampton counties. Some 27 counties today occupy its once vast area. Sunbury, the county seat, was laid out 1772. Site of Fort Augusta, a key post built 1756-57.

City type: Courthouse, 2nd & Market Sts., Sunbury. Dedicated July 13, 1982.

42 TULPEHOCKEN PATH

At Mahantango Gap, seen to the south, was the Double Eagle, a stopping place on the Indian path that ran from Shamokin (Sunbury) at the Forks of the Susquehanna to Weiser's in the Tulpehocken Valley, and on to Philadelphia.

SR 3016 (former LR 49008) N of Klingerstown. Erected Jan 11, 1950.

43 TULPEHOCKEN PATH
The Indian Ambassadors Road turned east near here over the hills to the Tulpehocken Valley. Used by Iroquois chiefs from Onondaga, now Syracuse, carrying peace wampum from the "Fire that Never Dies" to Philadelphia. Often traveled by Shickellamy.
PA 147 N of Herndon. Erected Nov. 10, 1950.

Entering Sunbury

44 SUNBURY
Laid out 1772 as the county seat of Northumberland on the site of Indian Shamokin by Surveyor-General Lukens and William Maclay. Borough incorporation Mar. 24, 1797. Here Fort Augusta was built in 1756.
On main highways leading into city. Erected Oct. 30, 1947.

44 DANVILLE-POTTSVILLE R.R.
Opened Sunbury to Paxinos in 1835, operated on wood rails by horsepower. Steam locomotive first used in 1838; and iron rails, 1853. The terminal was nearby and here anthracite was loaded on canal boats for shipment to Philadelphia-Baltimore.
PA 147 (Front St.), Sunbury. Erected Nov. 21, 1947.

44 WILLIAM MACLAY
Lived in the house opposite, 1773-86, and then moved to Harrisburg. Member of first U.S. Senate; wrote a famous Journal of its debates. A critic of Washington and Hamilton; pioneer leader of Jeffersonian democracy. He helped survey Sunbury, 1772.
PA 147 (Front St.), Sunbury. Erected Oct. 1, 1947.

44 FIRST ELECTRIC LIGHT
First successful use of a three-wire electric lighting system was made July 4, 1883, in the City Hotel building in Sunbury. Thomas A. Edison directed the work. The Edison Electric Illuminating Co. plant was at 4th and Vine Streets.
PA 147 (Front St.) at Market St., Sunbury. Erected Oct. 30, 1947.

44 SHIKELLAMY
Oneida chief and overseer or vice-regent of the Six Nations asserting Iroquois dominion over conquered Delaware and other tribes. He lived at Shamokin Indian town, Sunbury, from about 1728 until his death, 1748. Said to be buried near hear.
PA 147 (Front St.) at Fort Augusta site, Sunbury. Erected Oct. 1, 1947.

44 THOMPSON'S RIFLE BATTALION: CAPT. JOHN LOWDON'S COMPANY
Recruited from nearby points in June 1775, Lowdon's Company was a part of the first battalion in the colonies authorized by Congress. Among those who entered Continental service in this company was Timothy Murphy, whose many feats of marksmanship were to make him a hero of the Revolution.
PA 147 (Front St.) at Hunter Home, Fort Augusta site, Sunbury. Dedicated June 3, 1987.

44 FORT AUGUSTA
Built in 1756-57 by Cols. Burd and Clapham and the key frontier outpost of the region. Mansion built 1852.
PA 147 (Front St.) at site, Sunbury. Erected [1948].

44 FORT AUGUSTA
First selected as rendezvous for the Sullivan Expedition, Lt. Col. Adam Hubley's command. The only regiment quartered here to march against the Six Nations. Marked by the Pennsylvania Historical Commission, 1929.
Plaque: PA 147 (Front St.) at site, Sunbury. Dedicated July 27, 1929.

44 [SHIKELLAMY]
Erected as a memorial to Shikellamy, also Swataney, "Our Enlightener," the representative of the Six Nations in this Province. First sent to Shamokin (Sunbury) in 1728; appointed Vice-Gerent in 1745. Died Dec. 6, 1748, he was buried near this spot. This diplomat and statesman was a firm friend of the Province of Pennsylvania. Erected by the Fort Augusta Chapter, D. A. R., in co-operation with the Pennsylvania Historical Commission, June, 1915.
Plaque: PA 147 (Front St.), Sunbury, just N of Fort Augusta site. Dedicated Oct. 15, 1915.

44 THE BLOODY SPRING

Here, during the French and Indian War (1754-1763), one colonial soldier venturing from the garrison at nearby Fort Augusta, was fatally shot by an Indian foe. His blood is said to have crimsoned its waters.

N. 7th St. Extension between Shikellamy Ave. & Memorial Park, Sunbury. Erected June 14, 1967.

Leaving Sunbury

45 PENNSYLVANIA CANAL

The North Branch and West Branch Divisions, built 1828-34, joined here in Northumberland at a canal basin. Boats with coal from Nanticoke or lumber from Williamsport locked down into the river nearby and re-entered the Canal on the west bank.

US 11 Northumberland near E end of bridge. Erected June 17, 1952.

45 JOSEPH PRIESTLEY HOUSE

Home, 1794-1804, of the noted English scientist. Administered by the Pennsylvania Historical and Museum Commission.

472 Priestley Ave., Northumberland. Erected Sept. 19, 1963.

Joseph Priestley House, Northumberland

46 JOSEPH PRIESTLEY

The noted English scientist, discoverer of oxygen, and Unitarian theologian lived in Northumberland, 1794 to 1804. His home and laboratory along the river are now a Priestley memorial and museum.

US 11 NE of Northumberland. Erected Oct. 3, 1947.

46 WYOMING PATH

Section of the Iroquois Warriors Path, following the Susquehanna from the Wyoming Valley to Shamokin, now Sunbury. U.S. 11 follows its general route. South of here the trail crossed to Shamokin Island.

US 11 NE of Northumberland. Erected Mar. 23, 1949.

46 PENNSYLVANIA CANAL (NORTH BRANCH DIVISION)

This Division, built 1829-32, carried coal, until 1901, from Nanticoke mines to Northumberland, and from there to inland towns and seaport cities. From Lackawanna Creek downwards, there were 2 dams, 14 locks, and 7 aqueducts. Traces of towpath and canal bed can be seen here.

US 11, 3.5 miles NE of Northumberland. Erected June 17, 1952.

47 GREAT SHAMOKIN PATH

This Indian highway followed the West Branch of the Susquehanna to the Great Island at Lock Haven. From there it crossed the mountains by way of Snow Shoe to Chinklacamoose, Punxsutawney, and Kittanning.

PA 405, 3.9 miles S of Milton. Erected Oct. 1949.

47 CAPTAIN JOHN BRADY

Pioneer surveyor, Indian fighter and patriot resided here, 1769 to 1776, when he moved to Muncy Manor, later known as Fort Brady. He served in the French and Indian War, in the Pontiac War was Captain of the Second Pennsylvania Regiment, and in the Revolutionary War raised a company in the Twelfth Regiment Continental Line, of which he was Captain. Seriously wounded in the Battle of Germantown. He was murdered by Indians, April 11, 1779 on Wolf Run near Fort Brady while home on sick leave. Marked by the Pennsylvania Historical Commission and the Northumberland County Historical Society, 1928.

Plaque: PA 405 (E side) .5 mile S of intersection PA 45. Dedicated Sept. 22, 1928.

47 BUCKNELL UNIVERSITY
Organized in 1846 as the University at Lewisburg by the Baptist Church. Named Bucknell University in 1886, honoring William Bucknell, donor and trustee. Degrees first conferred upon women students in 1885.
Junction PA 405 & 45, 3 miles S of Milton. Erected Sept. 22, 1947.

48 SHIKELLAMY'S TOWN
The earlier residence of the noted Oneida chief was near here. As the Six Nations' overseer or vice-regent of the Delaware and other refugee Indians, he spent the most of his time from 1728 to 1748 at Shamokin, now Sunbury, where he died.
PA 405, .5 mile S of Milton. Erected Oct. 6, 1947.

48 JAMES POLLOCK
Governor of Pennsylvania, 1855-58, was born in Milton, 1810. State debt reduced during his term by sale of State-owned canals and railroads. As Director of Mint, prepared, 1864, the motto ''In God We Trust'' for coins. Died at Lock Haven in 1880.
PA 405, .2 mile N of Milton. Erected June 20, 1951.

49 WARRIOR RUN CHURCH
Named for Indian occupation of the region. Presbyterian landmark. A log church was here in 1789. The present building erected in 1835. Restored in 1947 by Warrior Run Chapter D.A.R., aided by descendants and friends.
SR 1007 (old PA 147) at site N of McEwensville. Erected Feb. 18, 1947.

49 COL. MATTHEW SMITH
Captain of Lancaster Co. militia with Col. Benedict Arnold on 1775 midwinter march to Quebec. In 1779, served as Vice-President of Pennsylvania Council. Died in 1794; buried here in an unmarked grave.
SR 1007 (old PA 147) at Warrior Run Church N of McEwensville. Erected Mar. 9, 1949.

49 FORT FREELAND
Mill built 1773, stockaded 1778 by Jacob Freeland. Attacked, captured and destroyed by British Tories and Seneca Indians; 108 settlers killed or taken prisoners, July 28, 1779. Marked by the Pennsylvania Historical Commission, 1929.
Plaque: SR 1007 (old PA 147), Warrior Run Church N of McEwensville. Dedicated July 27, 1929.

Snyder County

F SNYDER COUNTY
Formed March 2, 1855 out of Union County. The name honors Simon Snyder (Governor, 1808-17) who made his home in Selinsgrove. The county seat of Middleburg was laid out 1800, incorporated 1864. County was scene of the Penns Creek Massacre of 1755.
City type: County Courthouse, W. Market St. (US 522), Middleburg. Dedicated Dec. 1, 1982.

50 PENNSYLVANIA CANAL (SUSQUEHANNA DIVISION)
At this point, highway crosses Port Trevorton Canal Basin. Coal from mines about 15 miles to the east crossed the river on the Trevorton, Mahanoy and Susquehanna Railroad bridge from 1855-70 and was transshipped here to canal boats.
US 11 & 15 at Port Trevorton. Erected June 6, 1952.

51 SIMON SNYDER
Three times Governor of the State, 1808-17, and member Assembly, 1797 to 1808, lived in Selinsgrove during that period. Died Nov. 9, 1819, in his home on Market St., which still stands. Buried First Lutheran Church cemetery.
SR 2017 (old US 11 & 15) just S of Selinsgrove. Erected Sept. 30, 1947.

51 **[SIMON SNYDER MANSION]**

This house was built in 1816 by Simon Snyder, Governor of Pennsylvania, and was occupied by him until his death. Placed by the Pennsylvania Historical Commission and the Snyder County Historical Society, 1918.

Plaque: 121 N. Market St. (old US 11 & 15), Selinsgrove. Dedicated May 14, 1918.

51 **COXEY'S ARMY**

Jacob Sechler Coxey (1854-1951) was born here. In 1894 he led a march of unemployed workers, popularly known as ''Coxey's Army,'' on Washington. Public works programs and relief measures were asked. This focused attention on the plight of the unemployed.

814 N. Market St. (old US 11 & 15), Selinsgrove. Erected Sept. 9, 1966.

51 **PENNS CREEK MASSACRE**

October 16, 1755, a band of Indians ambushed and killed, wounded, or took captive some 26 settlers of this region. The attack was just west along Penns Creek, and first to follow Braddock's defeat.

SR 2017 (old US 11 & 15) just N of Selinsgrove. Erected Sept. 30, 1947.

52 **SCHOCH BLOCKHOUSE**

This pioneer refuge during the Revolutionary War era was located at a spring 300 yards south. Built on Matthias Schoch's tract about 1770 and in use until 1783.

US 522 at Kreamer. Erected Sept. 30, 1947.

53 **SUSQUEHANNA UNIVERSITY**

Founded 1858 by the Evangelical Lutheran Church as the Missionary Institute and Susquehanna Female College. The present corporate title was adopted in 1895.

US 522, .5 mile W of old US 11 & 15, Selinsgrove. Erected June 17, 1948.

53 **ALBANY PURCHASE**

The NE corner of the land deeded the Proprietors by the Six Nations in great council at Albany, July 6, 1754, was 1 mile north of Penns Creek. It ran thence ''North of the West as far as your Province extends.''

US 522 (old US 11 & 15) 1 mile N of Selinsgrove. Erected Sept. 30, 1947.

53 **[PENNS CREEK MASSACRE]**

In commemoration of the (John) Penn's Creek Massacre, which occurred along this stream on October 16, 1755, when the settlers were attacked by the Indians and about 26 killed, wounded or carried into captivity. This was the first Indian outbreak within the Province of Pennsylvania following the defeat of General Edward Braddock, in the French and Indian War. Erected by the joint action of the Pennsylvania Historical Commission and the Snyder County Historical Society, October 16, 1915.

Plaque: S end Old Trail (just E of US 11 & 15), Penns Creek N of Selinsgrove. Dedicated Oct. 15, 1915.

53 **[HARRIS AMBUSH]**

On October 25, 1755, John Harris, founder of Harrisburg, and a party of 40 men, who came up the river to investigate the (John) Penns Creek Massacre, were ambushed by a party of Indians near the mouth of this creek, at the head of the Isle of Que, about one-third of a mile south of this spot. Erected by the joint action of the Pennsylvania Historical Commission and the Snyder County Historical Society, October 16, 1915.

Plaque: on stone with previous plaque. Dedicated Oct. 15, 1915.

Susquehanna University, Selinsgrove

54 SUNBURY
Laid out 1772 as the county seat of Northumberland on the site of Indian Shamokin by Surveyor-General Lukens and William Maclay. Borough incorporation Mar. 24, 1797. Here Fort Augusta was built in 1756. Historic center of travel, trade and industry.
US 11 & 15, 4 miles N of Selinsgrove at Sunbury bridge. Erected Sept. 15, 1948.

55 SHIKELLAMY
Oneida chief and overseer or vice-regent of the Six Nations asserting Iroquois dominion over conquered Delaware and other tribes. He lived at Shamokin Indian town, Sunbury, from about 1728 until his death, 1748. Said to be buried near here.
US 11, 5.4 miles N of Selinsgrove, entrance Shikellamy State Park. Erected Nov. 30, 1947.

Sullivan County

G SULLIVAN COUNTY
Formed March 15, 1847 from Lycoming County. Named for State Senator Charles C. Sullivan, who was active in securing its creation. Laporte, the county seat, was incorporated 1853. County is home of Eagles Mere (long a noted resort) and Worlds End State Park.
City type: Courthouse, Main & Muncy Sts., Laporte. Dedicated Aug. 18, 1982.

56 WYALUSING PATH
An Indian path from Wyalusing on the North Branch of the Susquehanna, ran down Muncy Creek to the West Branch. Christian Indians, led by the Moravian Bishop Ettwein, came west over this path in 1772 to found a "City of Peace" on the Beaver River.
US 220 at Beech Glen 1 mile S of Muncy Valley. Erected Jan. 12, 1951.

57 CELESTA
Name of religious community founded by Peter Armstrong. Site is 2 miles west. In 1864, he and his wife deeded about 600 acres to "Almighty God and His heirs in Jesus Messiah, for their proper use and behoof forever." Armstrong died in 1884.
US 220 just NE of Laporte. Erected July 12, 1951.

58 OLD WOOLEN FACTORY
A short distance SE, along the Loyalsock, is the site of old factory established in 1810 by Samuel Rogers, Jr. During the War of 1812, it made kersey cloth for the army. Flood in 1816 stopped operation of the factory.
Junction PA 87 & 154, Forksville. Erected Jan. 12, 1951.

58 RURAL ELECTRIFICATION
In 1936 seventy-five percent of Pennsylvania farms had no electric service. During the next five years, with Federal support, 14 consumer-owned cooperatives were formed in this State. Sullivan County Rural Electric Cooperative, serving users in Sullivan, Lycoming and Bradford counties, was incorporated Dec. 3, 1936.
PA 87 just SW of PA 154, Forksville. Dedicated Sept. 25, 1987.

Tioga County

H TIOGA COUNTY
Formed March 26, 1804 from Lycoming County. The name, derived from an Indian word meaning "the forks of a stream," honors the Tioga River. Wellsboro, the county seat, was laid out in 1806; incorporated 1830. On Pine Creek is Pennsylvania's Grand Canyon.
City type: Courthouse Sq., PA 287 & 660, Wellsboro. Dedicated Mar. 26, 1982.

59 BLOSSBURG COAL

From 1840-90, ''Bloss'' coal from the mines of the nearby region was widely known and used as smithing and steam coal. Tioga in those years was a leading county in bituminous coal production in the U.S.

PA 287, 3.5 miles N of Morris. Erected July 25, 1947.

60 WILLIAMSON ROAD

At Liberty was located a storage depot known as the Block House. It was built of logs, about 20 x 40 feet in size. Supplies were kept there and bread baked for the road builders, 1792-96.

SR 2005 (old US 15) just S of Liberty. Erected July 25, 1947. (For background see Williamson Road, Lycoming County.)

61 COAL DISCOVERY

While acting as scouts for the Williamson Road party in 1792, Robert and Benjamin Patterson discovered coal at present-day Blossburg. The first drift to mine the coal was opened on Bear Creek by David Clemons about 1815.

US 15 just S of Blossburg. Erected 1975 (revised 1947 marker).

61 WILLIAM B. WILSON

First secretary of labor in 1913-21, Congressman, and labor leader, spent the greater part of his life here. He was born in Scotland, 1862, worked in the Arnot mines, rising to prominence as a labor stateman. His home is opposite. Died in 1934.

US 15 just S of Blossburg. Erected Oct. 29, 1948.

62 WILLIAMSON ROAD

Here the road builders late in 1792 ended work. After facing starvation, they were rescued by canoes and supplies from Painted Post. Canoe Camp derived its name from the incident.

Business US 15 S of Mansfield at Canoe Camp. Erected July 25, 1947.

63 CORNING & BLOSSBURG RAILROAD

One of the early railroads in the Northeast was completed in 1840 from Corning, N. Y., to Blossburg. It was built by the Tioga Navigation Company to connect the Chemung Canal, and the Erie Railroad, with the local coal fields.

City type: S. Main St. (Business US 15), Mansfield. Erected June 4, 1983 (revised 1947 marker).

63 RURAL ELECTRIFICATION

In 1936 seventy-five percent of Pennsylvania farms had no electric service. During the next five years, with Federal support, 14 consumer-owned cooperatives were formed in the State. Tri-County Rural Electric Cooperative, serving much of north-central Pennsylvania from Mansfield, was incorporated October 24, 1936.

N. Main St. (Business US 15), Mansfield. Dedicated Oct. 24, 1986.

64 WILLIAM A. STONE

Governor of Pennsylvania, 1899-1903; Congressman in 1891-99, was born two and one-half miles SW of here Apr. 18, 1846. Graduate of Mansfield Normal. Began law practice in Wellsboro, 1870. Moved to Pittsburgh, 1877. Died Mar. 1, 1920.

Courthouse Sq., PA 287 & 660, Wellsboro. Erected Sept. 1, 1948.

64 NESSMUK

Nessmuk was the pen name of pioneer conservationist and woodsman George Washington Sears (1821-1890), a resident of Wellsboro. Noted chiefly as the author of first book on woodcraft, Sears was also a poet, adventurer, canoeist and outdoor writer.

Courthouse Sq., PA 660, Wellsboro. Erected Oct. 10, 1972.

65 WILLIAM A. STONE

Governor of Pennsylvania, 1899-1903; Congressman in 1891-99; was born two and one-half miles SE of here Apr. 18, 1846. Graduate of Mansfield Normal. Began law practice in Wellsboro, 1870. Moved to Pittsburgh, 1877. Died Mar. 1, 1920.

PA 362, 3.5 miles SW of Wellsboro. Erected Sept. 1, 1948.

66 NESSMUK

The pen name of poet, woodsman, out-door writer and pioneer conservationist George Washington Sears (1821-1890), a resident of Wellsboro, Pa. From near this spot he wrote the first prose and verse descriptions of the Pine Creek Gorge.

End of PA 660, Leonard Harrison State Park. Erected 1972.

67 PINE CREEK PATH

A Seneca trail from the Genesee to the Susquehanna at Jersey Shore, forked one mile south of here. One branch ran through the gorge of Pine Creek; the other crossed the hills, following Darling Run and Baby Creek back to Pine Creek at Blackwell.

US 6 at Ansonia. Erected Nov. 2, 1951.

Union County

1 UNION COUNTY

Formed March 22, 1813 out of Northumberland County. Its name honors the Federal Union. The county seat was first Mifflinburg, and after 1815 it was New Berlin. Lewisburg, county seat since 1855, was incorporated 1822 and is home of Bucknell University.

City type: County Courthouse, 2nd & St. Louis Sts., Lewisburg. Dedicated May 10, 1982.

68 LEE MASSACRE

Major John Lee and his entire family, with the exception of a son Robert, were massacred near here by an Indian war party on August 16, 1782.

US 15 at Winfield, just S of PA 304. Erected Apr. 28, 1947.

69 DRY RUN CEMETERY

Opposite on the bluff at Penns Creek lay Buffalo Valley's pioneer cemetery. Abandoned 1791 after a generation of use, it held graves of veterans of the French and Indian War and of the Revolution.

PA 304, 1 mile W of New Berlin. Erected June 9, 1948.

69 EVANGELICAL CHURCH

The first church built by ''Albright's People,'' later the Evangelical Association, was erected in New Berlin in 1816. It was the first Evangelical Church in the United States. The site is marked by a monument.

PA 304, 1.2 miles W of New Berlin. Erected Sept. 22, 1947.

70 LEROY MASSACRE

Near here John Jacob Leroy was killed by Indians on Oct. 16, 1755, following the Penns Creek Massacre. This was the first Indian hostility in the region after Braddock's defeat.

PA 104, 1.5 miles S of Mifflinburg. Erected Apr. 28, 1947.

71 [LeROY MASSACRE]

John Jacob LeRoy was killed by the Indians near this spot during the time of the Penns Creek Massacre, October 16, 1755. This was the first act of hostility by the Indians of this Province following the defeat of General Edward Braddock, July 9, 1755. A daughter of John Jacob LeRoy, Marie, and Barbara Leininger were taken to the Muskingum in Ohio, from which they escaped several years later and returned to Philadelphia. Erected by the Pennsylvania Historical Commission and the Union County Historical Society, 1919.

Plaque: SR 3016 (former LR 59043) 1 mile E of Pa. 304, NW of New Berlin. Dedicated July 19, 1919.

72 EVANGELICAL CHURCH

Same text as Evangelical Church above.

Junction PA 45 (Chestnut St.) & 104 (10th St.), W end Mifflinburg. Erected Sept. 22, 1947.

72 FOUGHT'S MILL

The nearby mill is on site of the earlier mill built in 1771. The original Fought's Mill was a settler's refuge against Indians in Revolutionary days. Here was held Nov. 3, 1776, Buffalo Valley's first election under the Constitution of 1776.

PA 45 (Chestnut St.) at Buffalo Rd., Mifflinburg. Erected Sept. 22, 1947.

73 SAMUEL MACLAY

Member of Congress, 1794-97. U.S. Senator, 1802-09. Also member of the General Assembly, 1787-91; 1797-1802. Resident of Buffalo Valley after 1770 and died here in 1811. Buried in the nearby churchyard cemetery.

PA 45, 4 miles SW of Lewisburg. Erected Apr. 28, 1947.

73 BUFFALO CHURCH

Organized by Presbyterian pioneers, 1773; broken up by Indian raids. Resumed, with first regular pastor, 1787. Log church of about 1775 replaced by stone in 1816, by brick in 1846. It stands a mile to the north.

PA 45, 3.7 miles SW of Lewisburg. Erected June 9, 1948.

Entering Lewisburg

74 BUCKNELL UNIVERSITY

Organized in 1846 as the University at Lewisburg by the Baptist Church. Named Bucknell University in 1886, honoring William Bucknell, donor and trustee. Degrees first conferred upon women students in 1885.

US 15 in Lewisburg at stadium. Erected Sept. 22, 1947.

74 ROBERT LOWRY

The famed hymn-writer lived in this house, 1869-75. Here, some of his best known hymns were written. His music was sung in many foreign lands. One of his works is, "Shall We Gather at the River." Lowry died in 1899.

City type: 110 University Ave., Lewisburg. Erected Nov. 22, 1954.

74 UNDERGROUND RAILROAD

This old stable was a station on the Underground Railroad. Here fugitive slaves were hidden, fed, and aided in reaching the next station on their journey.

City type: University Ave., Lewisburg. Erected Nov. 22, 1954.

74 LUDWIG DERR

Founder of Lewisburg, 1785. Lived here in a log house incorporated in the present structure. Nearby, he operated a trading post and a grist and saw mill. Derr died in Nov. 1785.

City type: 34 Brown St., Lewisburg. Erected Nov. 22, 1954.

74 GENERAL TASKER H. BLISS

Chief of staff of the U.S. Army during the first World War and military counsellor to President Wilson at the Versailles Peace Conference, was born in this house on December 31, 1853.

City type: 115 S. Front St., Lewisburg. Erected Nov. 22, 1954.

74 LEWISBURG CROSS-CUT CANAL

Completed in 1833 as a part of Pennsylvania Canal. It was $5/8$ mile long and had 3 lift-locks. A dam provided slack water, enabling boats to cross the river, thus creating a great trade center here.

City type: PA 45 (Market St.), Lewisburg near bridge. Erected Jan. 3, 1955.

Leaving Lewisburg

75 ELI SLIFER

Home, 1861-1888, of Civil War Secretary of the Commonwealth, who as an assistant to Governor Andrew Curtin had leading role in mobilizing State's men and resources for war. Elected State Assemblyman, State Treasurer. Born 1818, died 1888. House is now office of Evangelical Home.

US 15 just N of Lewisburg. Erected Oct. 4, 1968. Evangelical Home is now United Methodist Homes.

76 BUFFALO CHURCH

Organized by Presbyterian pioneers, 1773; broken up by Indian raids. Resumed, with first regular pastor, 1787. Log church of about 1775 replaced by stone in 1816 and by brick in 1846.

PA 192, 4 miles W of Lewisburg. Erected June 9, 1948.

77 COL. JOHN KELLY

Outstanding Indian fighter of Buffalo Valley. Settled here about 1769; built log house to the north, now weather-boarded, in 1775. Col. Kelly served with distinction at the battles of Trenton and Princeton. He died in 1832. Buried at Lewisburg.

SR 1002 (former LR 59019) just E of Mazeppa. Erected Mar. 21, 1952.

78 SHIKELLAMY'S TOWN

Earlier residence of the noted Oneida chief located nearby. As the Six Nations' overseer of the Delaware and other refugee Indian groups, Shikellamy spent most of his time after 1728 at Shamokin — now Sunbury.

US 15, 3.6 miles N of Lewisburg. Erected Apr. 28, 1947.

78 [SHIKELLAMY'S OLD TOWN]

On the plain stretching south-east from this ridge was situated the village of Shikellamy's Old Town, which was visited by Conrad Weiser in 1737 when on his way to Onandaga. Shikellamy was appointed Vice-Gerent of the Iroquois Confederacy in 1745 and made Shamokin (Sunbury) his headquarters. Erected by the Pennsylvania Historical Commission, the Union County Historical Society, and the United Evangelical Church Historical Society, 1921.

Plaque: Central Oak Heights just off US 15 southbound, S of West Milton. Dedicated Aug. 2, 1921.

79 WIDOW CATHERINE SMITH

Built a stone house on this site in 1774, operating saw and grist mills that stood near the intersection of the present highways. During 1776, she completed the boring mill where a great many gun barrels for the Continental Army were manufactured.

SR 1011 (old US 15) at SR 1010 (former LR 629), White Deer. Erected May 25, 1967 (revised 1953 marker).

REGION XII

Coal Kingdom, Leisure Land

The wooded and leisure-time hills of the Poconos, the scarred landscape of the anthracite region, the commercial and industrial lowlands of the Wyoming Valley, and the rolling dairy country of the north reflect the various economies of the six northeastern counties of *Lackawanna, Luzerne, Pike, Susquehanna, Wayne* and *Wyoming.*

Due to charter conflict between Pennsylvania and Connecticut, the first settlers of European origin in this region were Connecticut families in the Wyoming Valley. In 1771 Pennsylvania responded to their ''intrusion'' by erecting Fort Wyoming, which was promptly lost in the First Yankee-Pennamite War. By 1776 some twenty-six hundred Connecticutites had come, crossing the Delaware River at such points as Dingman's Ferry and following such routes as the Wyoming-Minisink Indian Path. Wilkes-Barre was then the seat of Connecticut's Westmoreland County, a disputed claim that was settled finally in 1782 by the Continental Congress.

Settlement coincided with Pontiac's uprising in the west in 1763 and with the American Revolution. In both, settlers suffered the Indians' wrath, the frontier forts being an indication of their fear. In the Revolution, the Iroquois and their British allies struck at the Pennsylvania-New York frontier, and in retaliation, Major General John Sullivan marched in 1779 through Luzerne and Wyoming counties to New York to destroy Native American villages and crops.

Within this region is a portion of North America's largest deposit of anthracite coal, which to transport required canals and railroads. Completed in 1828 and 1837, the Delaware and Hudson and the Lehigh Navigation canals provided some necessary links. In 1829 the Stourbridge Lion, the first steam locomotive in the U.S., was tested on the Delaware and Hudson gravity railroad. Meanwhile, in Scranton, which arose on the introduction of the anthracite furnace for the smelting of iron, the first electric streetcar service in the U.S. was begun in 1886.

Much of the primeval forest was cut for timber, and in its place have grown vast stands of hardwood. To this land of forests and lakes, the Pocono Mountains have attracted many vacationers. Where the land permits, however, dairying is the principal enterprise. Anthracite has declined and communities have sought new employment for the shrinking number of their inhabitants.

When coal was ''king,'' it was also the source of unrest. In Luzerne County, a march of striking miners near Lattimer in 1897 resulted in the death by gunshot of twenty of their number. Conversely, Terence V. Powderly, leader of the Knights of Labor, greatest of the nineteenth-century unions, was elected mayor of Scranton three times from 1878 to 1884.

The presence of such visionaries, of one kind or another, adds color to the historical landscape: Galusha Grow, sponsor of the Homestead Act; George Gatlin, Indian-painter; Joseph Smith, the Mormon prophet; Zane Grey, western novelist; Gifford Pinchot, conservationist and governor; Horace Greeley, utopian and editor; and Charles Pierce, philosopher.

People and events form the web that distinguishes each of Pennsylvania's regions and the Commonwealth as a whole.

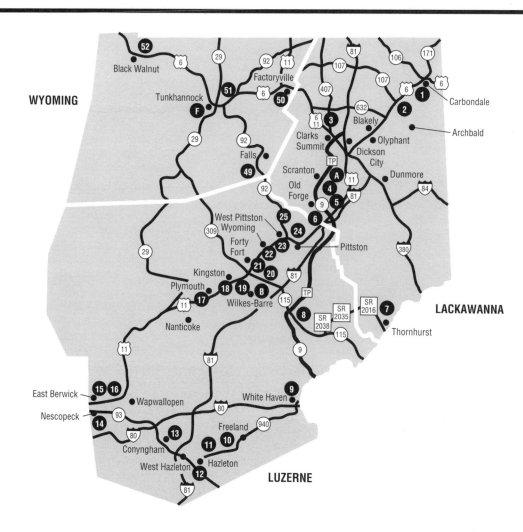

WYOMING

LACKAWANNA

LUZERNE

Black Walnut

52

6

29

92

11

Factoryville

51

51

6

50

Tunkhannock

F

29

92

Falls

49

West Pittston

Wyoming

309

Forty
Fort

29

25

24

23

22

21

20

Kingston

Plymouth

18

19

B

17

11

Nanticoke

Wilkes-Barre

115

TP

8

SR
2038

SR
2035

SR
2016

7

Thornhurst

115

9

11

81

East Berwick

15

16

Wapwallopen

White Haven

9

Nescopeck

93

14

80

13

Freeland

940

11

10

Conyngham

West Hazleton

12

Hazleton

81

81

80

81

107

107

106

171

92

11

407

632

6

11

3

Blakely

Clarks
Summit

Olyphant

Archbald

Dickson
City

Scranton

Old
Forge

TP

A

4

5

6

9

Dunmore

84

81

11

2

1

Carbondale

380

9

Pittston

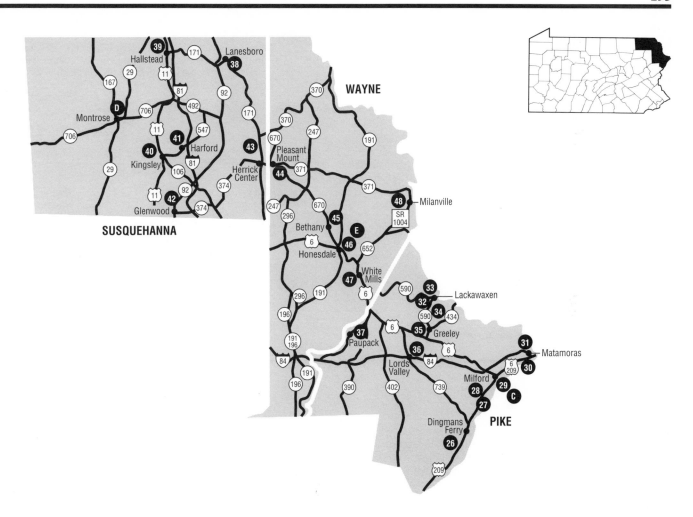

Hallstead
Lanesboro
39
171
38
29
11
167
92
81
492
D
706
171
Montrose
547
11
41
706
43
40
81
Harford
Kingsley
Herrick
Center
29
106
374
WAYNE
370
370
247
191
670
Pleasant
Mount
371
11
42
44
371
92
48 Milanville
Glenwood
374
374
247
SR
1004
670
296
45
Bethany
E
6
46
652
SUSQUEHANNA
Honesdale
47
White
Mills
6
33 Lackawaxen
590
296
32
191
590 34 434
196
35
Greeley
191
37
6 31 Matamoras
196
Paupack
36
6
6
84
30
209
196
191
Lords
Valley
84
Milford
390
402
739
28 29 C
84
27
Dingmans
Ferry
26
PIKE
209

Lackawanna County

(A) LACKAWANNA COUNTY
Formed August 13, 1878 from Luzerne County, it was Pennsylvania's 67th and last county created. The name is an Indian word meaning "stream that forks." Scranton, the county seat, was made a city, 1866. It became the anthracite coal mining capital of the world.
City type: Courthouse Sq., Spruce St., Scranton. Dedicated May 25, 1982.

(1) CARBONDALE
Founded by the Wurts brothers, pioneers in developing anthracite resources of the region, in 1822. Here the first underground mine was opened in June, 1831, near Seventh Ave. Chartered as a city in 1851.
On main highways leading into city. Erected 1947.

(2) FIRST AID PIONEER
Here in 1899 Dr. Matthew J. Shields organized first aid for mine workers. From it grew the plan of Red Cross industrial first aid, which he helped establish. Dr. Shields died in Scranton, January 23, 1939.
Junction US 6 & PA 107, Jermyn. Erected Nov. 18, 1947.

(3) ELDER MILLER
Pioneer preacher and teacher in Abington region, lived near this village. Born in Connecticut in 1775. Settled in Waverly about 1800; died here in 1857. The first church in the township, and the first school, were on his farm.
PA 407 at Waverly. Erected Sept. 14, 1948.

Entering Scranton

(4) SCRANTON
Ebenezer Slocum built his first house, and made the first iron here prior to 1800. Its founding, naming, and growth as a city were due to George W. Scranton and associates. Leader in iron and steel for 60 years after its founding, 1840.
On main highways leading into city. Erected Sept. 7, 1948.

(4) LACKAWANNA IRON
Iron was forged in Slocum Hollow by 1797. Nearby are remains of Lackawanna Iron Co. works begun 1840 by Scranton and associates. Iron rails for the Erie R. R. were made here, 1847. Steelmaking begun in 1875. Closed in 1902.
Cedar Ave. near Lackawanna Ave., Scranton. Erected Dec. 4, 1947.

(4) FIRST ELECTRIC CARS
The first street car system in the U.S. built entirely for operation by electric power was at Scranton. It began operation on Nov. 30, 1886. The initial run was between central Scranton and Green Ridge section.
Courthouse Sq., Adams & Spruce Sts., Scranton. Erected Sept. 15, 1948.

(4) THOMAS J. FOSTER
Pioneer in education by mail, editor, publisher, veteran, was born Pottsville, Jan. 1, 1843. Founded the "World Schoolhouse," the International Correspondence Schools, in 1891. An early advocate of mine safety laws. Died in Scranton, Oct. 14, 1936.
Wyoming Ave. near Ash St., Scranton. Erected Oct. 5, 1948.

(4) THE "PIONEER"
This gravity railroad car, used on the Pennsylvania Coal Company Railroad, was presented by the Company to the City of Scranton, Sept. 3, 1909. The car was used on the line from Hawley to Pittston from 1850 to 1884.
Nay Aug Park, Scranton. Erected July 15, 1948.

(4) [MUNSEE INDIAN VILLAGE]
This stone marks the site of a former Indian Village, occupied after 1743 by a band of Munsee, under Chief Capoose. About 150 feet east of this spot stood a famous apple tree, under which the Indians held their councils. This tree was designated as "the town sign-post of Providence" by the settlers in 1774. It was 13½ feet in circumference when it was blown down in 1885. Erected by the Pennsylvania Historical Commission in co-operation with the Lackawanna Institute of History and Science, May, 1916.
Plaque: wall near stadium entrance, Providence Rd., West Scranton. Dedicated May 26, 1916.

❹ CAPOOSE

On the nearby flat was located an Indian village under the chief, Capoose. It was settled by Munsee following their removal from the upper Delaware valley after 1743.

Providence Rd. & Diamond St., West Scranton. Erected Dec. 2, 1947.

❹ FIRST SETTLER

Nearby was located the first house in present Scranton. It was built by Isaac Tripp in 1771. He was born in Rhode Island; migrated from Connecticut. Member of Assembly. Killed by Indians on Dec. 16, 1778.

N. Main Ave., West Scranton. Erected Nov. 18, 1947.

❹ TERENCE V. POWDERLY

Noted labor leader. Born Jan. 22, 1849, in Carbondale. Grand Master Workman of the Knights of Labor, 1879-93. Scranton's Mayor, 1878-84. Later Federal immigration official. Died in 1924. His home was near here.

N. Main Ave. near Mears St., West Scranton. Erected Nov. 18, 1947.

❹ REV. WILLIAM BISHOP

Baptist clergyman and first ordained minister in Scranton, built a combined log church and house near here in 1795. There he preached and held services. He was born in England, 1749, and died in Scott Township in 1816.

Main Ave. & Price St., West Scranton. Erected July 14, 1948.

Leaving Scranton

❺ KEYSER CREEK

At this point was established the first white settlement in Lackawanna County. In 1769, Timothy Keys, Solomon Hocksey, Andrew Hickman, built homes here. In July, 1778, Keys and others were slain by Indians. The Creek is named for Keys.

Main St. (SR 3013), Taylor. Erected Sept. 2, 1948.

❻ OLD FORGE

On the south bank of the Lackawanna River opposite this spot was located the iron forge built 1789 by Dr. William Smith and James Sutton. The oldest forge in the region, the town was so-named.

SR 3013 (former LR 35055), Old Forge. Erected July 24, 1947.

❼ JAY GOULD

The first business venture of the noted speculator and railroad manipulator was in this village, then called Gouldsboro. Here, 1856-61, he owned a large tannery with Zaddock Pratt. The tannery profits became the basis of his fortune.

SR 2016 (former LR 665), Thornhurst. Erected June 19, 1947.

❼ JAY GOULD

The first business venture of the noted speculator and railroad manipulator was at nearby Thornhurst. Here, 1856-61, he owned a large tannery with Zaddock Pratt. Gould's tannery profits became a basis of his fortune.

River & Locust Ridge Rds., Thornhurst. Erected June 18, 1947.

Luzerne County

❼B LUZERNE COUNTY

Formed September 25, 1786 from Northumberland County. Named for Chevalier de la Luzerne. Wilkes-Barre, the county seat, was settled 1769. A center of the Yankee-Pennamite Wars (begun 1769) and 1902 Anthracite Strike, conflicts that changed America.

City type: Courthouse, N. River St., Wilkes-Barre. Dedicated Sept. 24, 1982.

❽ SULLIVAN'S MARCH

Gen. John Sullivan's army camped a short distance west from here on June 22, 1779. It was the fifth camp on the march from Easton. Next day the army reached Fort Wyoming, Wilkes-Barre.

PA 115, 6.3 miles SE of Wilkes-Barre. Erected Oct. 13, 1947.

9 WHITE HAVEN
Named for Josiah White (1781-1850) whose Lehigh Navigation system was vital to coal and lumber transport. This was the northern limit, 1837-1862, of the two-way navigation from Easton. Here it met White's 20-mile railroad to Wilkes-Barre with its inclined ''Ashley Planes.''
City type: PA 940 about 150 ft. W of bridge, White Haven. Dedicated May 25, 1985.

10 SAINTS PETER AND PAUL LUTHERAN CHURCH
The first Slovak Evangelical Lutheran congregation in the Western Hemisphere was organized mainly by Michael Zemany, pioneer Slovak Lutheran. The first service was conducted on February 22, 1883. Present church building, remodeled later, was erected in 1886.
Washington St. (300 block), Freeland. Erected June 18, 1971.

11 LATTIMER MASSACRE
Seeking collective bargaining and civil liberty, immigrant miners on strike were marching, in protest, from Harwood to Lattimer. Here, on Sept. 10, 1897, they were met by armed deputy sheriffs. The ensuing affray resulted in the death of more than twenty marchers.
Off SR 3028 (former LR 40088) ca. .5 mile E of Lattimer Crossroads. Dedicated Sept. 10, 1972.

12 ST. JOSEPH'S CHURCH
Organized in 1882 by the Rev. Ignatius Jascovich, pioneer Slovak Catholic priest, St. Joseph's is the oldest Slovak Roman Catholic parish in the Western Hemisphere.
City type: 5th & Laurel Sts., Hazleton. Erected Nov. 2, 1970.

13 SUGARLOAF MASSACRE
After an unsuccessful attack on Fort Augusta, Indians and Tories surprised a detachment of Northumberland [actually Northampton] Co. militia on Sept. 11, 1780. The site of the massacre is just beyond the town.
PA 93 ca. 5 miles NW of Hazleton, near Conyngham. Erected Oct. 13, 1947.

13 [SUGARLOAF MASSACRE]
Near this spot occurred the Sugarloaf Massacre. On September 11, 1780, a detachment of Captain John Van Etten's Company, Northampton County Militia, resting at the spring was surprised by a band of Indians and Tories led by the Seneca chief Roland Montour. Those who perished were Captain Daniel Klader, Corporal Samuel Bond, Jacob Arndt, Peter Croom, Philip George, Abraham Klader, John Kouts, James McGraw, Paul Neely, George Peter Renhart, Jacob Row, George Silhamer, Abraham Smith, Baltzer Snyder, John Weaver. Marked by the Pennsylvania Historical Commission, the Wyoming Historical and Geological Society, and the Sugarloaf Commemorative Committee, 1933.
Plaque: Walnut Ave., .2 mile W of Main St., Conyngham (just E of PA 93). Dedicated Sept. 9, 1933.

14 PETER F. ROTHERMEL
The noted painter was born in Nescopeck on July 8, 1812. His huge masterpiece, ''Battle of Gettysburg,'' ordered by the State Legislature, is on display at the William Penn Memorial Museum, Harrisburg.
PA 93 between Montgomery & Cooper Sts., Nescopeck. Erected 1970 (revised 1947 marker).

14 NESCOPECK
Name of Shawnee-Delaware Indian village located here. From Braddock's defeat in 1755 until Fort Augusta was built in 1756, it was a rallying point for Indians hostile to the English.
PA 93 E of bridge, Nescopeck. Erected Nov. 1948.

15 NESCOPECK
From the mouth of Nescopeck Creek an Indian path went east over the mountains by the way of present Hazleton to the Lehigh near Mauch Chunk; then to ''the Forks of the Delaware'' at Easton.
US 11, .5 mile E of East Berwick. Erected Apr. 1949.

16 WAPWALLOPEN
Name of the former Indian town near the mouth of the Wapwallopen Creek. Indian trails connecting old Wyoming, the "Warrior's Path," and the Juniata and West Branch Susquehanna valleys intersected here.
US 11 near Wapwallopen. Erected Nov. 1948.

17 ABIJAH SMITH & COMPANY
Established 1807 by Abijah Smith, who had bought 75 acres here on Ransom Creek and was later joined by his brother John. Their shipments of coal by ark down the Susquehanna, begun in 1807, continued for 20 years. This company was, in 1818, the first to extract Pennsylvania coal by powder blasting. In the same family almost 70 years, it was considered the first commercially successful U.S. anthracite firm.
US 11 (Main St) at State Armory, Plymouth. Dedicated June 4, 1989.

18 HENRY M. HOYT
Was born on this site in 1830. Governor of Pennsylvania, 1879-83; first to serve four years under the State Constitution of 1873. Advocated correctional institutions for care of youthful offenders. Died in 1892.
City type: US 11 (714 Wyoming Ave.), Kingston. Erected Oct. 1952.

Entering Wilkes-Barre

19 WILKES-BARRE
Laid out 1770 by a group of Connecticut settlers, on land claimed by that state. Seat of "County of Westmoreland," erected 1776. Near here took place the Wyoming Massacre, 1778, and the "Pennamite Wars" of 1769-72 and 1784.
On main highways leading into city. Erected May 5, 1949.

19 FORT DURKEE
First fort built by the Connecticut settlers; begun in April 1769. Used during the first Pennamite War against Pennsylvania authorities, 1769-71. It stood 1000 feet from Ft. Wyoming.
River St. near South St., Wilkes-Barre. Erected Oct. 13, 1947.

19 FORT WYOMING
Built by Pennsylvania, 1771; seized by Connecticut settlers. Rebuilt 1778. Mobilization camp for Sullivan's army, 1779. Destroyed 1784, after withdrawal of the Continental and Pennsylvania garrisons.
River St. near South St., Wilkes-Barre. Erected Oct. 13, 1947.

19 THE SULLIVAN EXPEDITION AGAINST THE IROQUOIS INDIANS, 1779
Fort Wyoming. Mobilization camp of Sullivan's army, June 23-July 31, 1779. Marked by the Pennsylvania Historical Commission and the Wyoming Valley Chapter, D. A. R., 1929.
Plaque: on River Commons, River St. near W. South St., Wilkes-Barre. Erected 1929.

19 GEORGE CATLIN
The great painter of Indian portraits was born here July 26, 1796, of Connecticut ancestry. Until 1823 he practiced law here and nearby. He began painting Indian pictures six years later.
River & South Sts., Wilkes-Barre. Erected Oct. 13, 1947.

19 WILKES-BARRE FORT
Completed 1778, enclosing the courthouse of the Connecticut county of Westmoreland. Surrendered with Forty Fort to the British in 1778.
W corner Public Sq., Wilkes-Barre. Erected Oct. 13, 1947.

19 REV. JOSEPH MURGAS
Pioneer in development of overland wireless telegraphy. In 1898 he began his experiments on these grounds. His first public transmission of sound was made here on Nov. 23, 1905. Pastor, artist, biologist, and a supporter of Slovak aspirations, he died 1929.
City type: at Sacred Heart Church, 601 N. Main St., Wilkes-Barre. Dedicated Nov. 25, 1990.

Leaving Wilkes-Barre

20 CONNECTICUT SETTLEMENT
The first Connecticut settlement on their Susquehanna Purchase, 1762. Following its destruction by Indians on Oct. 15, 1763, no further settlements were made until 1769.

River Rd. (SR 2004) N of Wilkes-Barre. Erected Oct. 13, 1947.

21 FORTY FORT
Named for the forty Connecticut settlers of 1769. Begun in 1770. The Wyoming Massacre followed its surrender to Major Butler's force of British, Tories, and Indians, July 4, 1778.

US 11 (Wyoming Ave.) & River St., Forty Fort. Erected Oct. 13, 1947.

21 DENISON HOUSE
Built in 1790, home of Col. Nathan Denison, Revolutionary Officer and Luzerne County Judge. Administered by the Pennsylvania Historical and Museum Commission.

At site, 35 Denison St., Forty Fort. Erected May 23, 1972.

22 BATTLE OF WYOMING
Nearby on July 3, 1778, 300 patriots under Col. Zebulon Butler were defeated by 1100 British, Tories, and Indians with Maj. John Butler. Captives were massacred; survivors fled to Forty Fort.

US 11 in Wyoming at monument. Erected June 1952.

22 THE BLOODY ROCK
On the night of July 3, 1778, after the Battle of Wyoming, fourteen or more captive American soldiers were murdered here by a maul wielded by a revengeful Indian woman, traditionally but not certainly identified as "Queen Esther."

City type: Susquehanna Ave. between 7th & 8th Sts., Wyoming. Dedicated July 22, 1962.

The Forty Fort Meetinghouse

Ralph Vivian, Ace Hoffman Studios, Plymouth

23 PITTSTON FORT
Erection begun 1772 by Connecticut proprietors. Forced to surrender to the British, July 4, 1778, and partially destroyed. Restored 1780, and used until after the end of the Revolutionary War.

Pittston Ave. & Parsonage St., Pittston. Erected Oct. 13, 1947.

24 JENKINS' FORT
Stockaded home of John Jenkins. Built by Connecticut settlers, 1776.
Surrendered to the British under Maj. John Butler, July 1, 1778, and was burned.
Junction US 11 & PA 92, West Pittston. Erected Oct. 13, 1947.

25 SULLIVAN'S MARCH
Gen. John Sullivan's army camped on the lowlands on the opposite side of the
river, July 31, 1779. It was the first camp on the march from Ft. Wyoming,
Wilkes-Barre, to Tioga.
PA 92, 1 mile N of West Pittston. Erected Oct. 13, 1947.

**25 THE SULLIVAN EXPEDITION AGAINST THE
IROQUOIS INDIANS, 1779**
Lackawanay, ten miles from Wyoming. First encampment of Sullivan's army on
its march from Wyoming to Teaoga, July 31, 1779, lay on lowlands directly across
the river. Marked by the Pennsylvania Historical Commission and the Dial Rock
Chapter, D. A. R., 1929.
Plaque: PA 92, 1.5 miles N of West Pittston. Erected 1929.

Pike County

C PIKE COUNTY
Formed March 26, 1814 from Wayne County and named for Zebulon M. Pike. Its
bluestone and lumber, carried by D & H Canal and by Erie R. R., helped build
our nation. Famed for its natural beauty. Near Milford, the county seat, is Gov.
Pinchot's Grey Towers.
City type: County Courthouse, Broad & High Sts., Milford. Dedicated Sept. 17,
1981.

26 DINGMAN'S FERRY
Here was located one of the earliest ferries across the Delaware. Andrew
Dingman in 1750 built the flatboat he used as a ferry with his own hand axe.
Dingman was one of the pioneer settlers.
US 209 at Dingmans Ferry. Erected June 1, 1948.

27 WYOMING-MINISINK PATH
Here, an important Indian trail connecting the Delaware and Susquehanna
Rivers ascended Indian Point to Powwow Hill. The path was used by Delaware
Indians in their migration to the Wyoming Valley, and later by Connecticut
settlers.
US 209, 3 miles S of Milford. Erected Apr. 17, 1951.

28 GIFFORD PINCHOT
The noted forester, conservationist and Governor of Pennsylvania two terms in
1923-27; 1931-35, had his ancestral home at Grey Towers, Milford. He is buried
in this cemetery. Born in Connecticut, 1865. Died on October 4, 1946.
US 209 S of Milford. Erected June 1, 1948.

29 GIFFORD PINCHOT
The noted forester, conservationist and Governor of Pennsylvania two terms in
1923-27; 1931-35, had his ancestral home at Grey Towers, Milford. Born in
Connecticut, 1865, of a long line of pioneers of this region. Died Oct. 4, 1946.
US 6 NW of Milford. Erected June 1, 1948.

30 CHARLES S. PEIRCE
The noted philosopher, logician, scientist and founder of pragmatism lived in
this house from 1887 until his death in 1914. America's most original
philosopher and greatest logician, a great part of his work was written here.
US 6 & 209 NE of Milford. Erected June 1, 1948.

31 OLD STONE FORT
Sometimes referred to as Fort Matamoras, this stone structure was built about
1740 by Simon Westfael, one of the earliest Dutch settlers in the region. It was a
refuge from Indians in days of frontier warfare.
1st St. (2 blocks S of US 6 & 209), Matamoras. Erected June 1, 1948.

32 ZANE GREY (1872-1939)
The prolific author of western novels lived on this property, 1905-1918. Among his books written here was the famed "Riders of the Purple Sage" (1912). He had a lifelong love for this area, and his remains now rest within view of the house.
City type: Zane Grey Museum, Scenic Dr. just N of PA 590, Lackawaxen. Dedicated Oct. 28, 1989.

33 BATTLE OF MINISINK
July 22, 1779, 300 Tories and Indians led by Joseph Brant, Mohawk chief, were attacked near Lackawanna by some 175 settlers. Brant was returning from raiding New York settlements. All but 25 of the patriots were killed. Brant escaped.
Old PA 590 N of Lackawaxen. Erected June 1, 1948.

34 SYLVANIA COLONY
The site of Horace Greeley's Utopian colony modeled on Brook Farm and the ideas of Fourier, French Socialist, was located here. Based on common property holding and equal labor, it failed in 1845 after July frosts had killed all crops.
PA 434 at PA 590, Greeley. Erected June 1, 1948.

35 SYLVANIA COLONY
The site of Horace Greeley's Utopian colony modeled on Brook Farm and the ideas of Fourier, French Socialist, was near here, 1842-45. The 300 members of the Sylvania Society abandoned it after July frosts killed all crops in 1845.
Junction US 6 & PA 434 NW of Milford. Erected June 1, 1948.

36 WYOMING-MINISINK PATH
The highway here follows closely the route of the Delaware Indian trail from Minisink Island to Wyoming. Refugees from the Massacre of Wyoming, 1778, camped by the "boiling" spring, which may be seen in the woods a few yards SW of here.
SR 4004 (former LR 51019) .3 mile W of Lords Valley. Erected May 4, 1951.

37 WYOMING-MINISINK PATH
Here the path from Minisink Island to Wyoming descended the hill to ford Wallenpaupack Creek, before the valley was flooded to make the present lake. Crossing the mountains to Capoose (Scranton), it descended the Lackawanna Valley to the Susquehanna.
PA 507 at Paupack. Erected Nov. 22, 1950.

37 WALLENPAUPACK
This region was the site of one of the earliest settlements in this area. Early Connecticut claimants built a fort here in 1773 and had a virtually independent government until 1798. The old Indian trail from Cochecton to Wyoming passed nearby.
PA 507 at Paupack. Erected Aug. 13, 1948.

Susquehanna County

D SUSQUEHANNA COUNTY
Formed on February 21, 1810 out of Luzerne County. Named for Susquehanna River. Home of Galusha A. Grow, sponsor of 1862 Homestead Act. Montrose, county seat incorporated 1824, was an early Abolitionist center and stop on the Underground Railroad.
City type: Monument Sq. adjacent to County Courthouse, Montrose. Dedicated July 5, 1982.

38 STARRUCCA VIADUCT
Built in 1847-48 by the Erie Railroad, it it the oldest stone railroad bridge in the State in use today. Viaduct is 1040 feet long, 100 feet high, and 25 feet wide at top.
R 1009 (former LR 296) at Lanesboro near viaduct. Erected Sept. 1951 & revised 1974.

39 JOSEPH SMITH

Founder of Mormonism, once lived a few miles east of here prior to 1830. Much of the translation of the "Golden Plates" for the Book of Mormon is said to have been done there. Site now owned by the Church of Latter Day Saints.

US 11 between Great Bend & Hallstead. Erected May 15, 1947.

40 GALUSHA GROW

Father of the Homestead Act, opening western lands to free settlement in 1862, lived at nearby Glenwood. Speaker of the House, 1861-63, and member of Congress, 1893-1903. Died in 1907; buried in Harford Cemetery a few miles from here.

Intersection US 11 & PA 547 N of Kingsley. Erected May 15, 1947.

41 GALUSHA GROW

Father of the Homestead Act, opening western lands to free settlement in 1862. Speaker of the House 1861-63. Returned to Congress 1893-1903. Educated at Franklin Academy, Harford, and buried in this cemetery.

PA 547 in Harford at cemetery. Erected May 15, 1947.

42 GALUSHA GROW

Father of the Homestead Act, opening western lands to free settlement in 1862. Speaker of the House 1861-63. Returned to Congress 1893-1903. Retired to his home, which stood on this site, until his death in 1907.

PA 92 just N of PA 374 at Glenwood. Erected May 15, 1947.

43 SAMUEL MEREDITH

The first treasurer of the U.S., 1789-1801, and Revolutionary patriot, spent the last years of his life at Pleasant Mount. Died here in 1817, on his estate called Belmont.

Intersection PA 171 & 374 at Herrick Center. Erected May 15, 1947.

Wayne County

E WAYNE COUNTY

Formed on March 21, 1798, from Northampton County. Named for Gen. Anthony Wayne. Site of test run of Stourbridge Lion, first locomotive in U.S. to run on a commercial track. Honesdale, county seat incorporated 1831, was western terminus of D & H Canal.

City type: County Courthouse, Court St. between 9th & 10th Sts., Honesdale. Dedicated July 8, 1981.

44 SAMUEL MEREDITH

The first Treasurer of the U.S., 1789-1801, and Revolutionary patriot, spent the last years of his life at Pleasant Mount. Died here in 1817, on his estate, called Belmont.

PA 371 & 670 just W of Pleasant Mount. Erected Oct. 21, 1949.

44 SAMUEL MEREDITH

This memorial is a tribute to the financier-patriot of the Revolution who was first Treasurer of the U.S., 1789-1801. George Clymer and Meredith were large landholders in this area. Meredith died at his estate, Belmont, in 1817.

Intersection PA 371 & 670, Pleasant Mount. Erected July 28, 1948.

45 DAVID WILMOT

The author of the Wilmot Proviso of 1846 barring slavery from territory acquired in the Mexican War, was born in this house Jan. 20, 1814. He died in Towanda, March 16, 1868, after a notable career in the State and Nation.

Wayne St. off PA 670 at Bethany. Erected May 29, 1947.

46 STOURBRIDGE LION

A replica of the famous Stourbridge Lion, first steam locomotive run on rails in the U.S., 1829, is housed here. Beside it is the Eclipse, original passenger coach on the D & H Gravity Railroad.

US 6 just W of Honesdale. Erected 1947.

46 HONESDALE

Named for Philip Hone, noted New York merchant-diarist, who pioneered in developing transportation and anthracite resources of the region. Laid out 1827 at head of D & H Canal. County seat since 1841.

US 6 & PA 191 entering Honesdale from W & SE. Erected Apr. 9, 1948.

46 LINCOLN NOMINATION

In May, 1859, Horace Greeley met with notable political leaders to create a boom to nominate Abraham Lincoln for President. The events that ensued at the Republican National Convention in Chicago paralleled the strategy planned at the parley held in this building.

115 9th St., Honesdale. Erected Aug. 26, 1968.

Stourbridge Lion locomotive, Honesdale

46 DELAWARE & HUDSON CANAL

Terminus of the waterway uniting the Hudson and Delaware rivers. Built in 1825-28. A gravity railroad feeder reached to Carbondale. For 70 years the anthracite trade outlet for the region.

US 6 & PA 191 (Main St.) at historical society, Honesdale. Erected May 29, 1947.

46 STOURBRIDGE LION

Here began the trial run of the first locomotive operated by steam on rails in the U.S., Aug. 8, 1829. The Lion was English-built for use on levels of the Gravity Railroad. It was piloted by Horatio Allen.

US 6 & PA 191 (Main St.) at Park St., Honesdale. Erected May 28, 1947.

47 DORFLINGER GLASS WORKS

Founded in 1865 by Christian Dorflinger on this site. Glass was made and cut here until 1921. Noted for the quality of Flint Glass, Dorflinger supplied the White House with sets of tableware through a number of administrations.

US 6 at White Mills. Erected June 28, 1951.

48 CUSHETUNK

The first Connecticut settlement on the upper Delaware was made here in 1755, under lead of Moses Thomas and Daniel Skinner, on lands called Cushetunk by the Indians. Settlement seized by Indians and Tories, 1778.

SR 1004 (former LR 63027) N of Milanville. Erected May 28, 1947.

Wyoming County

F WYOMING COUNTY

Formed on April 4, 1842 out of Luzerne County. The name, honoring the Wyoming Valley, is derived from an Indian word meaning ''extensive meadows.'' County seat of Tunkhannock was settled 1790; incorporated 1841. Sullivan's March passed through in August 1779.

City type: County Courthouse, Warren St., Tunkhannock. Dedicated July 9, 1982.

(49) SULLIVAN'S MARCH

Gen. John Sullivan's army camped on the lowland on the opposite side of the river Aug. 1-2, 1779. It was the second camp from Fort Wyoming at Wilkes-Barre en route to Tioga.

PA 92, 2.8 miles S of Falls. Erected May 1947.

(49) WYOLUTIMUNK

Across the river is the site of the Indian town. "King" Teedyuscung stopped here with Frederick Post, May 17, 1760, on his way to Tioga and the "great concourse in the West."

PA 92, 2.6 miles S of Falls. Erected Aug. 16, 1949.

(50) CHRISTY MATHEWSON

Famed baseball pitcher, was born in Factoryville, 1880. Attended Keystone Academy, 1895-98, and Bucknell University, 1898-1902. He played for the New York Giants from 1901 to 1916. Known to baseball followers as "Bix Six." Served overseas during World War I; Captain, Chemical Warfare Service. Christy died in 1925. Buried at Lewisburg, Pennsylvania.

US 11 near Factoryville, front of Keystone Junior College. Dedicated June 18, 1955.

(51) THE SULLIVAN EXPEDITION AGAINST THE IROQUOIS INDIANS, 1779

Tunkhannock. Twelve miles from Quialutimack on the march from Wyoming to Teaoga, August 3, 1779, lay on lowlands between this point and river. Marked by the Pennsylvania Historical Commission and Tunkhannock Chapter, D.A.R., 1929.

Plaque: US 6 (W. Tioga St.) at Warren St., Tunkhannock. Erected 1929.

(51) SULLIVAN'S MARCH

Gen. John Sullivan's army on Aug. 3, 1779, camped by the river. Third camp from Fort Wyoming. Part of the Clinton-Sullivan campaign ending in the rout of the Six Nations Iroquois. The Tory-Indian menace on the frontier was eliminated.

US 6 (W. Tioga St.) at Warren St.,Tunkhannock. Erected May 1947.

(52) THE SULLIVAN EXPEDITION AGAINST THE IROQUOIS INDIANS, 1779

Vanderlip's Farm. Fourteen miles from Tunkhannock, fourth encampment of Sullivan's army on the march from Wyoming to Teaoga, August 4-5, 1779, lay on the lowlands known as Black Walnut Flats. Marked by the Pennsylvania Historical Commission and Tunkhannock Chapter, D.A.R., 1929.

Plaque: US 6 at Bluestone Rd., Black Walnut. Erected 1929, relocated early 1970s.

(52) SULLIVAN'S MARCH

Gen. John Sullivan's army camped on the lowlands here Aug. 4, 1779. The fourth encampment between Fort Wyoming and Tioga Point.

US 6 near Black Walnut. Erected May 1947.

This is an index of historical marker titles that incorporates page references to the subjects of these titles that may be found in marker texts throughout this *Guide*.